NOISE:
The Unwanted Sounds

David M. Lipscomb

Professional/Technical Series

nh Nelson - Hall Company
Chicago

ISBN 0-911012-97-4

Library of Congress Catalog Card No. 73-89466

Copyright © 1974 by David M. Lipscomb

For information address
Nelson-Hall Company, Publishers, 325 W. Jackson Blvd., Chicago, Ill.
60606

Manufactured in the United States of America

Library of Congress Cataloging in Publication Data

Lipscomb, David M
   Noise: the unwanted sounds.

   (Professional/technical series)
   1. Noise pollution. 2. Noise—Physiological effect.
I. Title.
TD892.L56   614.7'8   73-89466
ISBN 0-911012-97-4

·Contents·

145
155
274
jumbojet:
148

· PREFACE ·

This book begins with an attempt to explain to the layman some difficult concepts in a rather technical subject; then somewhat more advanced material is added. Thus the book hopefully will add to the reader's knowledge not only facts and figures but also, most important, a broad understanding of the subject.

While the book necessarily conveys information, it also contains philosophic and speculative statements and theoretical considerations as well as a healthy sprinkling of humor. Some define humor as examples of incongruity. Some great incongruities, and hence hilarious anecdotes, stem from the multiple types of reaction man gives to sound stimulation. Noise produces tension, and tension is treated with laughter; so laughter may be one effective reaction in an overall consideration of the noise problem.

Such a broad subject as noise cannot be easily treated in a free-swinging running dialogue; neither should a book about noise read like a novel. One purpose it should serve is as a meaningful source for references. To this end the subject matter here has been largely compartmentalized and placed into relatively homogeneous chapters. If a reader wants information only on aircraft noise he can find that material without having to read the entire book. Skip-reading is entirely possible and may be encouraged for those not interested in an overview.

The most direct route to failure in an undertaking like this one lies in any attempt at exhaustive treatment. Other books on noise range from highly technical and mathematically oriented

1

classroom textbooks to extremely simple reviews; this book is intended to find the middle ground. Highly technical material has been eliminated, but with a conscious effort to avoid the trap of perpetrating erroneous concepts for the sake of simplicity. If a descriptive term must be applied to the book a preferable one might be *perspective analysis*. The immense and confounding subject of noise and its effects deserves a perspective.

Problems abound in the study of noise. Defined operationally as "unwanted sound," noise is an admixture of almost infinitely variable components. Sound is by nature transient, which, coupled with the widely varied human responses to sound stimulation, dramatically increases its complexity. Each technical point in this intricate subject will be discussed as it arises; hence the book has no long chapters on, say, the acoustics of sound, the anatomy of the ear; the psychology of perception; but, rather, covers each subject in the context of the discussion.

This book may be considered unique in that the writer is professionally involved in the study of noise and its effects on humans and animals. Most general treatments of noise have been books prepared by professional writers after a thorough search of available literature and frequent conversations with researchers. The book also may be unique in its extensive discussion of lay concepts as expressed in numerous letters received during the past few years. Additionally, a strong word of caution is voiced as an entire chapter devoted to discounting the frequent overstatements about the noise problem.

That noise, by virtue of man's abundant experiences with it, has become an increasingly popular study area is indicated in part by the dramatic rise in requests to our laboratory for information for term papers, class projects, and science fair exhibits. This interest should be served, and current information is the best servant.

I cannot conclude this preface without a personal note. Through several years of preparation for the profession of audiology (the scientific study of the ear and the measurement of hearing) I found a recurrent theme that has become what I like to regard as a sane obsession. No other area in the study of the ear has caught my fancy so strongly as noise. Hopefully the reader will sense some of my excitement for the study of noise and will be captured by its absolutely fascinating qualities.

One final word of caution: this book is not free of my biases. In such a broad area of study conclusions drawn from research results are not unanimous among those of us who in clinics and laboratories seek to ferret out bits of new information. Although one can express only what he holds to be true at the time he speaks, new discoveries in the future may dramatically alter some of the material here. At the present time this book represents what I consider the truest and most realistic approach to noise.

·1·

A Sound Beginning

Well begun is half done
Horace

A group of scientists, it is said, once fashioned a time machine in the form of a robot programmed to journey to a future year and collect samples of the culture of that time. When the robot returned from its maiden journey with empty collection bins one member of the development team commented dejectedly, "It didn't work!" The group's leader responded, "Oh, no! I'm very much afraid it did."

This anecdote contains some essence of the concern for conditions in the present environment and for the future of the "beleaguered" earth. Some have been inclined to warn of the dire circumstances that surround the overuse of valuable resources, but 15 years ago little thought was given to the possibility that needed resources were anything but infinite. The seemingly endless supply of fossil fuels, clean air, and pure water seemed to signal a cheery future for all our heirs. How different the picture appears today!

During the return trip of Apollo 13 in April 1970 the service module exploded, and most of the civilized world became acutely aware of the limited resources aboard the tiny damaged craft. This drama made Buckminster Fuller's spaceship principle a newly distinct reality in the minds of many who earlier had hardly considered such an idea. The dilemma aboard the Apollo spaceship can be thought of as a miniature enactment of the approaching problems of humans aboard the planet earth. The available resources and their uses determined the quality of the environment of Apollo 13. Certainly a smelly spaceship is not a happy one; one whose air causes its crew to cough, choke, and wretch cannot be a pleasant habitat; nor would a noisy spaceship be a cheerful place.

Nearly 4 billion inhabitants are on the spaceship earth hurtling through the solar system with abundant but finite resources. Continuing investigations already have pointed out that this terrestrial craft has badly fouled water and air, and most of its inhabitants have found their homes to be overly noisy. They are not happy about it. The situation can be colored pretty grim. In fact, if the threats to existence are not taken seriously the future does not appear to be altogether bright. Ecocatastrophe, a word in current vogue, promotes thoughts of an impending environmental contamination that will leave man poisoned by the water he drinks, gasping for a safe breath of air, half-blinded by the glare and reflections of metal skyscrapers, covered with garbage, and distraught by the sound around him.

As the types of pollution proliferate, more students of the environment have tended to classify noise among them because of the increase in the average amount of sound people are exposed to each day. Dr. Vern Knudsen, leading acoustician and professor at UCLA, has suggested that sound levels in some cities are up as much as 20 decibels (dB) over the level known 20 years ago, which represents a 10-fold increase in the sound pressure that bears in on the eardrums. Of course, it must be pointed out that not all communities have experienced noise level rises of such dramatic proportions, but virtually all growing communities are noisier today than they were two decades ago.

Quite clearly this gradual increase in noise levels cannot be allowed to continue. Many cities experience high sound levels at present, and further growth of noise is tantamount to destruction of the human way of life. During the high activity hours in downtown Tokyo the sound levels seldom go below 88 dB; in New York 90 dB sound is common at rush-hour times. These levels are so high that one would need to shout in order to communicate with a companion standing within three feet. Such levels also extend into the danger zone for hearing health, because long-term exposure to intense sound may cause partial loss of hearing.

Growth in urban sound levels at the previous pace of as much as one dB per year cannot be tolerated. Look at it this way. A tribe of cannibals—quite adequate hunters but terrible boy scouts—built a severely lacking fire under the missionary in their pot. This shortcoming meant that the water around the missionary warmed at the rate of only one degree an hour. That's not much, but eventually the missionary will cook. In like manner the slow but steady rises in urban noise levels will lead to the most undesirable condition of sheer cacophony if allowed to continue unabated.

Reaction to noise has led to the formation of several organizations whose goal is noise abatement. Congressmen have become interested in the federal government's role in finding workable solutions to the problems that result from high-intensity sound. Interested labor leaders see industrial noise as a serious threat to workers. Citizens are banding together to bring about control of the noise the transportation industry generates. Professionals warn of serious side effects to man if noise sources are not brought under rigid control.

Noise, defined as unwanted sound, has been known for a long time. The Bible alludes to loud sounds in the command, "be still and know" (Ps. 46:10). Ancient literature refers to some sounds as being unthinkable, and more recent writings have amplified the undesirability of excessive high-level sounds. In the name of progress, however, noise often has been regarded as an undesirable but necessary by-product. An example is the advent of air travel, whose accompanying noise many felt must simply be tolerated. The same attitude for years allowed noise from a multitude of other sources—lawnmowers, vehicles, tools, construction equipment, and sirens, to name a few. But in recent years the public has become remarkably less tolerant of noise.

A favorite story of hearing scientists concerns a village drunk whose body chemistry was such that excessive drinking was causing him to lose his hearing. Forcefully confronted with the option of sobering up and saving his hearing or remaining a sot and becoming deaf, he resolved to avoid the hard stuff forever. All went well for several days, but then his doctor happened on him, staggering down the street, obviously back into his previous pattern. Disgusted, the physician scolded his patient and asked if he had forgotten the terrible consequences of his repeated binges. "I tried, Doc," the man responded, "but when I was sober I didn't like what I heard." The drunk's problem, coupled with advances in noise control technology, has occasioned greater emphasis on noise abatement.

Early recognition that excessive noise exposure poses a hazard to the hearing sense cannot be cited with full accuracy. Surely an early connection was drawn between loss of hearing and industrial noise. In 1830 Fosbrooke observed that the work environment of the blacksmith was such that hearing handicaps resulted from prolonged tenure in that occupation. A short while later the boilermaker was seen to have a characteristic occupationally related hearing loss. Since those early days the effect of noise on the industrial worker's hearing capability has become an increasing source of concern among hearing health specialists. But noise damage is not restricted to those whose jobs include large doses of sound stimulation. Former President Lyndon Johnson once said: "What was once . . . described as 'the busy hum of traffic' has now turned into an unbearable din for many citydwellers. We dare not be complacent about this ever-mounting volume of noise."

Noise obviously has made itself known. Few causes for the deterioration in the quality of life are so common to so many persons. Although the federal government's commitment was formerly not so sizable as noise researchers would like to see, that noise is being included in recent legislation and environmental quality pronouncements of elected officials is somewhat comforting. It is encouraging to learn that the summit environmental pact signed in Moscow during President Nixon's visit in May 1972 included noise as one of the environmental contaminants whose control the United States and the Soviet Union agreed to work on together.

OUT OF THE PAST

Noise is not an altogether new area of concern. In their introduction to the proceedings of a conference on Noise as a Public Health Hazard, W. D. Ward and James Fricke speculated that the first noise problem may have occurred when Eve poked Adam in the remaining ribs and told him to stop snoring. Many years ago the Roman poet Horace fiercely denounced the "barking of the mad bitch and the squealing of the filthy sow," two environmental noises that quite obviously disturbed him. In a modern translation of the Old Testament the prophet Amos, condemning the court of King Jeroboam, says, "Your musicians played so loudly in entertaining the rich that you could not hear when poor folks cried out for help!" In 1788, the philosopher Schopenhauer wrote, " . . . the truly infernal cracking of whips in the narrow resounding streets of the town must be denounced as the most unwarrantable and disgraceful of all noises." This early invective against traffic noise was not the first, though, for some accounts mention that a few Roman officials were disturbed by the sounds of chariot wheels on cobblestone streets.

On some occasions sound was used intentionally in order to torment and defeat an enemy. A third-century Chinese proposal for defeating the enemy prescribed that flutes, drums, and chimes or bells be sounded without hesitation until the adversaries dropped dead. The author of this formula believed that noise trauma was the most agonizing death he could conceive. A well-known example of sound as battle strategy is Joshua's victory at Jericho.

Because sound is one of the most familiar and useful parts of the environment it stands to reason that throughout history some sounds have served to distract and irritate people. The value of sound lies in the information it provides. If it contains no information it usually is regarded as noise. Sometimes, however, the decision on whether a sound is information or noise is not easy; frequently it contains some elements of both. Consider the sound of a machine. To the machinist it carries information because it gives him a clue about the machine's functioning. But for the person at another work station the sound is noise, for the only useful information it carries to him is the news that the blankity-blank thing is turned on again. This concept gives rise to a nearly infinite complexity that can be lumped under one heading—the human response to sound.

THE NOISE PROBLEM

A common catch phrase in the popular literature is "the noise problem," but it is important to note that the subject has not yet been reduced to a definable entity. It is safe to estimate that no one professionally concerned with noise fully understands enough about it to encapsulate it with a single or simple description. So the noise problem continues to be a mystery because neither the parameters nor the depth and breadth of each factor involved are understood well enough to allow comprehension of the full effect of sound stimulation on humans (and animals).

In addition to the problem of definition one must consider the wide range of individual differences in responsiveness to various sound stimuli. It can be said, for example, that noise for the parent is music for the child. Mental set, orientation, experience, personality, health, and myriad other personal factors confound the attempt to fully and comprehensively recognize all of the ramifications of "the noise problem."

One cannot be absolutely confident in predictions about how increasingly greater noise levels will affect future generations. Some have issued serious warnings about devastating problems that will beset later inhabitants of this planet if noise, along with other environmental contaminants, is not controlled and reduced. These forecasts may or may not be viable, and that is part of the problem—we don't know. Because noise is a natural by-product of expanding human technology, and wherever humans go they take their technology with them, environmental noise increases with continuing technological expansion.

Today's vast technology was triggered by the industrial revolution, which has proclaimed the philosophy that the machine should serve to ease human burdens, raise the standard of living, and multiply productivity. From the beginning, precious little regard has been paid to the health and aesthetic problems technology may bring about, which is unfortunate because the great minds that have designed and built complex and purposeful mechanisms are fully capable of incorporating environmental considerations into their designs. these,)

From an acoustician's stance the technological revolution has been a blight. It has given rise to noise-generating devices that with some thought about sound output during the design stages could have been made to function more quietly. A hopeful sign is that some industries now are beginning to assess the noise potential of their products. These steps are long overdue.

In 1968 the then Surgeon General Dr. William H. Stewart said: "Calling noise a nuisance is like calling smog an inconvenience. Noise must be considered a hazard to the health of people everywhere." Dr. Stewart thereby put noise in the same category as a virus, something to be controlled and where possible eliminated. During his keynote remarks before the First National Conference on Noise as a Public Health Hazard, Dr. Stewart declared, "These movements [steps toward abatement] must become stronger in our jet age world than the noise they seek to abate. Noise is not something we are going to be able to live with. It must be controlled, on the drawing boards and in the courts."

Why is noise exposure an area of such concern? Why prepare a descriptive book rather than design more experiments? These difficult questions defy adequate answers, but a basic response can be given. Noise affects uncountable aspects of our lives. The word *noise* and the word *nausea* have the same Latin root. Further, is it just coincidence that *noise* and *annoys* rhyme? These not very favorable relationships connote much more than simple or superficial response. Noise reaches into the depth of man's being and disrupts the complex processes that strive to maintain physical and chemical balances in the body. Noise is important in understanding the quality of life; so it is important to step out of the laboratory long enough to bring some of the most recent information to interested citizens. The words of a *New York Times* headline, "America Waking Up to Noise Pollution," hopefully are prophetic in that people soon will realize that noise in the environment deserves adequate treatment and control, for it will not just go away by itself.

In a ABC television documentary on noise, "Death Be Not Loud," Jules Bergman observed: "America is getting noisier and noisier. If you're hearing more and enjoying it less you're in good company, and there are plenty of reasons why. Noise is growing by one decibel a year. Nearly 10 million Americans already suffer hearing loss from noise."Although the figures and data are open to some question and cannot be held to be absolute for all persons in all locations, the statement represents the type of "wake up, America" cry that is part of the attempt to bring the noise problem to the country.

Breadth of the Problem

In essence environmental noise, in the occupational environment or in the recreational milieu, affects us at two levels. One level, annoyance, is quite general; the other, physical damage to the ear, is very specific.

Annoyance As an adjunct to continuous exposure to noise, the keen balances maintained in the body become disturbed, a state made known at the conscious level as the feeling of annoyance or stress. Stress induced by perpetual noise exposure has been listed as the cause of numerous physiological reactions. Blood vessels constrict, giving rise to increased blood pressure; heart rate increases; muscles become tense; perspiration tends to increase; adrenalin output rises markedly; kidneys become more active; liver function changes measurably; the pupils of the eye dilate; breathing rate increases; and changes in brain chemistry have been observed experimentally. There is, in effect, a general bodily reaction to noise, which in turn contributes to feelings of fatigue, irritability, or tension. In addition, physiologic imbalance as a result of industrial noise exposure has been found to contribute to lowered productivity and increased worker errors. Evidence is accumulating in support of the thesis that an inordinately high environmental noise level plays a large part in causing industrial accidents.

Many researchers prefer to determine annoyance rather than loudness because loudness is not a fully satisfactory measure of the degree to which a sound will disturb persons. As will be seen later, however, attempts to design an annoyance measure have met with only limited success; largely because of the huge number of undetermined physiological factors, each of which may contribute to the effect a particular sound may have at a given time.

Ear damage The ear contains thousands of tiny and delicate sensory cells that are indispensable to the functioning of the hearing sense. High-intensity sounds have the proven capability of destroying these cells. This very specific effect of noise has been the subject of continuing research for several years in the laboratory, and a good deal will be said about it in Chapters 2 and 3.

The hearing sense shares fluid with the balance sense; so to a large extent—especially when something goes wrong with one of them—the two senses interact and may be affected by each other's problems. Ear damage and excessive stimulation of the ear structures, then, can cause a collateral effect in the balance sense.

THE QUALITIES OF SOUND

The severe temptation to lapse at this point into a detailed and extensive discussion of sound and its physical properties will be subverted as well as possible in order to maintain interest and move quickly into other subject matter. However, a few concepts can be covered in general terms in order to lay a foundation for understanding the material to follow. More sophisticated readers may want to consult some of the excellent introductory textbooks cited in the references. Some subjects are omitted in this discussion because they will be explained as they are presented.

THE PROPERTIES OF SOUND

Sound is common to the environment. The hearing sense is constantly in the "on" mode; so we are continuously aware of the sounds around us. Only the deaf have experienced total absence of sound. Even in specially constructed rooms some sounds, although soft, are audible to persons who have good hearing. One such room is called an *anechoic chamber*, a name that implies a lack of echo. Any sound created within the confines of the room is absorbed by the walls and not allowed to reverberate back into the room. A handclap sounds peculiar because one hears only the initial coming together of the hands. The familiar ring of the sound dancing from one surface to another is absent. Sound in the anechoic chamber is different to say the least, but sound is still present. When sounds are not being made within the room a listener can have such strange auditory experiences as hearing the blood surging through the veins and arteries of the head in the region of the ear. In addition, *Brownian noise,* sound caused by the random collisions of air particles, may be heard. Several dimensions of sound evoke different responses.

Three Dimensions

All sound is generated by vibrating bodies that move back and forth during vibration. This motion creates alternating positive and negative pressure waves that change their speed of vibration according to changes in the vibrating structure. The faster the vibrating body moves, the higher is its frequency of vibration and the more rapidly the sound pressure waves change from the positive to the negative phase. Frequency was once described as cycles per second (c.p.s.) but now has the international standard designation hertz (Hz). A tuning fork vibrating 1,000 times per second causes a 1,000 Hz sound. This first dimension, *frequency*, a physical attribute of sound, has the psychological correlate *pitch*. A rapidly vibrating violin string is perceived as being high in pitch; one whose oscillations are less rapid reaches the awareness as a lower pitched musical sound. Several physical properties of the driving force, such as mass, length, and thickness, create these frequency changes.

A second dimension of sound is *amplitude*. The speed with which a sound source vibrates does not directly determine the strength of the sound. Sounds of a single frequency can be heard to be very soft or very loud, depending on the energy behind the sound wave. The wave strikes the ear with a certain force; so if the amplitude of the sound is great, the force will be great also. This physical event is comprehended psychologically as loudness. A unit of amplitude is a decibel (dB), a term used often throughout this book. Named in honor of Alexander Graham Bell, the decibel is a logarithmic unit that expresses the ratio between two pressures or powers. A somewhat confusing sidelight is that the decibel is used as the unit of measure for over 60 physical phenomena, including voltage in electrical calculations.

In this book the decibel is the unit used to describe the sound pressure or the sound power present in a particular environment. Its meaning is often abstract and can be confounding to those not familiar with acoustic terminology. A better understanding of sound pressure levels may be gained from Table 1.1, which details the relationship between familiar environmental sounds and their relative sound pressure levels in decibels.

Early students of sensation learned long ago that since many sensations do not grow in a linear fashion, doubling the output of the stimulating source does not necessarily result in a doubling of sensation. In fact, loudness growth has been found to lag behind stimulus growth in a nonlinear fashion (logarithmic). The mathematics of this situation can be avoided by means of two rules of thumb that may assist in understanding the dynamics of sound pressure growth: (1) doubling a sound pressure results in a 6 dB increase in the sound, regardless of whether the original sound was high or low in amplitude; (2) a 10-fold increase in sound pressure is measured as a 20 dB rise. These features hold throughout the range of hearing from the softest audible sound to the most intense a human can stand.

When a sound increases in pressure from 134 dB to 140 dB (the pressure is doubled), the change in sound pressure is 1 million times greater than when that sound is increased from 0 dB to 6 dB. Thus reduction of high-level sounds by even a small number of decibels is a significant reduction in the sound pressure and may mean the difference between discomfort and acceptability.

The recurring use of decibel values in this and other writings requires a clear understanding of the unit. Table 1.1, a compilation of published figures and some laboratory measures, may be used as a reference throughout this book in order to more fully understand the decibel levels being discussed. The representations in the table must be understood to be average levels; for example, many trucks may produce less noise than indicated in the table, whereas others may be noisier than indicated (a

Table 1.1   Reference Levels of Familiar Sounds (dBA).

Sound Level	Industrial (and Military)	Community (Outdoor)	Home (Indoor)
0 — Threshold of audibility (Brownian noise)			
10 — Barely detectable			
20 —			Very faint whisper (20)
30 —			Audible whisper (30)
40 —			Quiet office (40) Quiet residence (45)
50 —		Light traffic (50) Large transformer (53)	Average office (50)
60 —		Air conditioner (60) Near freeway (64)	Conversation (60)
— Annoying (65)			
70 —		Inside auto at 65 mph (77)	Fairly loud speech (70) Television audio (70) Noisy restaurant (70) Vacuum cleaner (74) Dishwasher (75) Living room music (76) Clothes washer (78)

80 — Intolerable for telephone use

Ear damage possible (85)

90 — Speech interference

100 — Very loud

110 —

— Maximum under federal law (115)

Tabulator (80)
Lathe (81)
Cotton spinning (83)
Milling (85)
Cockpit, prop (88)

Newspaper press (97)
Farm tractor (98)

Heat furnace (100)
Air hammer (100)

Textile loom (106)
Loom room (108)

Riveter (110)

Compacter (116)
Scraper-loader (117)

Diesel train (83)
Diesel truck (84)
Prop flyover at 1,000 ft. (88)
Motorcycle at 25 ft. (90)

Rock drill (92)
Compressor (94)
Power mower (96)

Police siren at 100 ft. (100)
Snowmobile (100)
Loud outboard (102)
Jet flyover at 1,000 ft. (103)
Loud motorcycle (105)
Loud mower (105)

Diesel truck accelerating (114)

Chain saw (118)

Loud singing (80)
Garbage disposal (80)

Food blender (88)

Loud shout (90)
Subway (90)
Cockpit, light plane (90)

Loud subway (95)

Table 1.1   (continued)

dB				
120 — Discomfort threshold	Oxygen torch (121)	Turbine generator (120)		Rock music (120)
	Armored personnel carrier (123)	Thunderclap (120)		
130 —		Air-raid siren (135)		
140 — Pain threshold		Jet at 10 ft. (140)		
		.22 caliber rifle (140)		
150 —		Jet, near by (150)		
		Shotgun (158)*		
160 —	M-1 rifle (161)*	Toy cap pistol (163)*		
170 —				
180 —		Apollo lift-off, close (188)		
190 —				

Theoretic maximum for pure tones (194)*

*The gunshot measurements and theoretic maximum are not expressed in A-weighted values.

problem related to our earlier discussion of the transient nature of sound). A fascinating aspect of the table is the rather incongruous groupings that occur; functionally unrelated appliances and machines are found to be identical in the amount of noise generated. Also, there are some surprises. Noise from some household items often is found to exceed the noise of many industrial machines that have for years been known to create dangerously great noise levels. The table is ordered according to the levels generally regarded as border areas for hearing safety and irritation.

Individual differences will cause some persons to disagree that a particular noise should be described as irritating even though in the chart it appears in that category. They may note further that some sounds outside the irritating range are quite irritating to them. This difference in opinion points up once again the confounding variability of the noise problem.

The format of the table is after that used by Dr. Alexander Cohen and his colleagues in their very informative treatment of the concept of *socioacusis*, a term Dr. Aram Glorig coined to describe the loss of hearing as a result of nonoccupational noise exposure.

A third dimension of sound is its complexity. Two frequently used illustrations of sound are shown in Figure 1.1. The height of the waves indicates the amplitude and the horizontal distance is time, indicating that during the creation of a sound time passes.

The top drawing (A) shows the simplest sound possible —the *sine wave*. When a sound generator is set to produce a sine wave the result is a *pure tone*, which is seldom heard in the environment. Since pure tones are used to test hearing, many are familiar with their sound quality.

The bottom drawing depicts a complex sound. Unlike the sine wave, this sound has no readily apparent regularity; rather, it consists of many up and down variations in amplitude, and the first portion of the sound does not seem to be repeated in any of the later portions. The two illustrations do have something very much in common, however. The complex sound is composed of several pure tones. With the use of expensive and sophisticated electronic equipment and a complicated

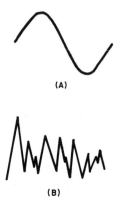

(A)

(B)

1.1   Examples of sound. The top illustration (A) is a sine wave, heard as a pure tone. (B) is a sketch of the type of picture street noise would give if shown on an oscilloscope.

mathematical formula complex sounds now can be separated into the various pure tone components.

The complexity of sounds made by various objects has its characteristic signature according to the way the pure tones combine, allowing persons to distinguish between, say, a violin and an oboe. Although both are playing the same note, their complexity (timbre) is specific to the instrument.

Though not to be considered one of the three characteristics of sound, *transience* should be mentioned. At a given moment in time a sound will be an admixture of a certain number of pure tones; then the next moment a completely different set of tones will comprise the sound. This transient quality gives sound an extremely complex nature. Sound measurement is difficult because sounds do not stay at the same level, but, as shown in Figure 1.1, are constantly changing.

Sound Propagation

Once sound has begun, the pressure wave travels away from the sound source. The most common example of *sound propagation* is the familiar view of ripples in a pool after a rock is dropped in the middle. To an extent this illusion is incomplete, for it must be remembered that sound waves radiate in all directions, not only in a single plane.

As the sound impulses move steadily away from the sound generator (a vibrating body) they move at certain rates of speed. The speed at which sound travels varies according to the medium through which it moves. For example, in air, at sea level, the speed of sound is given as 1,100 feet per second, or about 750 miles per hour. One common expression of this concept is that the speed of sound is *Mach 1*. An aircraft capable of flying at twice the speed of sound is called a Mach 2 plane.

Sound can travel through materials other than air. The density and elastic qualities of a medium combine to determine how rapidly the sound pressure wave can traverse the medium. The more dense a medium, the less speed the wave will have unless the elasticity of the medium is great. In steel sound travels much faster than in air (16,400 feet per second). Although steel is 6,000 times more dense than air it is nearly 2 million times more elastic; thus the speed of sound transmission through steel is considerably greater than through air. Sound travels 4,700 feet per second through water; so a sound pressure wave initiated by a boat will reach a nearby island approximately 4 times faster under water than through air. For this reason the chirps and whistles of dolphins and certain species of whales are a quite efficient means of communication. Sound will not travel in a vacuum, a fact readily demonstrated by placing a ringing bell in a bell jar and evacuating the air from the jar. The sound of the bell is steadily reduced as the vacuum becomes greater until no sound exists even though the clapper still moves.

Someone has suggested that the moon environment would have been improved had the astronauts set up a large speaker system and played contemporary rock music during their stay there. Of course, no sound would be emitted, except for the vibrations transmitted from the speaker case to and through the lunar surface. Perhaps the idea is not a good one, but such an environment might be considered a good one for loud rock music groups.

During propagation sound energy is dissipated so that the

level of a signal grows less as one moves away from the source. In an open area this reduction is 6 dB each time distance from the source is doubled.

SOUND MEASUREMENT

From the foregoing discussion it becomes obvious that the measurement of sound is a very complex matter. Several factors are included in sound measurement.

1. *Amplitude.*   Prior to a sound survey the major question concerns the strength of the sound present. Answers are supplied by means of special equipment that distinguishes the amplitude in decibels. Figure 1.1 shows some results of two amplitude measures.

2. *Frequency.*   It has been stated that sound is made up of a large number of tones. Some sounds have a concentration of low-pitched tones; others are primarily a combination of high-pitched sounds; still others have a representation of many frequencies, both high and low. Often one must know the frequencies a particular sound contains. Frequencies are especially important to the control engineer, for sound treatment varies according to the frequencies (pitches) a noise source generates.

3. *Duration.*   Sounds of longer duration are generally more irritating or dangerous than are briefer sounds of the same amplitude. The length of time a sound occurs is important to the acoustical analyst.

4. *Timing.*   Sounds that occur during the sleeping hours are more distressing than are identical noises during the waking period. A thoroughgoing sound analysis includes the amount of time the sound in a particular environment extends into the sleep hours. Recent federal publications favor a sound analyzing technique which considers the hours between 10:00 p.m. and 7:00 a.m. as nighttime hours. A 10 dB penalty is added to all nighttime sounds in calculating overall noise levels.

5. *Intermittence.*   The on and off effects of noises vary with the rapidity and regularity of the cycle. Irregularly interrupted sounds often are more disturbing, for one cannot ignore them so readily.

6. *Character.* The character of a sound depends on whether it is continuous (steady state) or impulse. The sound most machinery makes is steady state, whereas gunfire or other sharp reports are characterized as impulse sounds. Measurement of the two types of sound varies widely because of the requirements for test and measuring equipment.

The American National Standards Institute (ANSI) has developed guidelines for making and reporting sound measures. This standardization ensures that sound measures can be compared even though they were not made in the same location or by the same person, thereby allowing the compilation of data such as that in Table 1.1 with the free knowledge that no gross errors appear in the measures, depending on the source.

Measuring Equipment

The equipment manufactured for sound evaluations is made to conform to the ANSI standards of performance. The precision and flexibility of measuring instruments varies according to the purpose of the device.

Sensitivity of such units must be great, for they are required to be responsive to a reference sound pressure as small as one

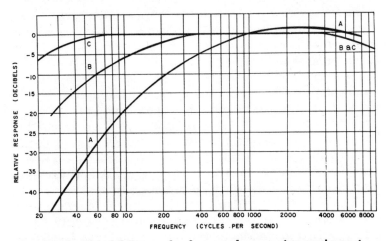

1.2   Standard weighting scales for sound-measuring equipment.

ten-thousandth of a millionth of normal atmospheric pressure (0.0002 microbar of 20 micronewtons/meter^2), a force Dr. Wayne Rudmose has described as "just about the push of a healthy mosquito." Translated to power this level of sound is one trillionth of a watt (10^{-12} watt). The range of measuring instruments must likewise be wide, for they are sometimes called on to respond accurately to sound pressure waves more than 100 million times greater than the reference pressure.

General-purpose sound meters are used to measure the sound present at or during a given moment or during a given set of event conditions. These devices consist of a good-quality microphone, an amplifying circuit, an indicating meter, and a power supply (usually a battery for portability). Most meters can be modified by manipulating a switch so that the responsiveness of the internal circuitry is altered to meet one of three standard weighting scales (see Figure 1.2). The "C" weighting scale allows a flat response in that the meter is equally sensitive to all sounds in its operating range. The "A" scale is regarded to approximate the human ear's frequency response by slightly filtering out the lower frequencies. The frequency response of the seldom used "B" scale lies in the midrange between A and C. In recent years the "A" scale has found favor as the measuring mode for determining human correlates of sound (again note Figure 1.1). Remember, however, that the "A" scale is only an *approximation* of the way a human ear responds; so "A" scale readings must be interpreted in that light.

The more sophisticated technology in the burgeoning instrumentation field has provided numerous additional ways to measure and analyze sound. The octave band analyzer is designed to utilize precisely tuned electronic filters in order to sample octave elements of a sound. Readings taken with this type of equipment yield information about whether the sound in question is primarily flat, high frequency, or low frequency. For more definition of the sound even more narrow filters can be used to measure 1/2, 1/3, or 1/10 octave bands. Computer technology has further refined the analytical capability of instrumentation so that some current versions of sound analyzers have the capability of measuring the acoustic pressure in very small bands, sometimes less than 1 Hz wide.

HUMAN RESPONSE TO SOUND

Physical measures of sound in the environment certainly can be made with exceptionally good reliability and accuracy as recent additions to the acoustician's wares have increased his ability to partially overcome sound's transient and unpredictable nature. Yet a most important factor cannot be overlooked: the receptor of the sound is a human, which creates another knotty problem as psychoacoustic factors (human psychological response to sound) enter the picture.

Not all people respond to sound in the same way. The range of human sensitivity to sound is wide; hence some perceive sound as being more intense than do others. Numerous psychological reasons account for additional variations among persons in responsiveness to sound stimulation.

The unit of sound amplitude (the decibel) can be well defined, but applying the decibel concept to noisiness is not an easy task. Psychophysical techniques have been developed with an understanding of the reality of individual variation in stimulus response. (University of Tennessee students learn this concept as the "Lipscomb Law of Individual Differences.") Regardless of the sensory mode, the sensation a given stimulus creates is modified by the state of the entire person. For example, very irritable persons will as a group be more bothered by aircraft noise than will low-key individuals. Persons engaged in precise activities will find aircraft flyovers more distracting than will laborers involved in gross tasks. It should be readily apparent that in the "perceived noisiness" category these variations severely limit attempts to scale psychological responses to given sounds.

If people were to be daunted and inhibited by such limits, however, the study of noise would be chaotic. Recognizing wide variations among individuals, several persons embarked on the arduous task of establishing methods and scales whereby human responses to sound amplitude and quality factors could be better understood. These attempts have had some degree of success in that several scaling methods have been developed and have served as springboards for development of the noy scale. When after an attempt to compare sound level measures of aircraft flyovers with loudness judgment it became apparent that the previously used methods did not hold at all levels, Dr. Karl Kryter and his associates established the noy scale by asking trained listeners to judge when a sound was twice as noisy as the previous sound. This judgment introduced into the scale the highly subjective but necessary irritation factor. Their scale was revised later to incorporate the use of octave measures, which provided the foundation for the *perceived noise level* concept.

During the early stages of commercial jet use the high-pitched whine of the engines seemed more annoying than the sound of propeller-driven aircraft. To account for this problem the noy scale was revised to give more weight to the higher frequencies in jet aircraft noise. This scale, *perceived noise level in decibels* (PNdB), provides a single-number value of the noisiness of aircraft flyovers. A further modification, effective perceived noise level (EPNdB), was given great play in the media during the SST controversy. Basically this new version takes into account the frequency of takeoffs and the time they occur.

Although these scaling methods are quite often used to determine aircraft noise levels they have not found much favor in other areas of environmental noise study. In aircraft studies, however, EPNdB calculations permit the plotting of noise level isocontours around airports in order to judge the irritation airplanes will cause in the surrounding communities.

Whereas the EPNdB represents here-and-now conditions, a further modification of the scale, the noise exposure forecast (NEF), is geared to predictive factors. Isocontours drawn around future airports are plotted according to NEF estimations and will serve to improve land use habits in neighboring areas of future airports.

The calculation of PNdB values is a rather arduous task, but a simple rule greatly eases the job. Although not fully accurate, the addition of 13 to the measured sound level using the "A" weighting scale (dBA) will yield approximately the PNdB. For example, a 92 dBA plane flyover would be nearly equivalent to 105 PNdB.

To assess human response to another very common environmental sound, traffic noise, the traffic noise index (TNI) was conceived. The level above which traffic noise monitored at a given location for 24 hours rose 10 percent of the time is combined in a formula with the level exceeded 90 percent of the time. The resulting number is compared to a chart in order to determine the dissatisfaction factor.

The concept of equivalent energy forms the framework for an important means whereby sound analyses are performed. The total exposure to a sound is calculated according to the energy exerted against the ear. For example, exposure to a 100 dB sound for 3 hours is equivalent to hearing a 97 dB sound for 6 hours. From this basis, equivalent loudness (Leq) can be used for scaling noise in the environment. The day-night loudness (Ldn) is Leq with a 10 dB penalty given to sounds which have occurred in the nighttime hours of 10:00 p.m. to 7:00 a.m. Recent trends indicate that Ldn is rapidly becoming a popular means of evaluating environmental sound.

As seen, the problem in using purely physical measures of sound as indicators of environmental quality is that similar acoustic events arouse widely differing reactions among individuals. Psychoacoustic techniques still entail so many variations that the physically based single-number environmental quality index remains a gleam in the psychoacoustician's eyes. To further cloud the issue a trading relationship exists between signal amplitude and its duration. This relationship is also affected by the frequency characteristics and recurrence of the sound.

All of the scaling methods described attempt to reduce the sound environment and human reaction to that sound to a set of numbers that can be plotted graphically. Therein lies a serious danger. A graph that displays noisiness characteristics of aircraft flyovers (or of any other sound source) leaves the impression that the levels are stabilized and fully predictable. Most presentations give little or no indication that the line of the chart is an approximation of an estimate of some midline determined by means of listeners asked to judge noisiness characteristics in some selected sounds. This observation is made to caution that EPNdB and all related single-number scaling devices are not so accurate that they can be discussed as absolutes. The range of variations is wide enough to cause serious questions about the appropriateness of these scaling methods in future planning of airports or other sources of community noise. Ldn scaling seems to be more promising in this respect.

HOW NOISE WORKS

Noise has been classified as insidious in our environment because its effects appear slowly. In fact, the effects of noise exposure may not become apparent until long after exposures have begun.

That noise is an undesirable element in the environment is readily apparent in the way unwanted sounds often impede the hearing of desired sounds. Life is spent in a world of competing signals, some of which are at times extremely important and at other times ignored. A sound one does not want to attend to can be considered noise; sounds a person is interested in are signals. Figure 1.3 is a schematic representation of the signal-to-noise concept. All three boxes carry a signal, the arabic numeral 1. The clear box leaves little doubt about the importance and availability of the signal. The other lines in the middle box represent noise. Since the noise is not too great, the signal is still quite easily discerned. The third box indicates an undesirable signal-to-noise ratio (S/N ratio) in that the noise, represented by cross-hatched lines, nearly obliterates the signal.

In like manner the audible sounds one wants to listen to or must hear may become lost in the background of interfering noise. This condition is called masking because the noise covers, or masks, signals. In general, the better the signal-to-noise ratio, the more clearly audible the desired sound will be.

Speech interference is one effect of excessive noise in the environment. In fact, when background noise levels reach a level of 80 dBA one's ability to hear conversation accurately is dramatically reduced. Most speech is understood by means of the vowels; the consonants contribute fine differences in content but, unfortunately, are more easily masked out by background noise, thereby impairing speech reception. Noise puts us in the same condition as the old person with hearing loss who responds "What's the time?" to the question "Are you fine?". One can hardly attempt to estimate the number of misconcep-

1.3   A schematic representation of signal-versus-noise conditions.

tions that have occurred in conversations because background noise precluded accurate speech reception.

The topic of this book is noise and its effects. However, extreme quiet in the environment also can be alarming, perhaps because man has been so accustomed to a noisy world that an abrupt interruption of noise is disturbing. A pilot taking off from Kennedy International Airport cut back on the throttle too much and apparently stopped the engines. The passengers experienced a loud quiet for a few seconds until the reassuring roar of the engines resumed. Few experiences can be more unnerving than that sudden onset of stillness.

When an anechoic chamber under construction at a midwestern university neared completion and the lack of echo and great quiet descended on the workmen, some found they could not stand the environment and became quite ill. To solve the problem a radio was brought in and played at near-maximum level until construction was completed. One day the radio gave out just before noon and no other was available. The rush to complete the room was so pressing that the workmen turned on a portable power saw and let it run the rest of the day so that they could stand to work in the room. In this case extreme quiet could be said to be disquieting.

THE END OF THE BEGINNING

Noise is a complex but fascinating area of study. Now we must discuss in detail some of the features that contribute to the overall noise situation. One can no longer pick up a newspaper without encountering comments, cartoons, or commentaries on noise. For example, in a popular cartoon the Senator asks his aide whether political speeches are exempt from a pending bill on noise pollution.

·2·

WITH EARS TO HEAR

He that hath ears to hear, let him hear.
Mark 4:9

In *The Virginians* W. M. Thackeray paraphrased the citation: "He that hath ears to hear, let him stuff them with cotton." The direction in which the environmental noise situation seems to be headed may make Thackeray's advice more true than humorous.

Auditory researchers have the great challenge of learning more about the ear and its function and the things that cause it to cease functioning. Director of the Kresge Hearing Research Laboratory in Portland, Oregon, Dr. Jack Vernon has stated this idea in beautiful terms.

> The overall aim of the laboratory is any investigation which will help preserve, restore, replace, or understand the ear . . . what we seek is to better understand hearing, a process understood only by nature and she destroyed all her records long ago. . . . To be allowed to investigate anything so sacred as the ear is indeed the all-time great honor. It is without doubt, the most exciting detective story of recorded time, but it unravels with appalling slowness and perhaps one of our greatest trials is to learn patience.
>
> The challenge of nature then, is the stuff and substance of research and we have presumed to tackle one of its most important and best hidden secrets.

Thus it is clear that the ear is a physical structure exciting in its challenging secrets and also one regarded with great esteem by those who attempt to uncover its mysteries.

This chapter is directed toward fostering a deeper appreciation of the ear and its qualities, but if one becomes dazzled by the intricacies and possibilities in the sense of hearing, so much the better. Possibly the best means of encouraging people to preserve something is to make them aware of how lost they would be without it. Ordinarily the ear comes with a lifetime guarantee of good or quite good working condition. If it is assaulted too often or too long by noise, however, the remarkable feats the ear is capable of are most certainly diminished in both number and quality.

A very brief introduction to the structure of the ear is necessary here. Figure 2.1 is a simplified drawing of the various parts of the ear, which is divided into four areas. The outer ear consists of the earflap and a tube that leads to the eardrum. Vibrations imparted to the eardrum are transmitted across the middle ear by three tiny bones. Then the innermost bone rocks in and out of its location, transferring the vibrations to the inner ear region. By a very complicated process the inner ear (cochlea) converts the vibrations into nerve impulses, which the fourth element, the nerve of hearing, carries to the brain.

Although auditory function appears to be blessed with an overabundance of components, the steady deterioration of these parts leads inevitably to a loss of communication skills; how grave depends on how widespread the damage becomes. Fortunately, in the scheme of creation the ear was held to be important enough to have a backup system. Thus with two ears a person may retain auditory capabilities if some untoward incident robs him of one of the hearing systems. Not uncommonly, diseases such as mumps result in total loss of hearing on one side, but fortunately the victim is not relegated to a lifetime of silence. Other factors, including heredity, also may result in the loss of one ear. Usually the person is aware of the loss, but not always. In our audiology clinic several years ago a tearful mother of a 15-year-old boy related how he approached her one day a short while before their visit with the comment, "Ya know, Mom, it is sure funny that God gives us two ears but only one of them works!" That was the mother's first indication that her son did not have bilateral hearing capability even though the results of the hearing test indicated that he had no usable hearing in one ear. Apparently this situation had existed from birth or early childhood, but the young man's adjustment to his condition had been so good that for 15 years his family was unaware of the deaf ear.

The value and irreplaceability of the ear is indicated again in the hearing mechanism's deeply sheltered position within the head and in its cover of bone, the densest in the body. The *petrosal* bone, a dense portion of the skull that lies directly under the middle side region of the brain, protects the precious and delicate portions of the ear from harm. Classes in the anatomy of the ear are cautioned that if they are called rockheads they shouldn't be angry but should compliment the name caller on his knowledge of anatomy.

Hearing provides man with the only distant 360-degree warning sense. The sense of touch, of course, also covers all sides of the body, but touch often warns too late. If a small animal could depend only on touch to tell him of the approach of a predator, the only message he would receive is, "He's got me!" Audition, a noncontact warning mode, alerts one to approaching danger or allows time to react to the warning shouts of others when one is in a potentially hurtful situation. Any hearing loss can be a serious handicap to safe living. Coal miners are conditioned (usually by sad experience) to recognize a certain cracking sound as the onset of a bump—a sudden dropping of coal from the ceiling or walls. This hazard has claimed many lives and has caused others serious injury. Continuous exposure to noise and the subsequent loss of hearing cause the miner to miss this warning signal.

Hearing is also a vital learning sense. Although all of the senses contribute to learning, communication through the auditory channels is extremely important, particularly to children. A school principal who decided to prove this concept asked teachers of the deaf, blind, and mentally retarded classes to bring their brightest student to a PTA meeting. At the beginning of the meeting the teachers were instructed to take their children to the classrooms and for the next 30 minutes use any resource they could muster to teach their student the concept *macroscopic*. During their absence the principal discussed the relative learning problems of each child. At the end of the instruction session when the children returned to the meeting the principal asked each child in turn to explain the term as best he could. The blind child quickly offered a definition and several examples alluding to hugeness. The mentally retarded child gave simple explanations of bigness and size, which also indicated that she had understood the concept. The deaf child, however, could not provide any indication of what the descriptive word meant to him, nor could he communicate any degree of learning. Such concepts as time, color, distance, which we take for granted, are immensely difficult to the severely hard of hearing or deaf person.

DEVELOPMENT OF THE EAR

The ear has had a long history of developments, modifications, and innovations as natural processes have worked to provide a more than adequate hearing mechanism. About 600 million years ago, with the beginning of life on earth in the form of tiny, single-celled water creatures, the history of the ear began. As these simple animals diversified and developed into multicellular types, some grew larger than others and became predators. In response to this imbalance protective spines and rudimentary armament took form on the smaller creatures of the sea. These spines continued to modify and became fins, which were primitive appendages. Early fishes developed a relatively simple ear structure, more important to the balance sense than to the response to sonic signals. However, advanced fishes developed a more sophisticated hearing and balance mechanism that apparently works adequately, for recent research findings at Princeton University give some indication that fishes certainly can hear tones.

An animal immersed in water does not need a highly complex ear, for sound waves carried through the fluid are quite capable of stimulating the fluid-filled inner ear. However, in the migration of sea creatures onto the land a hearing problem of great consequence developed. As an aside Dr. Merle Lawrence of the University of Michigan shows a delightful slide in which two early amphibians are half in and half out of the water heading onto the land. One turns to the other and says, "Well, here goes nothing!"

Airborne sound does not easily penetrate water. Anglers can talk to each other with little fear of scaring away their piscatorial prizes, for 99.9 percent of the sound bounces off the surface of the water, and the remaining amount, less than 0.01 percent, becomes waterborne vibrations, amounting to a transmission loss of about 35 dB. Thus early earth creatures may have had fish-type ears that consisted only of a fluid-filled chamber (inner ear). Since the airborne sounds were inadequate in driving the message to the ear, the amphibians would have had a hearing loss in the neighborhood of 35 dB and might have wished for a hearing aid. Then the earlier predator-prey situation recurred because the larger, more lumbering predators had little trouble in clumsily sneaking up on the smaller creatures, who could not hear them until it was too late.

To overcome this problem the ear underwent some striking modifications that resulted in the middle ear. Airborne stimuli were carried more efficiently to the inner ear so that land animals' auditory awareness improved by more than 25 dB. This process was gradual and can still be seen in a more rudimentary state in some animals such as frogs and other amphibians. Their middle ear does not house three bones; rather, a single columella spans the distance from the eardrum to the inner ear chamber. The importance of this development cannot be underrated, for it may well have been a major determining factor in man's continued existence. Without the middle ear man's predecessors could have been gobbled up centuries ago. This possibility has caused Dr. El Mofty of Cairo, Egypt, to speculate that the development of the middle ear was one of the most significant acts in the theater of evolution.

Development of the inner ear begins in a fetus only a few days after conception. By the end of the third month the inner ear is completed and is nearly adult size. Other parts of the ear are developed later, but the inner ear is one of the very earliest of the complex organisms of the body to reach completion.

HOW THE EAR WORKS

As sound travels through the ear it undergoes a series of transformations. The sites of these transformations can be seen clearly in Figure 2.1.

The acoustic vibrations borne by the air set the eardrum in motion. Here the first transformation takes place as the acoustic energy is changed into mechanical energy—the movement of the three tiny bones. At the base of the smallest bone another change takes place when the pulsing motion of the stirrup-shaped bone creates a type of hydraulic energy in the inner ear.

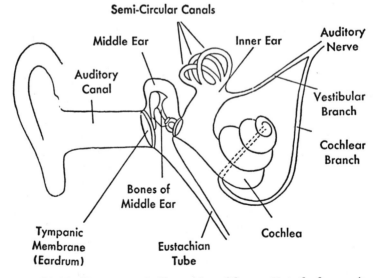

2.1   A highly diagrammatic illustration of the ear. Note the four major subdivisions—outer ear, middle ear, inner ear, and nerve pathways.

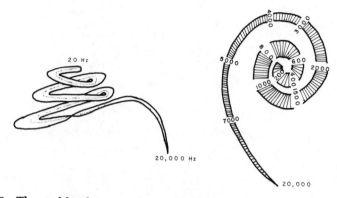

2.2 The cochlea has a central core around which a membrane revolves in spiral staircase fashion. This membrane supports the many sensory cells of the ear.

The final conversion takes place in the inner ear, where the cochlear activity generates chemical-electric events, triggering nerve impulses that are taken to the brain by way of the nerve of hearing. All of these transformations occur almost instantaneously so that the ear does not appreciably slow down the transmission of acoustic information.

For primarily acoustic reasons the ear is not equally responsive to all sounds. Low-pitched sounds—those below the middle C note on a piano—and high-pitched sounds—those above high C—are not so well received as sounds in the midrange. The middle frequencies carry the most important information to man, and the ear is most efficient in that frequency range.

The most familiar pathway for sound is that described during discussion of the ear's structure. This *air conduction* pathway is primary. Another pathway is called *bone conduction.* Some sound, especially the sound of one's voice, sets the bones of the skull in vibration, and these signals are carried directly into the inner ear. A person hears his or her own voice more by bone conduction, which gives the voice a sound slightly different from that in the air conduction mode. Since one is accustomed to his voice quality as he hears it, a voice recording is quite surprising. The usual exclamation is, "But that doesn't

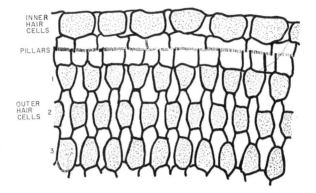

2.3   The sensory cell region of the guinea pig is shown in schematic form. Note the geometric cell organization.

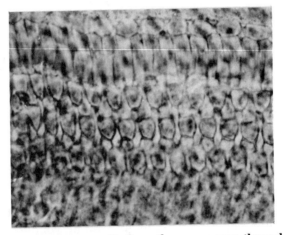

2.4   Guinea pig sensory cells from the ear as seen through a high-powered microscope (1000X).

sound like me!" The confusion occurs because modes of sound presentation to our ears are changed.

Although all parts of the ear are remarkably important to the ear's function, the cochlea (inner ear) deserves preferred treatment since that area receives the major destruction after intense noise stimulation. Figure 2.2 is a diagrammatic view of the cochlea as it would appear if the outer covering of bone were removed. The partition that looks like a spiral staircase is a membrane that holds the sensory cells for hearing. Each cochlea contains about 16,000 cells, which are responsible for converting the fluid vibrations into nerve impulses. A schematic view of these cells appears in Figure 2.3. Although these illustrations were drawn from animal ears, the similarities among mammal ears permit the use of animal tissues to show the effect of sound on the ear. The guinea pig inner ear, diagrammed in Figure 2.3 as if viewed from above, has a very regular organization that consists of a single row of *inner hair cells* and three rows of *outer hair cells*, so called because of the groups of tiny hairs atop the cells. These hairs play an important part in stimulation of the cell. The outer hair cells are staggered but remain geometrically consistent. The actual guinea pig ear tissue magnified more than 1,000 times is shown in Figure 2.4. It is possible to distinguish all of the rows of cells shown in Figure 2.3.

Aside from being the major site of noise damage, the cochlea is the only place where a total hearing loss can be caused. Removal of the middle ear will result in a hearing handicap but not a total impairment. Removal of the area of the brain responsible for giving meaning to the auditory nerve impulses will result in some degree of hearing decrement but not a total loss. If one suffered a severe infection or a fracture of the cochlea, however, the likelihood of a total hearing loss would be great. The cochlea, then, is a most valuable member of the hearing system and should be well guarded as Nature intended when it initially provided such great protection.

MORE REMARKABLE FEATURES

Most people know that too much noise exposure will cause permanent damage to the inner ear; yet, probably few people fully grasp the consequences of constant deterioration of the hearing sense. Therefore, we hope here to further establish the value of the ear. The ear does not come with an "on" or "off" switch; no earlids shut in order to provide some rest for these organs. They are always "on" and doing all possible to report on the sounds in the environment. That this state is both a blessing and a curse is abundantly apparent to those who have lived in the industrialized environment.

In a discussion such as this it is not possible to provide a detailed description of all the features of the sensory mechanism called the ear. Perhaps brief mention of several special characteristics of the *intact* ear will be sufficient.

1. The normal ear is extremely sensitive to sound. A signal can be perceived even though the force behind it is sufficient to move the eardrum only one one-hundred-millionth of an inch (less than one one-hundredth the width of a hydrogen molecule).

2. In the outer ear canal special cells secrete a foul, bitter-tasting substance that is toxic and repulsive to small flying insects. As a protective agent this ear wax fends off insects and traps dust or other foreign particles that otherwise might cause irritation of the delicate eardrum.

3. To discourage the overaccumulation of wax and other material in the ear canal, the skin layer of the canal migrates toward the outside. This physiological conveyer belt takes the old wax and its trapped particles out of the region of the eardrum. Occasionally a tiny tickling sensation at the ear announces the deposit of a small chunk of wax in the depression of the ear. The conveyer mechanism is keeping the ear canal unoccluded.

4. The ear structure holds several records. The hardness of the petrosal bone was mentioned earlier. In addition, the three bones of the middle ear are the smallest and hardest in the body. The smallest of these is the innermost bone, the stirrup, which measures only 3.3 mm high and 3.0 mm across at the base and weighs less than 3/1000ths of a gram. Attached to the stirrup is the body's tiniest muscle, which serves to make the stirrup's resistance greater, thereby partially protecting the inner ear from loud sounds.

5. To ensure proper functioning of the ear a venting tube connects the middle ear with the mouth cavity. This Eustachian tube allows air in or out of the middle ear in order to equalize the pressure of the middle ear with the outside world. As one travels to a high altitude his ears pop, a sensation that comes when air has left the middle ear through the tube. On returning to lower elevations the reverse occurs, and the air is equalized once again.

6. The inner ear is populated with approximately 16,000 sensory cells, and nearly 30,000 nerve fibers leave each ear to carry the message to the brain. But no simple two-to-one relationship exists between the nerve fibers and the sensory cells they serve. To allow the capability to perceive highly complex signals the innervation pathway to the brain must be likewise complex. It is so complex, in fact, that one student of the ear has estimated that a single nerve fiber leaving the inner ear has the potential to stimulate as many as 618,000 cells at the cortical level (in the gray matter of the brain).

7. To a certain extent humans can select what they hear. In numerous situations it is possible to attend to one sound in preference to another—if the ears are intact, that is. An early sign of cochlear damage is the noticeable deterioration of one's ability to hear conversations in somewhat noisy environments.

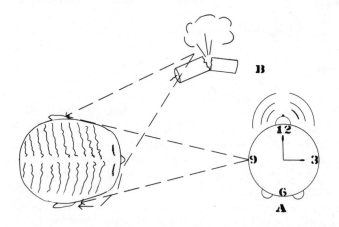

2.5   Auditory triangulation wherein the triangle drawn between a sound source and the two ears indicates the time the sound will arrive at each of the two ears.

8. The ears can determine the location of sounds by attending to the differences in arrival time of sounds at the two ears. Figure 2.5 depicts the concept of *auditory triangulation*. Note that the bursting firecracker is to one side, causing the sound to travel farther to one ear than to the other. The ears handle this time relationship and alert the brain to a sound occurring to one side. Because the alarm clock (truly one of the great noxious sound sources) is located at midline, the jangling sound reaches both ears simultaneously and is perceived as being on the center plane of the head. This capability, *auditory localization*, is made possible by our ears' rapid handling of the acoustic sounds. It has been determined that sounds arriving at the ears only 30 millionths of a second apart can be localized.

9. A quite recent discovery has indicated that the route between the ear and the brain is a two-way street. In addition to the nerve impulses that travel from the ear, a nerve pathway from the brain to the ear has been found. The pathway's function is not well understood, but some have speculated that it may serve to inhibit sensory nerve impulses. In this way the ear's response could be placed under control of the brain. This concept must wait for verification until further experiments have been completed.

10. The intact normal human ear can detect as many as 280 different intensity levels between the softest sound it can hear and the most intense sound it can tolerate. In addition, the normal ear can note over 1,400 pitch changes. These two types of auditory information combined allow the intact ear to distinguish as many as 300,000 to 400,000 discrete combinations of pitch and intensity—a feat that permits the human to be the communicating animal he is.

It must be added that when the ear has undergone modification due to damage, even slight damage, loss of these remarkable communication skills follows. Unfortunately, the damage that occurs in the inner ear is permanent in that no known mechanism can regenerate these damaged sensory cells. The point cannot be made strongly enough that noise damage will have a permanent and often dramatic effect on one's life.

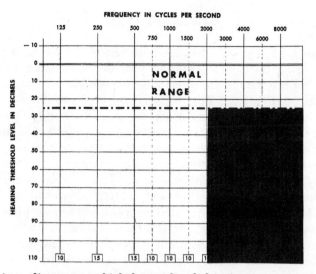

2.6   An audiogram on which the results of a hearing test are recorded. The darkened region locates the high-frequency impairment area.

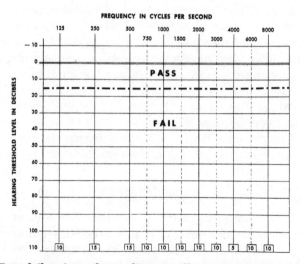

2.7   Pass-fail regions of an audiogram, illustrating the screening level of hearing surveys to be reported later.

HEARING TESTS

Some of the information in this book relates to the interpretation of hearing tests; so an introduction to the basic concepts of hearing test results and their interpretation will be useful. An audiogram, shown in Figure 2.6, is used to record the results of a hearing test. The vertical lines indicate the various test frequencies, ranging from a low-frequency tone at the left (125 Hz) to a high-frequency tone at the right (8,000 Hz). Each horizontal line represents sound pressure in decibels according to standards based on responses of the normal ear. The "0" line near the top of the audiogram is the "normal hearing" line.

In a hearing evaluation the subject receives pure tones, and the decibel value of the sound level where he barely heard the tones is recorded. A person is to be *clinically* within the normal range if he has hearing impairment no greater than 25 dB. A shaded area in the lower right corner of the audiogram is considered the range of high-frequency impairment. Noise exposure that caused permanent damage to the inner ear is reflected by a loss of hearing in the high frequencies. If the pathological condition persists, as might be so in continued exposure to noise, the resulting loss of hearing may not be restricted to this range.

In Chapter 3 results of hearing tests on several populations will be discussed. These tests were based on a criterion level of 15 dB, which is somewhat strict because it was the intent of the surveys to identify early hearing threshold shifts. The data indicate how many persons failed to respond in the pass region of the audiogram (see Figure 2.7). This interpretation was restricted to test frequencies at and above 2,000 Hz.

CONCLUSION

The ear is a truly magnificent structure. It was designed throughout eons by tests and trials in primitive animals and other forms of living creatures, and has become a remarkably efficient receptor sense in terms of preservation of life as well as the preservation of the quality of life. It makes good sense to protect this valuable organ with every means available.

•3•

Hurt without Pain

To destroy is still the strongest instinct of our nature.
Max Beerbohm

Max Born won the Nobel Prize in Physics in 1955. Two years later in the *Bulletin of the Atomic Scientists* he wrote: "The human race has today the means for annihilating itself—either in a fit of complete lunacy, i.e. in a big war, by a brief fit of destruction, or by a careless handling of atomic technology, through a slow process of poisoning and of deterioration in its genetic structure."

This great physicist's concern was that misuse of our resources might lead to ultimate catastrophe. Although not nearly so dramatic as the possibility of a life-ending holocaust, the threat of losing part of the human life quality may also loom ahead. Persons concerned about the environment have been issuing such warnings for some time. To the list of danger areas might be added the regrettable eventuality of hearing damage.

The inner ear, which suffers the brunt of destructively intense sounds, has no pain receptors, hence no sensation akin to the hurt felt after being cut or burned. To be sure, the inner ear has some means of warning of impending danger, but these warning signs are quite subtle and are missed most times. So the favorite adage of children at play, "Sticks and stones may break my bones, but words will never hurt me!" does not hold. Words or any other sound delivered with sufficient force to the ears can and will cause irreversible destruction to portions of the hearing

45

sensory mechanism. Even though they are located in the inner ear and protected by a dense shell of bone, the several thousand sensory receptor cells that play a major role in the normal functioning of the hearing sense are in jeopardy when noise levels reach ever-increasing new peaks.

Most people do not fully realize nor well appreciate the dangers in high-intensity sound. The ear is, however, a truly miraculous product of creative genius, which deserves to be protected from undue harm at all costs.

WARNING SIGNS

Noise not only can be disruptive, leaving one upset and feeling out of sorts, but also is destructive to the tiny and irreplaceable sensory cells in the inner ear. Several signs warn of the danger of intense sound to the ear structures.

1. When in the presence of high-level sound voice communication is extremely difficult or impossible, the sound level is dangerously high. One common environment in which this condition persists is the discotheque filled with the greatly amplified sounds of contemporary musical aggregations.

2. If on leaving a noisy environment the ears ring or buzz, exposure has been excessive and some degree of ear damage may have occurred, although normally it would be very slight. A single exposure to high-level noise certainly will not create a severe loss of hearing, but repeated exposure will bring about an accumulation of effect and can grow into a sizable problem.

3. Some persons notice a shift in hearing sensitivity after high-intensity noise exposure. That noise source should be studiously avoided. Although the hearing usually will return to normal after an appropriate rest period, repeated exposure may result in permanent ear damage.

4. During some episodes of extreme high-intensity noise exposure pain may be experienced. This tickle or piercing sensation arises when sound overstresses the eardrum; it is not related to inner ear sensations, where no mechanism for pain exists. When the pain threshold has been reached, damage cannot be avoided unless the exposures are for exceptionally brief periods of time and are spaced far apart.

5. The hearing and balance senses share the same closet —the inner ear; so high-level sounds may cause some effect in spatial stability and steadiness. Persons subjected to sounds that cause unsureness in locomotive capabilities, or downright dizziness and nausea, should avoid such episodes, for the sound may be causing ear damage as well as disrupting the balance mechanism.

6. After noise exposure some persons become highly disagreeable and tense. This nervous reaction may be occasioned by sound that over time may be hazardous.

7. In a New York medical college experiment women earlier found to be sterile were subjected to periods of quite intense sound stimulation. The sound was so intense that the women complained of numerous problems, including the onset of headaches. Although the experiment apparently gave favorable results in that several women began to ovulate, one must question whether the technique was advisable because of the duress it caused. The headache complaint is a rather nebulous one, because it is impossible to discern whether noise alone or a combination of effects caused the condition. If certain types of headaches can be traced to specific noise exposure events, the noise may be intense enough to have an otodamaging (ear destructive) capability.

Wide latitude must be given to interpretations of discussions of the warning signs of noise exposure, for the human's complex nature makes it exceptionally difficult to nail down specific cause/effect relationships with some simple formula or list of hazardous conditions. Individual differences in susceptibility to noise damage cause considerable problems. For example, most studies that have compared hearing losses among male and female factory workers point out that males as a group demonstrate significantly greater hearing impairment than do women who work in the same area. This factor gives some additional ammunition to those who espouse Ashley

Montagu's thesis that the female is the superior animal. It would be nice to say that the sex difference is environmental in that from boyhood men usually are exposed to greater amounts of sound than are women, and that the differences noted are thus simply an accumulation of the occupational exposure and preoccupational activities. However, our preliminary laboratory findings are also showing the same sex difference in noise damage susceptibility in guinea pigs, and it is known that the little boy guinea pigs have not been shooting cap pistols, firecrackers, and small arms or engaging in other similarly noisy activities. Perhaps this difference is a systemic one and will be explained only when the body's total reaction to noise as a stressor is better understood. Could it be that the female is better built for stress? This point will be discussed in considerably more detail in Chapter 4.

In addition to the apparent sex difference in noise damage susceptibility, wide ranges exist within each sex group in the degree of damage that occurs in response to a given set of noise exposures. This variation has led students of noise to summarize the condition as toughness or tenderness of the ears. Sometime ago Roberts Rings advertisements showed a huge man with bulging muscles, a cap, and a two-day stubble, daintily holding some automotive parts. The slogan was "tough, but oh, so gentle." One man may look like the character in the ad but have exceptionally tender ears. Another may resemble Casper Milquetoast but may be able to endure huge doses of intense noise exposure and never seem the worse for it.

A young woodsman scheduled for a hearing test asked for measures of the sound his chain saw generated because he was interested in knowing the type of exposure he was getting in using the saw almost constantly. He brought not only his two saws but also a thick log so that the noise of the saw under load could be determined. As indicated in Table 1.1 the larger saw was found to create a sound level of 118 dBA under load. The sound output of the smaller one was 116 dBA. His hearing test, which took place some time later, was a great surprise in that his hearing was absolutely normal in every respect. Other young men of his age who work in a nearby weaving mill were found to have a consistently great amount of hearing disability, especially for the higher pitches. Thus one can see that the range of individual variability makes impossible a universal rule about noise exposure.

SAFE LIMITS

The deleterious effect on the ear of high-intensity sound is ascribed to innumerous accounts throughout research literature. Considerable effort has been extended in attempts to objectify noise exposure data and to arrive at realistic damage-risk criteria (DRC), which aim at prescribing the amount of permissible exposure to high-intensity sound. Some of the criteria are quite complex and require thorough knowledge of the subject because the noise exposure condition is three dimensional: (1) the amplitude of the sound is important; (2) the frequency components are essential, for some pitches are more dangerous than others; (3) the duration of exposure adds further intricacies. In order to consider all three dimensions, each capable of wide variations, one must construct a three-dimensional model for damage risk. For simplicity many have dropped the frequency (pitch) dimension by converting the measures to the "A" scale, which takes into account the way a human ear might respond to the sound.

Conceivably, sound exposure levels in the 75 to 85 dBA range are the maximum safe for all but the most sensitive ears, although some researchers still maintain that sound exposure between 50 and 65 dBA can cause concern for hearing health. A compromise level might be established at about 70 dBA; that is, a person exposed to a sound continuously, day in and day out, would sustain no hearing damage if the sound did not exceed 70 dBA. Probably in no situation does a person receive this type of sound experience without some rest periods and consequently lower sound levels. Therefore, a higher upper limit, commonly set at 80 to 85 dBA, is possible without exceeding safe limits. Interpretation of 85 dBA as the safe level would include the stipulation that none of the widely varied levels in the sound environment exceed the safety level. It should be noted that we are discussing safe limits for avoiding ear damage. Sound levels constantly at or about 70 dBA might well be irritating to some persons.

LOSS OF HEARING

Damage to the sensory cells of the inner ear is permanent in that these cells never can be replaced. Thus when the ear loses some of its sensory structures it is less capable of performing complex functions.

Several common problems occur when one loses a portion of his hearing capability through noise exposure. (Note, however, that many of these conditions are present when the cause of the ear damage is not noise.) First, the ability to communicate with others deteriorates. Unfortunately, hearing aids are of little use in correcting this type of hearing problem; in fact, most hearing aid consultants agree that few cases of noise-induced hearing impairment have adjusted easily to the use of a hearing aid. We are not attempting to downgrade the value of hearing aids, but one must remember that the noise-related scattered destruction in the inner ear is not easily correctible, even with the good-quality hearing aids presently available. Certainly a hearing aid should be considered if communication problems become troublesome, because aid manufacturers now are designing instruments that more readily improve total communication ability. One such development that may afford additional help to persons with noise-induced hearing loss is front focus hearing, which is, in effect, a microphone designed to pick up sounds that come from the front and reduce the response to sounds in the rest of the environment. This situation will provide some relief for those who are bothered by background noise when listening to a sermon or lecture, for example.

Some of the specific problems in permanent hearing loss due to noise exposure are both frustrating and embarrassing. As the hearing sense becomes dulled, the ability to distinguish between many sounds of the language decreases, which can lead to a misunderstanding of orders at work or to the embarrassing situations popularly described in humorous stories. For the person who is experiencing the problem, however, it isn't funny.

The increasingly bothersome role background noise plays is one of the complaints most often heard from persons who have begun to notice a hearing deficiency from noise exposure. Normal ears can distinguish speech when background noise is nearly as high as the speech signal itself (sometimes even when speech is considerably softer than the ambient noise), but with deterioration of the sensory portion of the ear this capability continues to erode until the speech signal must be decidedly more intense than the background sound. Very old persons often have a great deal of difficulty in understanding speech if even a slight bit of background noise is present. This problem is no longer confined to the elderly, however. In recent years many young persons have experienced the same problem because their ears have sustained a sizable amount of permanent damage.

One other major effect of noise-induced hearing impairment, probably the most distressing, is that many important sounds simply are not heard. A ringing telephone in the next room may be missed; children may not be heard or understood, especially when they are speaking from a distance; women's soft and high-pitched voices may be impossible to hear and understand. The old gentleman who complains that he cannot understand women may not be speaking only of the mystique problem. The end result of such difficulties may be a downcast and withdrawn person who, frustrated by the difficulties in attempting to communicate with others, may cast himself in the role of the outsider and begin to give up trying to be a social creature.

Temporary and Permanent Loss

Hearing tests before and after noise exposure reveal the existence of temporary threshold shifts (TTS), or the amount of reversible reduction in hearing sensitivity (threshold). Any sound capable of causing a TTS of 30 dB or greater generally is regarded as dangerously intense, and exposure to such sounds should be avoided. Of course, one cannot constantly give himself hearing tests; so the previously mentioned damage-risk criteria were developed.

Repetitive or continued exposure to dangerously high sound levels probably will result in a permanent threshold shift (PTS). A TTS is totally reversible when the noise ceases and sufficient time has elapsed for the ears to recover. A PTS, however, is irreversible and connotes damage to the inner ear sensory cells. Once those cells are destroyed no known mechanism can regenerate them; so repeated exposures to high-level sound will result in the cumulative destruction of the sensory cell population, thereby increasing the breadth of effect. The first indication of such an occurrence is persistent reduction in hearing acuity for the audiometric high frequencies noted in Figure 2.6 (2,000 Hz to 8,000 Hz). As the PTS increases in magnitude, loss of hearing acuity for some lower frequencies will occur.

Damage-risk criteria, which serve as indicators (quite good ones) of the danger level for most continuous noise exposures have been established by determining the amount of TTS caused by sound of known amplitude and duration. If sound stimulation exceeds the allowable amount established in the DRC it is anticipated that the ear will have sustained some damage, which may not be measurable by means of hearing tests nor even noticeable to the subject himself but can nonetheless be present and pose a problem later as the effects of many such exposures accumulate.

HEARING TESTS

How does one determine damage to the ears as a result of noise exposure? The warning signals listed earlier *may* give a clue to the likelihood of damage. We know something about how partial loss of hearing structures occurs, but there is question about how well this information signals harm to the ear.

Auditory pathology in the wake of intense acoustic stimulation is measured in a variety of ways, the most used being the pure tone hearing test. In specific conditions and with a selected population, prevalence studies can detect the cause/effect relationship between certain types of noise exposure and the hearing loss measured in the population. Another approach might involve large-group testing of people who meet certain criteria; then test results would be considered the norm for that population and could be compared with the result of similar studies in other groups. A type of factor analysis can assist in detection of the degree of involvement the sound environment had in causing hearing ability differences between groups.

One of the most convenient and informative means of observing the effects of high-intensity noise is the testing of characteristically exposed populations, such as military and industrial personnel. Military leaders approached the problem of noise-induced hearing loss among the ranks by the formation of the Armed Forces National Research Council Committee on Hearing and Bio-Acoustics; and the armed forces have actively supported research geared to reduce the deleterious effects of noise. A very important event in the history of hearing surveys for this purpose was publication of the results of the 1954 Wisconsin State Fair Study, in which visitors at the fair were invited to have a free hearing test. Because fair visitors are quite responsive to the word "free," large numbers of people were tested. The results gave strong evidence of a correlation between occupation and the incidence of hearing impairment. Numerous surveys have taken place since then, but the basic information has been quite similar.

In the fall of 1967 a colleague remarked that more cases of high-frequency hearing impairment apparently existed among the incoming freshman class at the University of Tennessee. He was making a comparison of the students seen for several years in an abbreviated hearing screening check of those who reported concern about their hearing. We speculated that environmental noise certainly was a possible cause in that present-day young people are exposed to myriad high-intensity sounds unknown to youth one or two generations back.

In aging, the decrease in hearing ability for high-frequency sounds, *presbycusis*, grows steadily. The cause of presbycusis generally has been laid to the accumulative effects of all ear-damaging influences during a lifetime, coupled with decreased blood flow to the ear region in old people who have hardening of the arteries (arteriosclerosis). However, excepting hearing loss because of disease or heredity, young persons between the pre-teen and young adult years should have normal hearing throughout the audiometric test frequency range. Measurable hearing losses in the high-frequency range among many young persons could indicate the existence of inordinately high levels of environmental sound.

High-frequency hearing impairment among young persons once was considered a relatively rare phenomenon, but several recent studies have indicated that such impairment in people under 21 is increasing rapidly. A group in Colorado tested 1,000 school-age children and found that older children had significantly greater loss of hearing acuity than did younger ones. Also, the incidence of impairment among males was considerably higher than that among girls, a result found in populations noted earlier.

In the spring of 1968 three studies were begun in the Knoxville, Tennessee, city school system. In each study the hearing ability of 1,000 students was tested. Each study used children from only one grade level; so a combination of the studies provided a cross-section of three grades. The children were given a modified hearing screening test in order to determine the number of children who failed to demonstrate hearing within the normal range as shown in the pass region of Figure 2.7. Of particular interest to us was the condition of their hearing for the high-frequency tones (above 2,000 Hz). Of the sixth-grade pupils seen, only 3.8 percent of the students failed the high-frequency screening criterion (15 dB, based on the international standard established in 1964). This figure rose to 11 percent for the ninth-grade population and held at approximately the same level for high school seniors (10.6 percent).

This apparent trend to greater failure rates in older school-children was the impetus for similar hearing surveys of incoming college students. In the fall of 1968 a total of 2,769 incoming freshmen between the ages of 16 and 21 were given the same modified screening test used earlier in the public schools. It was disconcerting to note that 32.9 percent of the students failed to pass the hearing screening test. To confirm this astonishing finding, a portion of the incoming class (1,410 students) was screened for hearing in the fall of 1969. Contrary to the expectation of lower prevalence figures, the 1969 survey yielded an incidence of 60.7 percent. These percentages are shown graphically in Figure 3.1.

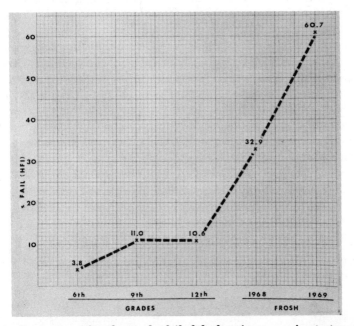

3.1   Percentage of students who failed the hearing screening tests and were classified as having a high-frequency hearing impairment. Note the upward trend in the figures, especially among college populations.

These data offer evidence, based on measurements of hearing levels among 7,179 young persons under 21, of an awesomely great undesirable trend toward a loss of high-frequency hearing acuity. Certainly most of the young people did not manifest serious hearing impairments, and most of those who failed by a slight degree actually were totally unaware of any loss of acuity. The point remains, however, that the population from the age range tested should have shown a considerably smaller number with measurable high-frequency impairment. The data also revealed that males in the studies demonstrated considerably greater incidence of hearing impairment than did females, a finding that correlates with research that preceded these studies (Table 3.1).

Of course, it is not feasible to attribute the rise in prevalence of high-frequency hearing impairment to noise exposure alone. One can reason, however, that the popularity of high-intensity recreational sound sources—live rock music, sport shooting, motorcycling, sport racing—coupled with the apparent rise in community noise levels should be considered to have a distinct effect on young persons' auditory acuity. To test this theory we used a questionnaire that considered four popular intense sound sources for young persons: motorcycles, school dances, gunfire, and school bands. Some trends indicated that the group with more exposure to these sounds had the greater prevalence of high-frequency hearing loss, but this relationship was statistically significant only for gunfire in one segment of the population.

Table 3.1   Comparison of the rates of high-frequency hearing loss males and females in five hearing surveys. The multiplication factor indicates the amount by which male failures were greater than female failures.

Group	Total Number	Male	Female	Multiplication Factor
6th grade	1,000	2.9	0.9	3.2 ×
9th grade	1,000	8.9	2.1	4.2 ×
12th grade	1,000	8.4	2.2	3.8 ×
1968 freshman	2,769	40.4	23.5	1.7 ×
1969 freshman	1,410	73.3	52.1	1.4 ×

These hearing test results are quite startling, especially when one realizes that the International Standards Organization audiometric reference levels were established with the use of "young nonpathologic ears." Apparently many of the students cited here certainly do not have nonpathologic ears as did the same age group only a few years ago when the standard for normalcy of youthful ears was established.

Most of the information of the audiometric effects of noise has been determined by testing with high-frequency tones. A method being developed allows use of the extra high tones to determine how well persons can hear in the upper reaches of man's audible response range. It is said that human beings possess ears that can respond to frequencies between 20 Hz and 20,000 Hz; yet for many good reasons conventional hearing tests include only those frequencies between 125 Hz and 8,000 Hz. Perhaps information in the upper frequency range can provide an early warning of approaching hearing deficit from various types of noise exposure and from other causes. Some reports have speculated that extra high-frequency hearing shifts may signal certain types of physiological conditions,-such as renal (kidney) disease and cardiovascular problems. These relationships are yet to be drawn and must be kept in the realm of speculation for the present. It stands to reason, however, that future tests of the extra high frequencies will provide us with more information about the way in which the ear deteriorates in reaction to damaging stimuli.

IMPLICATIONS

It is appropriate here to consider the future effects of noise-induced injury. Remember that noise in itself will not cause total deafness, although one could conjure up a wild set of circumstances, begun by some type of intense sound stimulation, wherein a person would develop an infection in the inner ear and lose the hearing sense. This occurrence would be most rare; so it is best to think of noise as causing problems less severe than total deafness.

Noise damage may result in disqualification from certain vocational interests. The person who wants to become an airplane pilot may never pass the physical exam because hearing difficulty, caused by excessive exposure to high-intensity sound, precludes response to test tones. The person who has always dreamed of being a surgical nurse may never realize such ambitions because hearing impairment shuts out the physician's requests for instruments. Doctors do not look too kindly on receiving scalpels instead of requested suture material.

Hearing loss of the type described here is not severe enough to disqualify persons from most professions, but it may have an impeding effect on their success. Consider the trial lawyer who misses a few words now and then. He may lose some of the key messages that would help him to win his case, and if word gets out that he doesn't hear well his clientele probably will diminish. The same problem exists in many other fields that require relation to and communication with others.

Increasing high-frequency hearing impairment in young adults poses a severe problem for management. Although most young persons in industry are considered to be in good health and basically intact when hired, quite possibly some already have sizable hearing impairment. In order that employers may be aware of such injury and hence protect employees from further hearing damage from high-level sound exposure in the work environment, the pre-employment hearing evaluation is a must. This step makes sense in that an industry cannot be held responsible for a hearing loss that was, in fact, incurred before employment. The pre-employment hearing evaluation also provides a mechanism whereby high-risk employees can be recognized early and assigned to less noisy plant areas.

An audiologic consultant to the Environmental Protection Agency has stated: "Although presbycusis (old-age deafness) is usually associated with the normal process of aging, nowadays it's thought that the continual din of our environment is probably a significant contributor." Knowledge that the hearing sense dulls with the passing years causes serious concern for the large number of young people with measurable hearing losses so early in life. When the progressive hearing impairment due to aging is heaped on the losses some young persons have already received, the result must be the dire prediction that this generation will experience considerably more hearing trouble at age 60 than do current 60-year-olds. In fact, 14 percent of the male college freshmen in the 1969 survey were found to have hearing equivalent to that of 50–60-year-old men.

FROM THE LABORATORY

We have found that in experimental animals (guinea pigs, chinchillas, rats) high-intensity sound with energy in a broad range of frequencies is capable of causing widespread destruction of the irreplaceable sensory cells in the cochlea (inner ear). After formation of scar tissue, cochlear tissues were dissected from the temporal bones of animals systematically exposed to high-intensity sound. In normal tissue the regular geometric configurations are as shown in Figures 2.3 and 2.4. In animals exposed to high noise levels the cell patterns are interrupted, and damage is readily seen. Figure 3.2 is a schematic representation of abnormal cochlear tissue. Note the interruption of cell patterning and visible damage. Several cells are bisected by a fine line, indicating the early stages of structure collapse, and spaces left by other cells, now completely missing, are filled with X-shaped scars. Once a cell has degenerated its loss is permanent in that no

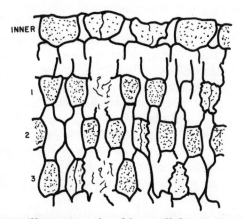

3.2 Schematic illustration of cochlear cell destruction as a result of intense sound exposure. There is no apparent pattern to the destruction. In the second row of outer cells is a scar, denoted by the X configuration.

known process can replace these highly specialized sensory cells.

In experiments to investigate the extent of anatomic damage to the ears of animals subjected to such sounds as intense rock music, animals received sound stimulation approximating that measured in discotheques. Extensive damage to the cells in the inner ear was discovered after a relatively short exposure to high-level rock music (peaking at 122 dB). The analysis of damage for an animal who listened to music for a total of 88 hours and 6 minutes over a 57-day period in 27 stimulus sessions revealed that the ear region that responds to frequencies around 1,000 Hz sustained more damage than did the inner ear area that serves the higher frequencies. This observation indicates that destruction to the cochlear cell tissues is not singularly a high-frequency phenomenon, although the early audiometric signs of noise damage occur with the loss of hearing for the higher pitched tones.

The actual tissue removed from one of the "rocked" guinea pigs appears in Figure 3.3. Clearly visible are several areas in which sensory cells are totally collapsed, shriveled, or missing. Figure 3.4, a composite view of normal and abnormal cells, affords some insight into the patterning of noise damage in the ear. The arrows point to two collapsing cells that appear to be shriveling like peas drying in the sunlight, but note that between the two dying ones is an apparently healthy sensory cell. This very random effect of cell destruction in the inner ear, rather than widespread destruction of a single area of the cochlea, often occurs. A section of the ear tissue damaged by noise exposure is shown in Figure 3.5. Darkened cells are the dead ones.

The results of additional studies with high-amplitude contemporary rock music supported the earlier findings. Animals given less stimulation were noted to have less destruction, but, interestingly, susceptibility to ear damage in guinea pigs also varies rather widely.

The growth of damage in the low-frequency ranges, where no destruction should occur, was observed by exposing guinea pigs to signals that had a shortened frequency width (called octave bands). Some were exposed to an intense low-frequency

band of noise; others received the same amplitude of midfrequency noise; a third group was stimulated by a high-frequency
sound. The results of this study, shown in Figure 3.6, reflect the
percentage of cells damaged by the sounds. For the low- and
midfrequency stimulated animals the damage appeared in the
cochlea at about the expected places—that is, at the top and in

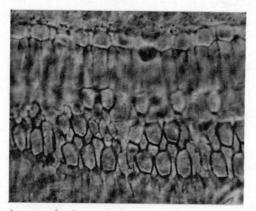

**3.3 Photomicrograph of ear cells removed from a guinea pig exposed
to rock music. A total of 19 percent of the sensory cells in this specimen
were irreversibly destroyed.**

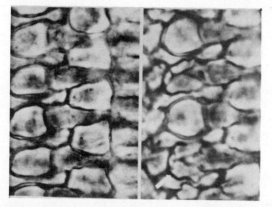

**3.4 Composite photomicrograph showing undamaged cochlear cells
removed from a control ear and typical collapsed cells (arrows) removed from a guinea pig ear after exposure to high-level sound.**

the middle of the cochlea respectively. The high-frequency sound, however, caused damage throughout the cochlea over a much broader range than did the other two stimuli; in fact, the greatest amount of damage occurred in the low-frequency rather than the high-frequency area of the cochlea. Destruction was more extensive than that caused by the low-frequency stimulus.

This is a very puzzling observation and the reasons for it are not entirely clear. Some acoustic reasons might explain the condition, but they are very complicated and beyond the scope of this book. Suffice it to say that noise can cause widespread damage in the cochlea, giving rise to the concern that in the wake of noise exposure greater hearing destruction occurs than one might see in the results of hearing tests. If these data can be

3.5 This cochleogram represents the extent of damage noted in the tissue shown in Figure 3.3. Damaged cells are represented by filled circles.

generalized to all mammal ears the implications can be rather startling. Since noise stimuli create destruction throughout the cochlea rather than at a specific or circumscribed region, it must be assumed that pure tone audiometric tests do not signal the loss of cochlear integrity in the upper reaches of the cochlea (low-frequency region). Thus when one sustains a permanent hearing disability from noise exposure such that the typical high-frequency hearing impairment is noted, cell destruction in the apical half of the cochlea may be even more prevalent —destruction not noted with the use of conventional pure tone hearing testing.

Widespread, irreversible inner ear damage in the cochleae of animals exposed to sounds comparable in amplitude and duration to sounds young people hear is quite alarming. Caution

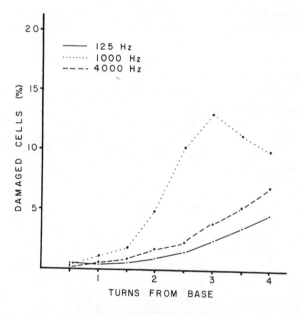

3.6 Percentages of damaged cells in ears of guinea pigs exposed to differing sounds. Note that all of the sounds caused greater damage in region 4 (low-frequency region). The midfrequency sound (1,000 Hz band) caused the most destruction.

must be exercised, of course, in relating observations from experimental animals to humans—especially guinea pigs, for these little animals seem to be slightly more susceptible to high-level sound damage than are humans. The inference is clear, however, that the typical discotheque sound environment is intense enough to be extremely hazardous to the health and well-being of the sensory cells.

Several years ago audiologists attempted to determine if in hearing screening they could use a simple pure tone device capable of generating only one tone. The idea was that persons who were beginning to lose their hearing would show the first loss at about 4,000 Hz; therefore, a screening device set for that frequency would identify the person without the need for extensive hearing testing. This beautiful theory was smashed by the ugly fact that not even full-scale audiometry indicates the extent of ear damage, much less a highly abbreviated method.

This cursory review of recent investigations lends considerable support to the thesis that high-intensity environmental and recreational sounds pose a potential threat to young people's hearing. However, that audiometrically obtained measures of hearing acuity may not necessarily reflect accurately the presence and extent of cell damage is indicated in the surveys that revealed a rather high percentage of young people who had a slight drop in hearing acuity in the high-frequency region, and in animal experiments in which intense sound stimulation caused extensive inner ear cell destruction.

THE RESULTS

The findings in the hearing surveys combined with laboratory data are reasons for concern. Although high-level noise cannot be singled out as the only factor in this apparent auditory epidemic, it must be considered a significant contributor to a seemingly sizable degree of auditory deficit in persons whose age group only a few years ago comprised subjects for the current audiometric norms.

In fact, a normative study to establish or validate audiometric standards now is virtually impossible in the major industrial areas of the civilized world because of damaged hearing within the population on which norms should be established.

These factors affect research in speech and hearing science in that the lack of qualified subjects seriously hampers projects. Many such projects require trained listeners to judge certain aspects of speech signals, but listeners (especially male listeners) who meet the necessarily stringent auditory criteria are difficult to find.

ANOTHER SOURCE OF DAMAGE

One of the physiologic responses to high noise stimulation, mentioned earlier, is constriction of the veins and arteries, and recent studies have shown that the blood supply of the inner ear region also is reduced. Dr. Merle Lawrence observed that noise can noticeably reduce the number of red blood cells (erythrocytes) in the inner ear of an experimental animal. He concluded that the reduction of blood supply in the vicinity of the inner ear sensory cells may account for temporary threshold shift, which of course may revert to permanent damage if the blood supply is cut off for long periods.

In some work related to the stress studies to be discussed in Chapter 4, studies of the presence of blood cells in the capillaries of the auditory and balance sense end organ regions revealed several interesting anomalies.

1. The number of red blood cells in the capillaries immediately under the auditory sensory cells are considerably reduced in the noise-stimulated animals. Figure 3.7, a composite photomicrograph, shows how the content of tiny capillaries appears to dwindle when noise stimulation occurs. At the top is a capillary in one of the control animals which did not receive noise exposure; at the bottom is the same region of the ear in an exposed animal. Note that the bottom capillary is nearly vacant, and blood cells that are present do not appear normal.

2. In an experiment with guinea pigs, exposed males

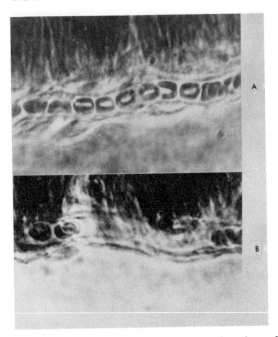

3.7   Comparison of capillary content of tissue taken from the ears of rats. Part A was removed from a control (non-noise-exposed) animal. Note the large number of blood cells. Specimen B was found in the ear tissue of a noise-exposed rat. The number of blood cells is severely diminished.

showed somewhat greater reduction in the presence of red blood cells than did females. This observation may offer a partial reason for the sex difference in susceptibility noted earlier.

3. Rats exposed to noise demonstrated a reduction of red blood cells in the capillaries adjacent to the balance sense as well as in the auditory portion of the inner ear. A common complaint in noise exposure is the feeling of imbalance. Such unsteadiness may be a vestibular side effect of the auditory overstimulation and concomitant reduction in blood supply for the entire inner ear region.

The apparent mechanism for this reduction in blood cells noted in the inner ear capillaries is the development of masses in the capillary walls in response to sound stimulation. These tiny areas of irritation and inflammation serve to thicken the capillary walls, thereby reducing the internal diameter of the passage. The result is the choking off of the capillary, creating sizable gaps between red blood cells and bringing blood flow to a near halt in some capillaries. A greatly magnified view of these swollen capillary walls is shown in Figure 3.8. Note that the internal diameter of the capillary is reduced to about half the normal size, and that a blood cell can be seen trying to ooze through the swollen area. This response to noise stimulation has the effect of interrupting the distribution of oxygen to the sensory cells and their supporting tissues, thus creating havoc in portions of the inner ear.

As evidence on the effect of noise on the hearing and balance mechanisms continues to accumulate it becomes increasingly apparent that measures must be taken to reduce sounds at the source when possible. When the source cannot be muted, ear protective devices must be advocated.

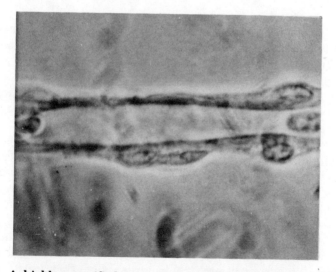

3.8 **A highly magnified view of a capillary taken from a noise-exposed rat. Note the swelling in the walls, which causes a reduction in the internal diameter of the capillary.**

MECHANISMS OF NOISE DAMAGE

How does ear damage occur after noise stimulation? Here are several suggestions.

1. *Physical force.*   High-intensity sound creates quite a stir in the fluids and tissues of the inner ear. These tiny and delicate membranes may yield to the force the sound exerts so that damage occurs as a gradual weakening of the tissues from continuous manipulation by acoustic driving forces.

2. *Heat transfer.*   One of the commonest health-related causes of inner ear damage stems from illnesses with sustained high fever. The temperature rise causes sensory cells to expire, leaving the individual with a hearing impairment. It has been suggested that tiny but significant forces within the ear created by extremely high sound levels can result in the generation of compartmentalized areas of temperature elevation; then cells immediately in the vicinity of the rise in temperature are damaged.

3. *Structural damage.*   Just as a hurricane will uproot trees and smash houses, sudden blasts of acoustic energy may tear and dislodge the tiny components in the inner ear. The tensile strength of the tissues also may be weakened, giving rise to permanent structural damage.

4. *Vasoconstriction.*   Blockage of the delivery capacity for the oxygen-bearing blood cells may play a role in damaging the inner ear.

All of these factors in various combinations may ultimately be found to contribute to noise-induced ear disability, or future research may find that none is as responsible as some yet-to-be-discovered feature. How many mechanisms of noise damage exist is not fully known. Two other suggestions are grouped separately, for they are entirely speculative.

1. *Hereditary predetermination.*   Dr. Ole Bentzen and his Danish colleagues at the State Hospital in Aarhus have noted an interesting group of physical features, which they are attempting to relate to sound injury susceptibility. Labeled the *ectomesodermal insufficiency syndrome*, these symptoms are

classified together because all of the affected structures arise
from the outer layer of the developing fetus. Interestingly, the
inner ear also arises from the outer sheath of a newly conceived
baby. Such conditions as triangular face shape, bluish sclera
(whites of the eye), skin pathology, consistent general health
problems, frequent miscarriages and difficulty during birth,
very thin or very coarse hair, and other similar anomalies are
being found to be related to possible susceptibility to hearing
damage due to noise. Bentzen and his group speculate that
certain numbers of these physical conditions may be useful
predictors of persons who should avoid noise exposure. Much
must still be done to prove the validity of this concept, but it
deserves serious consideration and experimentation.

2. *Lack of rest.*   All parts of the body demand periods of
rest. The nerves fire very rapidly, but at some time during the
cycle a nerve cannot fire, for it is taking its very brief siesta. The
ear, however, is always on and will respond to the driving force
of acoustic stimuli; so in order to achieve any rest the ear must be
taken into a quiet environment where the stresses caused by
constant sound bombardment can be put aside. Rising environmental noise levels, though, make quiet places more difficult to
find, and we may thus speculate that the ear tissues undergo
slight, almost imperceptible modifications due to lack of rest,
which make them more likely to sustain damage in high-level
sound conditions. This problem may further partially explain
the variation among persons in susceptibility to noise damage.
Some less susceptible people may spend time in surroundings
quieter than those for people found to be more threatened with
noise-related ear damage.

Both of these suggestions are not presently supported with
hard research data, although the second concept is currently
being tested in the laboratory.

A PROBLEM

Studies conducted in our laboratory and in many other institu-
tions have given strong evidence that rather extensive damage to
portions of the inner ear may not show up in hearing tests. A

common client complaint in audiology clinics is that communication is difficult, especially in noisy environments. Often the results of hearing tests are misleading because the client may demonstrate normal or near-normal hearing for tones and for speech; so perhaps the temptation (if not the tendency) has been to consider that the person is overreacting to his hearing condition. Sometimes he is classified as otoneurotic, and his subjective observations are dismissed as being inaccurate.

Yet there is good reason to believe that the amount of damage to the ears will not be adequately reflected in hearing tests, and audiologists are becoming aware that the subjective experience of the hearing-impaired person is to be counted and believed. Conventional tests may prove inadequate as predictors of the success one may achieve in living with noise-induced hearing impairment.

The following case history emphasizes the problem in satisfying the needs of noise-affected people. A 72-year-old lady complained that she could no longer hear well during her visits with friends and relatives. As shown in Figure 3.9, her pure tone test results indicated a slight-to-moderate hearing loss in both ears, with the decrease in hearing ability most extensive in the high-frequency response range. Her ability to understand speech in a quiet situation was excellent. In short, the test results did not indicate a significant hearing difficulty; in fact, her responses seemed better than might be expected for a person of her age. On finding that she had operated a sewing machine in a noisy garment factory for many years before her retirement, we decided to evaluate how well she could hear words when background noise was introduced. A small table in Figure 3.9 shows the results of that brief test. The S/N symbol indicates the relationship between the speech signal and the background noise. With a 50 dB S/N ratio her ability to repeat the words was excellent (100 percent). As the noise was increased and the S/N ratio decreased, her ability to discriminate the speech sounds was gravely reduced until with a S/N ratio of 10 dB she could repeat only 20 percent of the words. In this condition a person with no ear damage would be expected to respond accurately to 100 percent of the words.

The conclusion was that this patient had suffered extensive damage to the cochlea, but routine audiometric tests did not indicate the gravity of her receptive communication problem. Therefore, it is emphasized that persons who have been exposed to intense noise for much of their work life may sustain rather extensive inner ear damage that will not be recognized in routine hearing tests. The hearing health community has begun to recognize this situation and to offer more comfort and understanding to these persons.

Audiogram

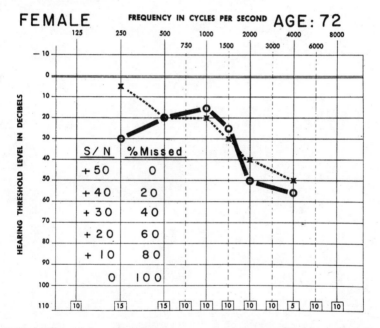

3.9 Audiometric test results for a 72-year-old female who had been exposed to garment factory noise. In the lower left-hand portion of the audiogram are the results of a simple S/N ratio speech test (see text for explanation).

·4·

A Health Hazard

But human bodies are sic fools,
For a' their colleges and schools,
That when nae real ills perplex them,
They mak enow themsels to vex them.
Robert Burns

A point of reference was to define noise as unwanted sound, but one might well ask, "Unwanted by whom?" Human complexity does not allow for universal agreement on sounds as being acceptable or unacceptable.

Aircraft noise near a metropolitan airport may disgruntle many on the ground below, while others are seemingly unaffected by the whir and whine of the jets. Even the theoretically soothing sounds of background music may perturb one who cares for total quiet.

In April 1971 the National Conference on Technogenic Disease, jointly sponsored by The State University of New York at Buffalo and Rachael Carson College, posed an interesting concept. It was pleasing to note that planners of the sessions included a discussion of noise. The term *technogenic diseases* provides a vivid description of the effects the increasing number of noise sources around us can have on several aspects of physical and mental function.

A medical dictionary defines "disease" as "literally the lack of ease; a pathological condition of the body that presents a group of symptoms peculiar to it which sets the condition apart

73

as an abnormal entity differing from other normal or pathological body states." Here the concept of noise as a source of technogenic disease can become confused, for no *single* group of symptoms for *a* disease can be attributed to noise exposure, per se.

A person exposed to unnecessarily loud sound over an extended period may develop internal physical problems; he may become stressed, with resultant personality maladjustment and interpersonal problems; his productivity and thought activities are likely to become disrupted. All or any of these untoward problems are potential aftereffects of distressing noise exposure.

BODY RESPONSE

Continuous exposure to noise disrupts the keen balances maintained in body physiology. This disturbance is made known at the conscious level as the feeling of annoyance or stress. It generally holds that the annoyance characteristics of a sound increase with the loudness level of the sound, but there is a frequency-dependent aspect as well. Those sounds whose energy is in the frequencies at and above 2,000 Hz are usually more annoying than are sounds whose spectrum contains mostly low-frequency energy. Because of the great range of individual variance discussed earlier, these responses are highly unpredictable.

Numerous studies have been undertaken to observe the internal reaction of the human in exposure to intense sound for long durations. Some results are still to be supported and strengthened by further research; other data will be found inaccurate and will be either modified or discarded. The trend, however, leads one to feel that potentially body function undergoes a very dramatic change during noise exposure.

One indication of physiologic reaction to noise is constriction of veins and arteries. In Germany Dr. Gerd Jansen at the Max Planck Institute has found that measurable decreases in blood flow through the veins and arteries of the hand can be noted very soon after the onset of loud sound. This reaction also can be seen by shining a strong light through the earlobe as the person is exposed to noise. Often a gradual whitening will be noted, indicating that the blood supply to that area of the skin has been reduced. We noted earlier that constrictions also are seen in tiny capillaries of the inner ear.

These changes in blood flow signal a reaction of the total cardiovascular system. When the diameter of the blood passageways is reduced, back pressure is set up, causing an increase in blood pressure—a reaction measured in experimental subjects who have undergone specific noise exposure. When the supply of available oxygen-carrying blood is cut, the breathing becomes deeper and somewhat more labored in order to provide more richly oxygenated blood to the body.

Other body reactions to noise stimulation include digestive system upsets, which in some cases might lead to such severe symptoms as stress ulcers. Skeletal musculature tends to increase in tension and may affect motor control, especially in fine manual tasks. Dr. Jansen has also observed that noise stimulation causes dilation of the pupils. Some reports have noted that inordinate pupillary dilation may cause a form of color-blindness, which may be a cause of some concern about safety from a perceptual standpoint.

During the restive condition the skin offers a certain amount of resistance to the passage of electricity from one point to another. This resistance can be measured with a *galvanometer*. When something happens to cause a stress reaction, perspiration appears quickly on or near the surface of the skin. These briny beads have the effect of allowing electricity to travel more efficiently across the surface of the skin, thus causing a noticeable deflection of the recording device on the galvanometer. The principle forms a part of the lie detector, a long-used police device now creeping into politics as candidates offer to "take a lie detector test" to prove opponents' misstatements. In the presence of disturbing noise the galvanometer indicates a stress-related reaction by detecting a noticeable change in skin resistance—a positive indication that alterations in some aspects of body function have taken place.

Endocrinologists have noted that the adrenal glands become quite active in the presence of noise as low as 68 dBA. The many forms the endocrine glands can take to alter the chemical content of blood provides another area of concern about the physiologically damaging impacts noise may have on the body.

Essentially, reaction to noise leads to a condition in which the counterrelevant forces within the body compete for control, altering the emotions and the general health and stability of human organisms. Such reactions contribute to feelings of fatigue, irritability, or tension. Continuous exposure to noise that has an irritating quality cannot facilitate good health. It remains to be proven whether it is as deleterious to health as some have suggested, but no support exists for any notion that noise is good. Exposure may not culminate in a definable illness, but it creates stress in the body, often without one's conscious awareness of being stressed.

Caution in these interpretations is essential. As shall be seen in Chapter 5, many are willing, even anxious, to hop onto the cry-wolf bandwagon and rant about all of the grave problems that noise or other environmental contaminants will cause.

A much-quoted comment that bears repeating here is the warning from Dr. Samuel Rosen of the New York Mt. Sinai Hospital. "You may learn to ignore noise, but your body will never forgive you." That observation remains to be proven in the future, but meanwhile it is an appropriate warning to approach noise stimulation with caution in anticipation of its adverse effects on the body.

STRESS AND EAR DAMAGE

It is interesting to ponder the interrelationships that may exist between stress reaction and ear damage. It certainly is not wise to propose a direct cause/effect situation in which ear damage will occur each time a person becomes upset. More than a chance correlation exists between the two aspects, however.

There are some confusing findings about the hearing status of some individuals who engage in extremely noisy occupations. Although the damage-risk criteria would lead us to believe that they should have remarkable hearing deficits, they do not. Although at this point it is mere speculation, eventually it may be discovered that the less stressing a sound is, the less prone is the recipient of the acoustic signal to develop a hearing shift.

Later we shall discuss the growth and impact of highly amplified rock-and-roll music. Amid a general expression of concern for the hearing health of persons who engage in these musical flights into the never-never land of audioeuphoria, statistics indicate that rock musicians as a group do not exhibit hearing damage commensurate with the type of sound exposure they are receiving. Remember that the high-level sound is their baby! They have nurtured and produced it. The pulsing, throbbing, screeching expression of their innermost being comes back to their ears as a balm (not bomb). If any bodily stress occurs it is most likely from unadulterated ecstasy. Make no mistake about it, some ear destruction probably occurs, but the additive effects of extreme internal distress are not there. Consequently, since the musicians are not negatively stressed their ears may not be so extremely jeopardized as they would be were they forced to endure a sound they could not tolerate. If this theory is ultimately borne out it will be another indication of the forethought that must have gone into creation of the human body. This *pleasure principle* simply adds another dimension to the already crowded list of factors that bear on the human response to sound and the prospects of ear damage from immersion in high-level sound environments.

AGING

Medicine recently has become much more aware of the geriatric patient as physicians suddenly are confronted with old people in ever larger numbers. Most of these persons present a complex set of symptoms that have motivated medical science toward concerted attempts to unlock some of the secrets of the aging process.

According to Dr. Hans Selye, a baby is born with a reservoir of stress-combating ability. The amount of this mystical capability varies; therefore some age more rapidly and expire sooner than others. This summary is, of course, an oversimplification of some very sophisticated research Dr. Selye has reported, but it does lend itself to a brief word about the possible contribution of environmental noise in accelerating the aging process. Noise is a stressor; so the more a person is overstressed by noise exposure, the more he is dipping into the precious reservoir of life-extending, stress-combating potion. When noise stress is linked with all the other forces that cause stress reaction it seems to pale into insignificance. We must recall, however, that unwanted sound is one of the major components of our environment, and when we are repeatedly disturbed with the stimulus it is to be regarded as more than a miniscule contributor to physical deterioration.

NOISE AS A STRESSOR

Noise has long been known as an irritant. Unnecessary and uninvited sound gives rise to the physical reactions just discussed. Noise often has been treated as a stressor, but in order to determine whether noise is a stressor in the classic sense rats were exposed to noise and then observed for the stress reactions Selye described: (1) shrinking of the thymus gland, a lymph gland situated immediately above the heart; (2) stress ulcers in the duodenum or other portions of the intestinal tract; and (3) swelling and discoloration of the adrenal glands, located just above the kidneys.

Small groups of rats were placed in a sound-treated enclosure, and a broad-band noise called *white noise* was set for a level of 110 dB. The animals were left in the noise continuously for 48 hours, then terminated still in the presence of noise in order to avoid the possibility of spontaneous recovery on being removed from the sound. One group of control rats was placed in a quiet enclosure for the same period. This exposure is, of course, rather extreme in order to quicken the stress reaction. The 2-day period was patterned after the studies Selye conducted by placing rats in extreme cold for 48 hours. In that period they developed the symptoms of stress alarm reaction.

Autopsy examination of the internal organ systems of the

noise-exposed rats yielded convincing evidence as every animal
demonstrated at least one abnormality in the stress reaction triad
and most were found to manifest all three. The thymus of noise-
stimulated animals was found to be affected in virtually all of the
specimens. Figure 4.1 shows a healthy thymus removed from a

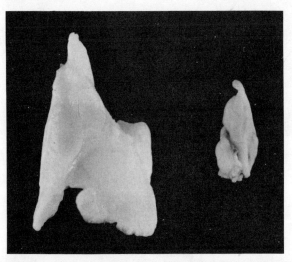

**4.1   Comparison of thymus glands removed from two rats. The large,
healthy specimen was found in a control animal. The shriveled gland
came from a noise-exposed rat.**

control rat and the small thymus removed from one of the
noise-stressed animals. These thymuses are extremes in a wide
range of effect.

Duodenal stress ulcers were found in over half of the rats,
and many of the animals developed ulcers in other regions of the
digestive system. In Figure 4.2 a one-inch length of intestinal
tract from a rat is shown. The important point here is the abnormal appearance in the specimen removed from a noise-exposed
rat.

Normally the adrenal glands are encased in a sheath of fat
and are somewhat difficult to visualize, but the noise-stimulated
animals presented no problem because that sheath of fat had

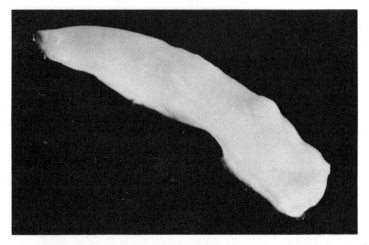

4.2   Surface aberrations in a one-inch length of duodenum removed from a noise-stimulated rat.

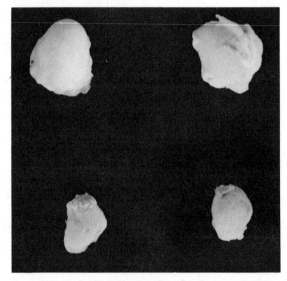

4.3   A comparison of adrenal glands. The larger glands at the top were removed from a noise-stimulated rat. The smaller ones in the lower portion of the photograph were taken from one of the control animals.

been dissolved away and the adrenal glands exposed. The outer covering of the adrenals, the *adrenal cortex*, is known to secrete as many as 500 different chemicals in response to a signal from the *pituitary*, the master gland of the body. When the body is overstressed the adrenal glands become excessively active, swell, and occasionally become slightly discolored. Some swollen adrenals are slightly lighter in color than are those of the control animals. Figure 4.3 compares adrenal glands removed from two rats. The larger, swollen glands at the top are a sign of noise-induced stress reaction.

A third group of animals, littermates to the experimental group, were used to indicate reaction to 48 hours of restriction in the quiet chamber. No pattern of differences could be noted between the two control groups.

A few other abnormalities were observed in the noise-exposed rats. The intestines were found to be generally more constricted than those in the quiet group, although both sets of animals fasted during their experimental period. One rat gave the appearance of having sustained a coronary thrombosis, supposedly during the noise exposure. Immediately prior to termination the noise-exposed rats were subjectively noted to be more subdued than were the other animals.

Although these irregularities were fully expected, it was still startling to note that such conditions could be seen in animals after only 48 hours. From the evidence we may conclude that in the sense of the classical definition, noise is a stressor.

A word of caution is necessary here. It is tempting to project the results of these experiments into some form of doomsday prognostication, and some find the temptation irresistible. Remember, however, that most studies of noise as a stressor have been conducted with nonhuman subjects, and therefore the projection to human reaction cannot be made directly. The most appropriate interpretation of the data is the realization that inordinately great exposure to noise has a potentially damaging effect on vital physiologic processes and must be avoided if one is to remain free of the types of disturbance such exposures might cause.

PSYCHOLOGICAL ASPECTS

That mental state is greatly influenced by physical well-being needs little argument. Therefore, if reaction to sound stimulation disarrays the internal functioning of the body, psychological condition can be expected to undergo some modifications that may or may not be overt. Psychological reactions can be related to the noxious aspect of the sound source, the relative pleasure–displeasure an individual is experiencing at the onset of the noise, the person's basic anxiety level, or his evaluation of his total situation at the time noise occurs.

Not many hard facts about the emotional concomitants of noise exposure are available. Allusions are frequently made to the frustrations, fatigue, vexations, irritations, and immobilizing qualities of high-level sound, but most of the projections are quite subjectively based. A fortunate accident in a series of studies undertaken to learn more about family communications allowed Dr. Jack Westman, psychiatrist at the University of Wisconsin, to describe the role of noise as a disruptive influence in the home. The data were collected by means of voice-activated tape recorders that turned on automatically when a family member began to speak. Early in their data analysis the Wisconsin researchers noted that the tape recorders had been turned on by noises in the home far more often than by the spoken word. From this base Dr. Westman made some observations on noise in the home.

> . . . [T]ogetherness at the supper table is hampered by household noises and by the general tenseness fanned by the daylong din. . . . We don't understand that noise makes us less efficient, less effective and more tense. Instead, we scapegoat. We take our tensions out on each other. Mothers yell at the youngsters. Parents bicker.

These factors indicate the psychological aspect of fear, annoyance, and irritation. In a report on community attitudes toward various aspects of aircraft noise Dr. Paul Borskey discussed *misfeasance*. The term was used to describe responses from persons who felt the noise could be controlled, but controls were not exerted. This group's concern about aircraft noise in the community was greater than that of those who did not hold the feelings of misfeasance.

Sudden noises, such as slamming doors, shouts, gunshots, or car backfires, are more alarming because of the lack of warning prior to the shock of the noise. After experiencing such a noise sensation the internal workings of the body usually are notably upset. Some persons whose psychological adjustment is not the best tend to react to such situations in bizarre ways, often with feelings of extreme anger or frustration. Heinous crimes have been spawned by sounds that created in an individual the urge to kill or maim.

PAST THE BREAKING POINT

Undue noise and the frustrations that often come with it may press shaky personalities over the brink. In New York City a man shot and killed a boy who was playing outside his window. The man, a night worker, related to the investigating officer that the boy's shouting and noisemaking had kept him awake. In Memphis, Tennessee, a young babysitter unloaded a shotgun into a group of six small children, critically wounding three of them. Her explanation was that they had disturbed her with their loud play. A Japanese student reportedly trying to study for an examination while a pile driver pounded near his room apparently become so distracted and disinhibited that he lost his senses, ran outside, and placed his head between the pile and the hammer to end it all.

Some are inclined to take the law into their own hands in attempts to abate certain noise sources. In France on a bus a woman's loud portable radio proved to be very disturbing to a fellow passenger, who finally grabbed the radio and smashed it over her head. Interestingly, the court listened to the case with a sympathetic ear and acquitted him. A later survey indicated that all but 1 of 300 persons asked agreed with the action the man had taken. Perhaps the single dissenter was the lady who had been struck.

In Kansas City a physician upset by the incessant clatter of a jackhammer in front of his home sauntered out into the street and began to chat with the workers. Suddenly he produced an ax and began to hack away furiously at the compression hose that supplied air to the machine. The court fined him and charged him with, of all things, disturbing the peace.

A New York businesswoman, interviewed on a national network related this tale.

> I got out at 40th Street and Madison after sitting 20 minutes in a traffic jam. And there was a car there from New Jersey blowing his horn. I walked over to him and said, "Will you please stop that, it's impossible to get through, the traffic jam is from here as far as the eye can see." He looked at me and blew his horn. I took off my shoe and hit his car. He did it again and I put another dent in his car. He turned to me and said, "You're crazy, lady!" I said, "I am and you did it." Whereupon he blew the horn again and I had the shoe on this time and I kicked his car. I really thought I was certifiable that day. But he stopped blowing his horn.

Of course, not all such stories border on the macabre. In Munich artist Helmut Winter, distressed by the droning sounds of low-flying Luftwaffe and USAF jets over his home, formed a king-sized slingshot and used it to fire potato dumplings at the planes. Apparently his aim was good, for one report indicated that the flight path was changed. The story got out, and Herr Winter was dubbed *Kartoffel Werfer* (potato slinger)—a hero of sorts. A similar story is told of an Idaho potato farmer who was arrested for standing in his field and hurling spuds at landing military planes. Fascinating how frustration can lead to overt action.

The mind is a marvelous entity at peace, but when ruffled the torment can be indescribable. Noise tends to stimulate the minds of some individuals to nervous peaks, apparently to no good cause. Man needs acoustic stimulation to enjoy life, but severe overloading of the auditory input channels poses a threat to his mental health. A British ear specialist, Dr. John A. Parr, speculates that "If repeated again and again, noise can ultimately cause a nervous breakdown."

EFFECT ON PERFORMANCE AND EDUCATION

The effect of noise on learning and performance is a fruitful, albeit difficult area of study. The previously mentioned physiological and psychological reactions may be considered to adversely affect motor performance and productivity. Research evidence in this realm is not conclusive so that background sound is sometimes described as having a good effect, at other times seems to pose restrictions on performance, and at other moments seems to have no effect at all.

Noise interference has been demonstrated in tasks that demand great concentration and rapid reaction. In studies of vigilance it was noted that subjects who were monitoring complicated racks of dials and gauges were less vigilant when noise was introduced into the environment. Such disturbances apparently stem from noise-induced lapses in attention or the creation of a condition of brain overarousal that results in reduced behavioral control. These observations have been translated to indicate that work efficiency could be reduced by high noise levels.

In one study sound-reducing earplugs were found to increase weaving mill workers' efficiency by 12 percent. Not only were the workers protected from ear damage but they also rewarded management with better performance. Much is to be learned about the relationship between noise exposure and quality of workmanship. One can intellectualize, however, that desirable work environments will optimize individual performance.

The effects of noise on pupil performance has been a subject of some study with understandably differing conclusions. Some have observed that noise does not seem to hinder pupils in the classroom; others have concluded that school work is negatively influenced. Again, intellectualizing would lead one to accept the second view simply from past experiences with interruptions caused by various noise forms.

Students in a school outside London near Heathrow Airport produced academic work well below the norm. Since a study of the intellectual and cultural backgrounds of the students gave no insights into such poor performance, it was assumed that the recurring sound of jets coming and going posed a significant impediment to the conduct of school business. Of particular note is that several public schools have been closed in recent years as a direct result of aircraft noise originating from major air terminals. Perhaps these closings are sufficient evidence that high-level noise that seems to be encroaching on the educational units in the community has a deleterious effect on some aspects of human performance and on the learning process as well. Certain noises, by their intensity, interest factor, or rhythm, must certainly be considered to be interfering agents, and they will be disruptive to normal educational situations.

·5·

A Word of Caution

They draw the longbow (exaggerate) better now than ever.
Lord George Gordon Byron

The comedian Norm Crosby, a master of the misused word, tells a story that has some bearing on the subject of this chapter. Here is an abbreviated version (Mr. Crosby's delightful style cannot be duplicated in print). A student in a university psychology department that had hit on a way to make fleas respond to word commands was performing a routine physical examination on one of them under his microscope. At some time during the exam the student whispered, "Fly flea," and the flea flew! He retrieved the tiny insect and repeated his command softly, "Fly flea." Once again the flea flew. This action went on for some time until curiosity got the better of the student, and he very carefully dissected the wings from the flea's body. After surgery was complete the flea huddled in the light of the microscope, and the student whispered, "Fly flea." This time the flea didn't move. "*Fly, Flea,*" the erstwhile researcher exclaimed in a louder voice, but still no movement. In a very loud voice the young man shrieked, "*FLY, FLEA.*" But, alas, no movement. A wry grin slipped over the student's face, and he noted in his lab workbook the observation: "When you remove the wings from a flea, he goes deaf."

Now, that is bad research, and the only thing worse than bad research is the biased or misplaced interpretation of research results. Concern for an area that poses a real or imagined threat can breed careless overstatements that result in an unfortunate dilution of factual evidence. As in the classic folk tale "Cry Wolf," alarmists create a credibility question that fosters contemptuous disregard for new and important knowledge about a problem. In the pages following are some of the overstatements, misstatements, rants, and raves of those we may regard as chronic bogeymen who surreptitiously with malice or blindly with good intent do the cause of quiet a disservice by casting unsupported dire predictions and unquantified research results into the media. Such forebodings do irreparable harm.

The serious student of the noise problem is beset with myriad statements about the possible effects of noise. Some of these statements are valid and can be believed; others must be disregarded. The problem remains: Which purported facts are viable? Examples of material that might be classified as unbelievable are offered here not to criticize persons who may have made the statements but to allow the reader to develop an appreciation of the facts that surround the noise question.

In essence this chapter is concerned with the philosophic question about how much the public should be stirred up in order to begin to combat a problem. The better philosophy in this matter is to educate but not to knowingly overstate. The philosopher A. N. Whitehead observed, "The chief error in philosophy is overstatement." It is our intent to try consciously to avoid that error.

The remainder of this chapter is comprised mostly of statements gleaned from a large number of sources. The only guideline in selecting them was that the sources be of recent vintage, a reasonable rule in that the past few years have provided an abundance of material for a treatment of overstatements of the noise hazard. Authors or sources usually are not cited because it is not deemed necessary nor fair to cite statements of professionals or journalists who were laboring under a temporary misunderstanding. Further, we hold these statements to be inaccurate, but some may disagree with many of the interpretations of the accuracy quotient in the concepts cited.

Finally, the possibility of change is always predominant. New data may give great credence to some of the comments downgraded here. Then the interpretation of truthfulness of the ideas will be accepted, and the statements will be reclassified.

Please realize that we do not intend to poke fun; the subject is far too serious for that little game. Although funny things are said, this matter is considered with the utmost seriousness.

POPULAR THEMES

Two or three popular themes crop up in news stories and articles about noise. One periodical titled an article, "The next sound you hear may be just too much." That wasn't too bad, but the subtitle stated: "Is the rising din around us making everybody deaf?"

Use of the word *deaf* is overworked in articles of this nature. As mentioned earlier, in virtually no way can a person sustain sufficient hearing loss from noise exposure to become deaf —that is, *deaf* as defined to be the absence of any usable hearing. This is not to play down the gravity of the loss of hearing that comes as an unfortunate aftereffect of excessive noise exposure but simply an appeal to keep things in perspective.

The subtitle of another article on noise poses the second overworked theme: "A great big fact of life—that's liable to drive you crazy!" Granted, noise can make one irritable, and on occasion one can lose his sense of personal equilibrium in the din of environmental racket; yet the likelihood of a large nation of many people going crazy from environmental noise is considered a gross overstatement. It is an eyecatcher, but it doesn't really sell the concept of the noise problem.

The third major overworked theme relates to the health aspects of the noise problem. "Noise will kill you!" "Noise is headed for the fatal level." "Expert claims noise is the cause of almost every known disease." "House mayhem deforms rats, rabbits." "Noise taking heavy health toll."

The headline writers cannot be held fully responsible, for the contents of each article quoted a person reputed to have some expertise in making statements that coincided with the headline.

PREDICTIONS

Grave warnings about the future are issuing forth from many of the popular sources of information on noise. The following appeared in a religious newsletter. "But will the harsh sounds of this world finally reach the crescendo envisioned by ———, chairman of ——— Noise Abatement Society, when he said: 'It is not inconceivable that we shall become a race of shouting maniacs'?"

A similar observation was found in an economics-oriented periodical. "Noise awakens us in the middle of the night, it interferes with concentration by day and it frequently makes us shout to be heard. Will it drive us crazy, too?"

Perhaps this question is a good one, but it is unduly unsettling as well. Consider the next citation as a way to ease the minds of the churchmen this religious periodical reaches.

> Truly, "noise pollution," as it is now called, is a serious and growing problem in the highly mechanized world in which we live. The extent of the problem was well summed up in the words of Dr. ———, an internationally known physicist: "If noise levels increase in the next 30 years as they have in the past, it could be lethal."

COMMENTS AND OBSERVATIONS

A United States senator was quoted as saying to a Senate subcommittee, "America now has the dubious distinction of being the noisiest nation on earth." He continued, "It will not be too many years before noise levels in the United States become lethal unless things are quieted down."

On a national television broadcast laymen made some interesting observations that reflect the confusion in their thinking spawned by media misgivings. In response to the inquiring reporter's question: "Has the construction noise caused many people in the neighborhood to move out or change their lives?" one resident replied, "Well, I wouldn't be surprised that it has. One woman was partially deaf and has gone almost completely deaf." On the same broadcast another resident near a busy airport made the following statements:

> I live across the street here at _____. There's never no peace and quiet in this community. The children go around with their ears clogged up, people are getting nervous breakdowns, other people with heart attacks. All suffer from this tremendous noise. We cannot sleep, we cannot rest properly. And we cannot listen to our television. When we get visitors, we have to stop talking and so forth. This is unbearable. How people can live under these conditions and the federal government don't do anything about it is beyond me.
>
> Yes, the people's health has been affected by it. I know a boy that's hard of hearing. When he moved here he had perfect hearing.

Concerning the noise problems of the citizens quoted above, their state congressman said:

> I've gotten interested in noise pollution for just what you hear now. It's a din that is belaboring our entire society; and the way we're going now we're all going to be a nation of deaf people by the year 2000, if we don't do something about it.

SONIC BOOM

During the height of the battle over funding the Boeing version of the commercial supersonic transport (SST) a host of citations, quotations, and predictions were coming into the media hard and fast. These tidbits of misinformation were not used by one side alone; both proponents and opponents of the project provided their share of overstatements about the blessings or curses of the proposed craft. One news service's report of a professional meeting was headed by this lead paragraph: "Violent noise, such as sonic booms, may have permanently damaging effects on unborn babies, a scientist warned yesterday."

A book written by a knowledgeable person included a post-mortem statement on the SST that may be flavored just a mite too strongly in view of the dearth of factual evidence to support the claims:

> If and when commercial supersonic flights are authorized over land, the probability of extensive damage, particularly to delicate geographical features, historic structures, and older dwellings in need of repair will be increased. As long as the noise problem persists, it will be a challenge to the survival of society's artifacts.

STATEMENTS ON HEALTH

We might be classified as a nation of worriers; so it follows that health might be an area of worry in which to indulge one's self. When strongly worded statements about newly discovered threats to our health come out in the media we are naturally most attentive; hence it is no wonder that eyecatching phraseology related to the imminent loss of health due to noise exposure has been a recurring theme.

Newspaper coverage of an international meeting of scientists who pooled their research findings in noise was a particularly fertile field for such material. One article stated: "So a noisy life might lead to injury to arteries, and to an increase in fatty materials in the bloodstream that make arteries clog up in the heart or brain." Another related that ". . . exposure to noise seemed to make jet pilots more susceptible to heart attacks." Still another report said: "Other specialists pointed to disturbed sleep in humans, and to upsets in the menstrual cycle of animals exposed to loud sounds, and to fatal seizures induced in animals by intense sound, and said maybe humans suffer similar costs."

One article concerned a researcher who, on observing that laboratory rats became ill after a series of thunderstorms, designed an experiment in which other rats were exposed to recordings of thunder. These findings gave rise to internal upsets that included a form of disarray for the pituitary gland. The data presented is not being questioned, only the way in which details were omitted, leaving the impression that being caught in a thunderstorm possibly may result in severe trouble even though one remains dry and is not struck by lightning.

Still another newspaper report cites noise as " . . . a cause of some instances of defects or mental retardation in newborn infants." We are sincerely concerned about the reactions of parents of defective children in reading such statements. If they have difficulty in accepting the reality of their personal tragedy can such comments be of any help? Conversely, is there justification in possibly misleading those who are grasping at any explanation of their baby's condition?

A choice example of the type of journalistic purple prose we can very well do without appeared in a nationally distributed tabloid. The particularly offensive comments have been lifted from the text and are quoted in series. Embellishing commentary is not necessary.

> "Noise is the cause of almost every known disease in the medical books," says the head of the _____ Noise Abatement Society.
>
> "Everyday noise like that from trucks or airplanes," he told the _____ , "can cause injury to tissues, can rattle the kidneys, cause inflammation of the stomach lining and inflammation of the brain.
>
> "The whole body comes under bombardment from shock waves emitted by noise and suffers daily from it."
>
> "As noise increases, so does our mental illness rate," _____ claimed. "The incidence of mental illness in people living around airports is eight times greater than that of people living in other areas," he said.

"We cannot protect ourselves from noise because we cannot shut our ears. Noise smashes into the finer points of the hearing follicles and they become deadened until we are deaf."

"Watch the youngsters of today when they go dancing. The noise is so loud that it creates deafness until they have to have the music at the highest possible point."

"Directly and indirectly," _____ summed up, "noise is responsible for every known disease . . . from the wearing down of tissues and organs so that we are more prone to disease to the actual creating of disease and hurt to our bodies by shock waves."

The preceding example hopefully was an overzealous reporter's distorting of words from an official of one of the many noise abatement groups that have sprung up around the globe. If the statements attributed to him are truly his, one might question just whose side he is really on.

A local paper ran an intriguing column in which it cited some research results. "A _____ medical researcher reported Monday short doses of the same noise levels American housewives endure all day long cause pregnant rats and rabbits to produce deformed offspring at least 25 percent of the time." One might wonder what type of reaction expectant mothers had when they read that information just after vacuuming the house?

During the United Nations International Conference on the Environment in Stockholm in 1972 the report of the World Health Organization reported, "Man rapidly is driving himself crazy with noise although it is the easiest form of pollution to control." The report described noise as "the curse of modern times and a major environmental problem," and said further that doctors now attribute one in every three cases of neurosis to noise and blame noise for one in every five headaches. In giving a frame of reference for decibel levels, the report stated that 140 dB "produces insanity."

At this point a small incident in the laboratory may show how researchers sometimes are tempted to come forth with some shocking and newsworthy claims. In order to study the combination of population density and noise exposure in their effect on the hearing and physical well-being of rats, a group of rats was allowed to overpopulate the cage so that the number became fairly good-sized. After several months of this crowding the rats were placed in a noise exposure chamber (described in Chapter 4). A group of control rats placed in a similar chamber had a quiet rather than noisy environment.

After the 48-hour stimulus period had ended, the door of the chamber was opened and three of the four rats were found dead, their white fur turned a sickly yellow. Immediately the thought came to mind, "Could the combination of overpopulation and noise have such a terribly drastic effect?" Naturally it is easy to consider a finding like that real news, to both the scientific community and the population in general. On reaching into the chamber to pick up the cage and more closely examine the animals, the mystery was solved. The extreme heat in the chamber indicated that the animals had sweltered. Because an associate had failed to turn on the ventilating fan, a great discovery became a dud.

Many have seized on the popular phrase coined by a leader in the study of noise: "Noise is the slow agent of death." This idea may be borne out in part, but others have "drawn the longbow" in respect to the concept. The final example is a classic. From its headline nearly to the last paragraph the types of undesirable material alluded to earlier are abundant. The article makes much of a comment from a local professional in the hearing health community: "Slayer's in _____ County now." Here are some of the more significant portions of the article.

> _____ is director of _____ at _____ Hospital in _____ and disagrees with acoustical physicist _____ of the University of _____ who says, "noise is slowly killing us."
> This disagreement is one of degree. "Noise is killing us," declares _____ . "Faster than we think," he adds. "The body can't take it—it dies. NOISE killed it."

Because it is concrete, Interstate _____ ricochets sound all over the county.

"It may not be damaging now to the human body but the sound actually tears up the highway itself," _____ says.

Black asphalt absorbs sound considerably better than concrete, and _____ notes it is the noise that wrecks the highway.

"What do you think causes wear on bridges and bridge abutments?

"It is the weight and vibration of the vehicles PLUS the sound that wear out the bridges and overpasses," _____ points out.

He paints a graphic little picture of a tradesman who has one of the noisiest jobs in the world—the man who handles the jack-hammer.

"They have to pay them more you see.

"They don't last very long. They die early."

It is the noise, you hear?

After this example we hardly need elaborate that papers, television, radio, and periodicals are being glutted with misinformation in the name of education. Hopefully these examples will assist the reader in obtaining some idea of the real and imaginary treatment of noise pollution.

·6·

THE FORTY-HOUR DIN

*The Constitution does not secure to anyone liberty to conduct
his business in such fashion as to inflict injury upon the public
at large, or upon any substantial group of people.*
Owen J. Roberts, Former Justice, U.S. Supreme Court

Reports on some forms of occupational noise exposure go back
to the days of the Babylonian Empire and to the construction of
the great ziggurats (towers of Babel). Through the centuries
certain industries and occupations have been recognized as
ones in which significant numbers of workers lose hearing as a
result of sound in the working environment.

In effect, hearing disability can be classified as an occupational hazard. One report has established that workers not in
noisy industries are considerably less prone to hearing deficit.
Hearing tests of 55-year-olds revealed that 22 percent of those
who did not work in noise had a hearing impairment, while the
incidence of hearing depreciation among those exposed to noise
was 46 percent. More than twice as many of those working in
noise sustained measurable damage to the hearing mechanism.

The problem with noise in the occupational environment,
and in the community as well, stems from the changes civilized
man has undergone as a result of the industrial revolution.
Machines, marvelous mechanized servants of mankind, have
taken a nearly unchallenged place in the civilized world. But
with the positive aspects of mechanization have come some
undesirable side effects in the form of various types of environmental contaminants.

NOISY INDUSTRIES

Back-saving equipment is the source of gigantic amounts of sound in such industries as steel foundries, steel rolling mills, knitting and weaving plants, boiler factories, paper mills, lumber sawmills, and aircraft factories. The construction industry also has a high degree of noise in the work environment.

The farmer, too, is exposed to high-intensity sound on a regular basis. A colleague who has described the "plow-ear syndrome" has found that one can tell with good reliability in which direction a farmer turns to watch the plow in its furrow. If the farmer consistently turns to the left, his right ear will sustain the greatest hearing impairment because that ear is oriented toward the noisy exhaust pipe of the tractor.

Although not an industry in the strictest sense of the word, the military still has a noise problem. According to a survey of 2,726 military men in different arms of the service, some rather disturbing relationships seem to exist between military noise exposure and incidence of hearing impairment. In the study it was found that 52.8 percent of infantrymen with 10 years of active duty had substantial hearing damage. An even greater number of armored personnel (63.3 percent) with more than 10 years in the service possessed noise-damaged ears. In the infantry and armored divisions more than 2 percent of the men tested failed to meet retention standards. In effect, the men are mustered out because of hearing disorders that probably resulted as a part of job exposure. Finally, the military report stated that 42.1 percent of the commissioned officers tested were found to have substantial hearing deficits. As many as half of these men might be considered candidates for hearing aids.

The Veteran's Administration spends huge sums of money each year (more than $8 million) in compensation to former servicemen whose hearing has been judged to have been permanently damaged during active duty. Not all of these cases are noise-induced in that some sustained infections, fungus conditions, and other forms of direct injury to the ear, but the best explanation for large numbers of the hearing deficits among veterans is noise exposure. Armored personnel (tanks, etc.) and artillery have been particularly noted as noisy subsections of the military services.

To provide, in addition to compensation, diagnostic and rehabilitative services for the veterans, the Veteran's Administration maintains hearing and speech service clinics in most of the VA hospitals. In a plan seriously considered in November 1971 the clinics would serve the speech and hearing needs of families of veterans with service-connected disabilities as well as those of the veteran. According to Captain Vincent J. Hyams, MC of the Armed Forces Institute of Pathology, the cost of the VA programs is $50 million. Although not the only factor in creating a need for this program, military noise exposure plays a significant role.

Some of the professions are not immune to excessive noise exposure. Newly developed high-speed dental drills have been cited as a threat to dentists' ears. These drill heads, capable of a speed of 100,000 revolutions per minute, permit faster work with less discomfort to the patient, but the high-pitched whine proves to be excessively loud for the dentist who is near the sound for long periods. Although the drills are not excessively noisy by other industrial noise standards, the dentist necessarily holds his head near the head of the drill. At this distance the sound has been measured to be roughly equivalent in amplitude to the noise a jackhammer generates when measured from a distance of 10 feet.

The National Bureau of Standards conjectures that in computer laboratories relatively simple programmer errors have been laid to high noise levels. We noted earlier that thought processes and logical mental activities can be disrupted by noise, and the levels in computer rooms range from 89 to 94 dB in areas where highly trained computer programmers attempt to concentrate.

With the exception of the Veteran's Administration activities, compensation for occupationally related hearing impairment has been slow in developing. In recent years workman's compensation in most states has included payment for hearing loss that can be attributed to occupational noise exposure, but documentation of the cause of hearing impairment still is a difficult problem. Compensation laws still vary widely in the type and amount of compensation allowed. In one state, total loss of hearing function is compensated to the tune of $28,500. The same injury in another state would bring only $3,000. These inequities must be resolved.

It has been estimated that 6 million industrial workers are engaged in occupations where the noise level is dangerously high. Some have estimated that if 10 percent of the people eligible for compensation were to bring suit, and if the average award were $1,000, the cost of legal action to industry would be approximately $450 million—a conservative estimate, for the average award has been nearer $2,000. This figure, while significant, takes a different perspective when it is noted that the World Health Organization has estimated that noise causes industrial worker inefficiency amounting to $4 million each workday. The value for this figure is found in the problems of quality control and labor malaise. The National Institutes of Health has estimated that each year industry loses $4 billion in compensation claims, production loss, and absenteeism.

A problem in industry has been, until recently, the lack of appropriate and enforceable standards as various ideas and philosophies have each competed for acceptance. Some have favored the use of temporary threshold shifts (TTS) as the guide to industrial damage-risk conditions, while others have attempted to integrate the PNdB concept into industry as well as in the measures of aircraft flight noise. Another concept has been that of speech interference, for some feel the extent to which communication is canceled serves as a sufficient warning of excessive noise. Refuting all of the above, another group has argued for enactment of physiologically based standards wherein the total state of the noise-exposed person is considered.

AN ADDITIONAL FACTOR

The primary problem of industrial noise lies in the bothersome sounds generated from within the plant, but disruption also may occur as a result of outside noises. For example, the staff of a quiet factory in an industrial park adjacent to an airport may find that frequent jet flyovers cut down on the ability to concentrate. Or a quiet plant may be located in an industrial area close to a very noisy industry. Then the racket from one plant drones into the other, affecting workers at both sites.

Until the shell of a new structure is completed construction noises adjacent to working areas disturb neighbors for seemingly endless periods of time—a condition that occurred in our laboratory during the first half of 1972. The research quarters and seminar room for the academic department are located under the west stands of the University of Tennessee football stadium. When an extension of the upper deck was begun, construction activities occurred directly outside the offices and labs. Almost immediately the staff was made aware of the type of life it would lead for the next several months when three large air compressors were brought in and allowed to run nearly the entire day thereby raising the sound level inside the offices to a point where telephone conversation was nearly impossible. On hearing the noise over the telephone, and having the situation explained to her, a caller said, "Well, I was going to complain to you about the noise problem we are having in our neighborhood, but I see you have a worse one"; whereupon she hung up.

Those raucous compressors were left running, even for lengthy periods of time when the devices they supplied with air were unused. Noting this, and seeing that the compressors were still operating while the workmen were at lunch, we approached the foreman to attempt a compromise on use of the machines. Mentioning that the compressor noise sure was bad brought the foreman's response, "Oh, you ain't heard nothin' yet!" When we mentioned that the telephone could not be used and that we would appreciate having the compressors stopped during the lunch hour so that the staff could at least have some quiet then, the foreman extended his echoic response. "Well, you ain't heard nothin' yet, wait 'till the big drills get here to dig for the pilings." That terminated the conversation, but he proved to be a latter-day prophet. When the big drills came on the scene and located next to our windows the show was over—a move had to be made. That move was approximately a quarter-mile around the horseshoe of the stadium to quieter quarters—hopefully

—but it was soon evident that this solution might have been more of a problem. Not only were the offices located a considerable distance from the other segments of the department but we also suddenly discovered that the new spaces were immediately adjacent to a railroad overpass. Attempts to carry on class in the newly arranged seminar room were frustrated as the train whistle covered up all efforts to communicate. Interestingly, in this location a new course, "Noise in the Environment," was taught for the first time. That the students felt it was a most adequate location was made abundantly clear as the construction noise began to move around the stadium toward our new location.

It was soon obvious that the move was ill-planned and that the old quarters would be better. The incongruity was that the noise study laboratory staff and others in the communication sciences were forced to vacate their work areas because construction noise made communication impossible.

During a local television talk show when this incident was mentioned, viewers were asked to call and try to convince the staff that construction people are not the most inconsiderate people in the world. To date, no one has.

GOOD NEIGHBOR POLICY

Industrial noise problems are a two-edged sword in that within the plants noise creates problems among the workers and noise broadcast into the surrounding area also causes problems. It is necessary, therefore, to consider industrial noise in terms of in-plant and outside-plant levels.

Communities are beginning to deal with the second problem by initiating legislation that sets permissible sound levels as measured at the boundary line of the industry property. In Knoxville a resident complained about the stamping noises emanating from a large metal fabricating plant. The authorities were notified, sound measures were taken at the property line, and the industry's management was notified that noise levels exceeded the permissible amount. The industrialists took steps to muffle the sound that escaped from the work area, and the resident's noise problem was solved. This little vignette had a happy ending because a spirit of cooperation existed among all those concerned.

In another incident a property-owner adjacent to an extraction industry that has large pieces of outside machinery talked with the office staff about the noise that radiated to the neighborhood. One young man volunteered the information, "Yeh, we wait until Mr. _____ calls us and we know it is time to oil the equipment again." Unfortunately, that does not seem an adequate solution to the community noise problem caused at the industrial setting.

FEDERAL CONTROLS

The federal government took a major step toward developing meaningful hearing conservation procedures in industry with the 1969 revision of the Walsh-Healy Public Contracts Act. This legislation provided guidelines for the maximum noise allowable in plants as a function of duration of exposure. If the guidelines are exceeded the plant then must reduce the noise at the source and/or provide workers with ear protection devices. This particular act related only to those approximately 70,000 industries that held contracts with the government in the amount of $10,000 or more annually, thereby excluding the numerous industries that do not deal directly with the government and leaving the hearing conservation of their workers to the option of management.

Largely based on the previously established damage-risk criteria, the guidelines incorporated in the Walsh-Healy Act and reported in the *Federal Register* on May 20, 1969, were predicated on the assumption that most workers can safely sustain continuous occupational exposure to sound of 90 dBA. The allowance exposure is adjusted accordingly as shown in Table 6.1. Industries that had measured sound levels with the use of octave-band meters rather than with the more simple A weighting scale could still use their previous measures by means of a conversion chart provided in the act.

Compliance is not easy to determine. Sound varies widely so that even high noise areas often are found periodically to have

Table 6.1   Maximum permissible exposures according to sound level of the acoustic environment as established in the federal guidelines.

Exposure Duration (hours)	Sound Level (dBA)
8	90
6	92
4	94
3	97
2	100
1½	102
1	105
½	110
¼ or less	115

Table 6.2   Analysis of noise exposure for two machinists located in different areas of a manufacturing plant.

Name	Exposure	Daily Exposure	Level	Ratio (D/P)	Exposure Value
T. S.	Milling machine	2 hr.	92dBA	2/6	0.333
	Bench grinder	1 hr.	95dBA	1/4	0.250
	Lathe	1 hr.	97dBA	1/3	0.333
	Workbench	4 hr.	90dBA	4/inf.	0.000
		Total			0.916
A. B.	Work station	6 hr.	92dBA	6/6	1.000
	Air jet	2 hr.	100dBA	2/2	1.000
		Total			2.000

sound levels within acceptable limits according to the federal guidelines. These multiple-exposure levels for industrial personnel are calculated for a single eight-hour shift; then a ratio between the exposure duration (D) and the permissible duration (P) is calculated for each exposure level. If the sum of this ratio exceeds unity (1), the worker's exposure is excessive. Table 6.2

cites examples of exposure figures calculated for two industrial plant workers. The first worker (T. S.) sustains exposure to noise in doses that total less than 1; thus in view of the federal guidelines he is operating within safe limits with respect to hearing hazard. The second worker (A. B.) is exposed to an acoustic environment that results in an accumulative exposure twice the allowable amount. It is therefore mandatory that A. B. have access to ear protection at least until his noisy work environment is brought under control.

The Walsh-Healy Act has had a marked impact on industrial hearing conservation programs; however, an additional factor is commonly overlooked in assessing the extent of noise exposure industrial workers sustain. An unfortunate paradox exists in modern-day living. Whereas considerable effort is being extended to bring the working environment under control with respect to industrial noise exposure, the otohazardous characteristics of recreational and environmental noise are becoming increasingly apparent. A worker whose occupational noise exposure index is marginally acceptable according to the guidelines may still suffer ear damage from partaking in noisy nonoccupational activities. Quite possibly one's occupational noise exposure is insufficient to cause permanent ear damage; possibly the same person's nonoccupational activities alone are not otohazardous; but if the two types of exposure are combined regularly into the same 24-hour period, the accumulative effect of noise exposure may be sufficient to result in damage to the hearing mechanism.

The guidelines proposed by the Threshold Limits Committee for Physical Agents of the American Conference of Governmental Industrial Hygienists provided the nucleus data on which the federal action is based. These figures are predicated on the assumption that the off-job hours for a given worker consist of low-volume acoustic resting level recovery time. Therefore, if a worker engages in noisy recreational activities after work this exposure would be considered in the computation of his daily exposure index. In effect, industrial or personal hearing conservation is a 24-hour concern.

In April 1971 the Williams-Steiger Occupational Safety and

Health Act (OSHA) generalized to all workers the Walsh-Healy guidelines for noise. This bill extended the requirements for industrial hearing health activities to include over 57 million workers. Specific limitations in the guidelines are identical to those of the Walsh-Healy Act (see Table 6.1).

The entire OSHA as printed in the *Federal Register* appears to contain more words than the Bible. It is a comprehensive compilation of a wide range of safety guidelines for such areas as temperature, handling of noxious gases, floor surfaces, safety guards on machinery, radiation safety, sanitation, and a host of others. Most of the safety guidelines were already in existence, but this act served to gather them into one reference and to make their enforcement necessary across the whole of business and industry. The Department of Labor is charged with enforcing this monumental act of Congress.

Although the OSHA statements about the initiation of hearing conservation procedures are contained in only slightly more than one column of this huge manual, their impact has been much more far-reaching than is indicated in the guidelines.

Floyd Van Atta of the Department of Labor has observed that the 90 dBA value is not "safe" in the absolute sense. He points out estimates of workers who will still suffer some hearing deficits even though they are within the 90 dBA level. These "unprotected" people number between 11 and 16 percent of the work force exposed. If an 85 dBA level were maintained, the number of overexposed workers would drop to an estimated 3 percent. At this writing speculation is that a revision of the interpretations of OSHA will include reduction of the baseline sound level to the more appropriate 85 dBA figure—appropriate in that the damage-risk criteria discussed earlier all seem to have established that level as the maximum safe limit for continuous exposure.

A BIT OF PHILOSOPHY

"Well, the word's out," the downcast young man remarked. "Our industry is one of the targets for enforcement of the noise regulations in the new Occupational Safety and Health Act." Then he asked how to begin the involved and seemingly mysterious process of meeting the regulations set forth by the act.

Perhaps the answer will come as a surprise, for he was not immediately given the outline of a program of plant procedure alterations that would lead to full compliance. Rather, the response was intended to foster in him an appreciation for the reasons behind the rules and regulations. Millions of words will be written about OSHA and about methods whereby effective noise control can be initiated. Perhaps too little will be said about the law's underlying objectives as they relate to the protection of the precious and irreplaceable hearing sense of the work force. The following comments to the young man are offered here so that others may become motivated to bring plant noise problems under control, not because the law says so but out of compassion for the employees.

The underlying purpose of OSHA noise guidelines is not to harass and embarrass industry but, rather, to provide a working environment free of the myriad contaminating influences of high-level sound. The estimates of huge financial losses due to noise interference provide good reason for forward-thinking management to rid their plants of noise and protect their employees from the devastating effects of continuous exposure to high-level sound. Hopefully, noise control programs will be initiated because management has compassion for employees. If that is the motivation, the mechanics of establishing a meaningful and effective program of noise control will be forthcoming.

MEETING THE GUIDELINES

The requirements of the law can be divided into three major areas. The order in which these areas are listed in the act is maintained here.

Sound Measurements

The act stipulates that sound-level measures must be taken to determine the extent of the noise problem, if any. These measures should be taken with standard sound-level measuring equipment utilizing the "A" scale, as outlined in Chapter 1. It is desirable, when possible, to obtain the readings at ear level of the workers involved. When purchasing appropriate sound-level meters it is best to stay with some of the well-established manufacturing firms. A number of inexpensive sound-measuring devices have hit the market lately, but most of them have a serious shortcoming in that they are not easily calibrated.

It is most important that sound-level measuring equipment be easily calibrated so that the accuracy of the readings is assured. In addition to a measuring device it is equally important to have an accurate calibrator. Although the calibration device adds significantly to the total cost of sound-measuring equipment, it will give the equipment its value. It is difficult to get worked up about new and innovative sound-measuring devices that cannot be calibrated with a known sound source (calibrator).

Noise Abatement

The normal inclination is to say: "Well, with the present situation we can't do anything about the noise levels; we'll get ear protectors and solve our problem that way." The Department of Labor inspectors are not likely to take kindly to that attitude, however. Usually, steps can be taken to abate the noise, at least to a degree. Efforts on the part of industry to make reductions in the overall sound levels will be scrutinized and evaluated, according to recent reports.

Granted, noise abatement can be a very expensive proposition, but it needn't be. Some programs call for the use of numerous specialists and consultants, but not always. Noise abatement procedures can cause expensive inroads into efficient material preparation by necessitating the rearrangement of factory layouts, but that seldom happens. Noise reduction can be a terrible headache for the plant personnel in charge, but they needn't feel they are against a stone wall.

Some smaller industries are forming a hearing conservation cooperative to provide equipment and personnel for an ongoing program in all their plants. Such a program usually can be underwritten for approximately $45,000 per year and can handle as many as 12 plants with full services.

Compared to the estimated losses incurred in industry as a function of noise-related problems the NIH figure of $400 million to bring industry into compliance seems relatively small. Of course, that amount is only an estimate and may be quite short of the ultimate total cost.

The growth of the industrial noise problem can be compared to the flooding of a river. Overnight the water can reach flood crest stage, but the waters take considerably longer to recede. Likewise, industrial noise problems seem to have reached a dangerous peak very rapidly, but we cannot expect an immediate reversal of the trend. In time, though, industry can be quieted. With the Department of Labor's insistence on abatement there will evolve a new and quieter generation of equipment that also will be less in need of frequent replacement, because taking cognizance of noise control in the design necessitates better engineering.

Hearing Conservation

Last but certainly not least in the triad of considerations is the hearing protection of industrial personnel. This program is necessary only because many industries find it absolutely impossible to sufficiently engineer noise out of their plants to bring the noise levels into concert with federal requirements. A successful, ongoing hearing conservation program consists of several important elements.

Hearing tests A joint committee comprised of representatives of five major organizations concerned with hearing health has adopted a program for training industrial nurses to administer hearing tests. This training includes an introduction to the anatomy of the ear, some discussion of things that go wrong with the ear, basic acoustics, and audiometric technique. At the end of the training period the nurse or audiometric technician is considered prepared to test hearing among plant personnel. Training programs may consist of a three-day short course, or the option for individual training of technicians may be available in some areas.

One precaution is necessary. Industrial noise consulting has become a very attractive business for some people who are not capable of adequately conducting services. Before industrial management contracts for services it should be sure that consultants possess appropriate credentials. Noise questions and those problems that border on acoustics are best dealt with by persons who hold full membership in the Acoustical Society of America. Almost anyone can obtain an associate membership in that organization in order to receive the journal, but the Acoustical Society is quite careful about allowing full membership. Therefore, if a consultant holds this credential he has demonstrated to the society's screening committee that he is sufficiently knowledgeable to be a member in good standing.

If the major area of work involves the administration of hearing tests or the interpretation of their results, the highest credential one may obtain is the Certificate of Clinical Competence in Audiology, which is awarded by the American Speech and Hearing Association. To obtain this credential the consultant must hold a master's degree in audiology with an academic background that meets rigid specifications. He must complete one year of paid professional clinical work under direct supervision of a certified audiologist, and then he must pass a written examination. The person who holds this certificate is quite qualified to deal with the audiometric questions in industry.

Increasing numbers of training programs for industrial audiometrists are being conducted around the country. As a service to industry the National Safety Council keeps an up-to-date listing of these training programs and on request will give names of instructors in various areas.

An integral portion of a hearing conservation program is the physician, and in many large plants the resident physician oversees the hearing test program. Since numerous medical problems can occur in the ear, medical consultation in the inauguration of a hearing conservation program is wise.

When the technician is trained and the appropriate hearing testing equipment acquired, the testing can begin. All testing must be conducted in a quiet area so that background noise will not interfere with reception of the test tones and cause the appearance of one having hearing worse than he really has. Acquisition of equipment appropriate for each setting is such an individual problem that an attempt here to discuss that part of the program does not seem profitable. Most audiologists and acoustic consultants can provide guidance, and some hearing aid company consultants sell the company's hearing test equipment.

All new employees should have a preemployment hearing evaluation to establish an audiometric baseline. The degree of hearing impairments many job applicants show may be astonishing, and young persons are no exception. As noted earlier, the results of hearing surveys among high school and college students revealed that a high percentage of young people already demonstrate significant hearing impairments.

Some time ago we received a request for measurements of sound levels in a nearby plant. When the measures had been made we were asked whether these levels were high enough to cause the onset of a severe hearing loss after a half-day exposure. The 95 to 98 dBA values were not great enough to have warranted an affirmative answer. The plant manager, though, told us about a man who worked one morning, walked off of the job during the lunch hour, and a few days later, had his attorney inform the plant superintendent that the man was bringing suit for loss of hearing. Detailed hearing tests confirmed the hearing impairment, and it was not possible to testify unequivocally that a hearing deficit could not be caused by some unique twist in a four-hour exposure time. The consulting physician suggested that the company settle, although the injury they were being held responsible for was highly unlikely. Lack of a missing preemployment hearing test here proved expensive.

Every employee whose work environment contains noise in excess of the OSHA guidelines should be tested annually. Appropriate steps must be taken if the hearing test reveals that a workman's hearing is deteriorating as a function of his noise environment. Often a good policy is semiannual hearing tests for persons located in areas of excessively high noise. The formula for retest procedures and relocation of personnel is another of those highly individual situations that must be tailored to the plant and its needs.

A final consideration in establishing a hearing conservation program is the distribution of ear-protective devices, which range from very ineffective, cheap earplugs to very effective earmuffs or combinations of plugs and muffs. It is not feasible to purchase only one type of ear protective device for all employees because the needs for ear protection are many and varied. Some workers just cannot wear the heavy muffs for long periods of time; others cannot stand plugs in the ears. Because ears differ greatly in size and shape, one style of plug that seems appropriate for some employees will be quite unsatisfactory for others.

Variations in noise levels and other factors, such as room temperature, mobility of workers, individual preferences, will dictate that a number of ear protector styles be used. A well-stocked safety equipment distributor can be valuable in helping industrial safety personnel select appropriate ear protectors. Hopefully, someday such devices will be museum pieces, no longer needed in industry.

A current problem in the use of ear protection devices is worker approval. Unions have been pressing for the development of good hearing conservation programs, but many workers have resisted ear protectors. Some regard earplugs as sissy stuff; others, having adjusted over the years, are reticent to change the sound around them by inserting earplugs. Some industries have resorted to a get-tough policy on ear protection wear; others have gotten good results with education programs.

Most people know that airline ground personnel are required to wear earmuffs in the vicinity of jets—a requirement estimated to have spared the hearing of many thousands of workers. A 10-year study conducted in the Midwest showed that only 2 percent of the workers who wore ear protection were found to have hearing changes, while more than 50 percent of the unprotected workers had significant hearing sensitivity changes.

Occasionally a worker who has seen the dangers of noise has, on his own, purchased or fabricated some form of ear protection. In a syndicated medical question-and-answer column a New York girl commented: "My fiance, who works in a noisy factory, uses flashlight bulbs as earplugs. John claims they fit so well that they seal off most of the noise. Are these safe to use?"

Because of their glass content the physician did not recommend the use of flashlight bulbs, but it appears to have been an effective means of stopping the ingress of unwanted sound. Wouldn't it be an interesting twist if one could buy flashlight and photoflash bulbs in assorted ear sizes?

FINAL THOUGHTS

The advent of noise controls in industry has been a welcome innovation in most cases. Some industrialists were afraid that controls would precipitate a flood of legal action, but thus far that fear has not been realized. In fact, plants that have inaugurated noise control measures have reported higher worker morale, and in some instances there has been tangible evidence of increased productivity and quality control.

It is always a nice surprise to fear something and find that it wasn't half bad. So it has been in some industries where the fear of virtually insurmountable noise problems has dissipated after a sound-level survey has shown the problem to be really only in the mind. Of course, others have stuck their heads in the proverbial sand and have discovered that the problem still would not go away.

A local manufacturing firm asked for an evaluation of the noise output of a large piece of machinery it was about to deliver to a customer. The sales manager had been asked about the sound the device generated and was told that if it did not conform to OSHA-prescribed levels the sale was canceled. Several concerned members of the sales staff who observed the measures being taken heaved an audible sigh when the noise level was discovered to be under the 90 dBA figure. They had never before been asked to consider noise levels, but they were confident that they would be asked again. At present, steps are under way to modify the device so that it will meet an 85 dBA level.

It has not been our intent to provide a comprehensive working guide for controlling industrial noise. This presentation should serve as a springboard into further consideration of the problem. It is imperative to realize, however, that industrial workers are entitled to appropriate protection from noise trauma. When a program to provide a satisfactory work environment has been initiated all factors tend to move upward. Workers enjoy a safer, more meaningful life, and industry experiences less turnover, fewer labor problems, and reduction of other negative influences on productivity.

An appropriate summary of the ways in which industrial noise can be approached is given by Professor Paul D. Emerson of the North Carolina State University Textile Laboratory: "One man can't put out the fire by himself. Each man has to stand and fight on his own little acre."

·7·

Dangerous Playthings

Men cannot labor on always. They must have recreation.
Orville Dewey

In observing that "the machine age has given us more leisure time in which to play," Stewart Chase offered a remark central to the theme of this chapter.

In recent years overall sound levels in many nonoccupational and recreational environments have increased dramatically. For example, motorcycle riding has become an immensely popular pastime. The exhaust noise of trail bikes has been disturbing to those who want an unspoiled and quiet wilderness as well as to those concerned primarily for the riders' hearing health. Recreational shooting, another popular activity, can result in damage to the sensory portion of the ear. Modern dance music augmented by high-powered amplification systems sends the sound level literally soaring to dizzying heights.

The list of noise-producing devices in the nonoccupational milieu appears to be growing. Included are such appliances and tools as lawnmowers, snowblowers, chain saws, blenders, sink disposals, clothes washers and dryers. The hobbyist encounters noisy gasoline-powered model airplanes and cars, loud racing car engines, raucous snowmobile exhaust noise, and high-level cockpit noise. Children commonly are exposed to such familiar toys as firecrackers and cap pistols as well as innumerable noisy toys of more recent vintage. Perhaps not all are damaging to the child's hearing, but all at least take their toll in frayed parental nervous systems. Getting to and from recreational activities also can be a source of noise exposure if the participant uses some of the more noisy forms of public transportation to be discussed later. The appearance of off-the-job noise exposure signals an end to the days when a worker could leave his job and retreat to his quiet rest environment.

The growth in popularity of noisy nonoccupational activities has created new problems in modern life. Military and industrial settings have long been plagued with the ongoing enigma of high-intensity sound, but the threat of legal action from employees and federal agencies has encouraged management to institute hearing conservation programs for their work forces. Paradoxically, the home and recreational surroundings are becoming glutted with racket-producing gadgets and activities. Most of the noise exposures cited thus far are occasioned with relative infrequency; thus it is presumed (hoped, at least) that persons who engage in some noisy activities on an irregular schedule have not encountered a serious hearing threat.

IMPULSE SOUNDS

One of the most dangerous sounds from the standpoint of ear safety and health is the impulse sound. Sometimes called impact sound, this type of noise is characterized by a very sharp report as in the crack of gunfire or the pop of exploding items such as firecrackers. In extensive surveys of sound levels generated by small-arms fire researchers have found maximum peaks of as much as 150 to 165 dB, but this level must be placed into perspective. The transient nature of impulse sounds is such that one generally can be subjected to higher peak levels for the brief duration of the impulse. If, for example, one were exposed for a minute or more to 161 dB sound he would surely suffer considerable ear damage. Fortunately, the peak sound of guns is sustained for only a small part of a second.

The danger in this type of sound lies in its speed of entry into the ear. It has been pointed out that when loud sounds occur two small muscles in the middle ear can contract, which tends to slightly reduce the ear's responsiveness to sound and thus directly provides a form of protection for the inner ear. Impulse sounds occur so briefly, however, that the pressure of the sound has already entered the inner ear and begun to overstress the tissues there before the tiny muscles have time to react and function protectively. Fortunately, the danger of impulse sounds is modified by their transient quality and their inability to hold high levels very long. It can be assumed, however, that repeated exposure to these sounds certainly would result in ear damage.

In a study completed at the University of Illinois, guinea pigs exposed to 500 rounds of impulse sounds peaking at 153 dB sustained total sensory cell destruction in one area of the inner ear. This destruction would not be manifest as a total loss of hearing but would result in some measurable effect over time. Figure 7.1 shows the sensory cells of a guinea pig exposed to 25 gunshots peaking at 161 dB. The animal's ears were prepared for

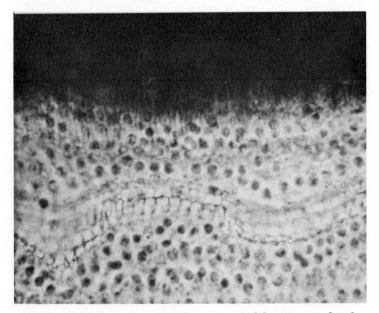

7.1 Guinea pig inner ear structures stressed by 25 rounds of an impulse sound peaking at 161 dB.

microscopic observation immediately after exposure, rather than after the normal period allowed for development of scar tissue, because of the interest in observing any effects that might show just after the impact signal stimulation. That the inner ear tissues seem distended and misshapen is readily apparent in the figure. In undisturbed specimens the tissue is seen to shape a very graceful curve as it forms the arc of one of the turns in the cochlea. This illustration quite clearly indicates the sizable distortion of the tissues after exposure to high-level impulse sounds. Other animals studied several days after being exposed showed considerable sensory cell damage, but the wavy distortion of the structures had disappeared. Apparently such distortion is visible only a short while after exposure; then the tissue regains its form in the living animal.

That frequent human exposure to gunfire sounds without adequate protection will cause measurable hearing deficiency has been well demonstrated. One of the most widely quoted studies was conducted in Jacksonville, Florida, comparing the hearing ability of shooters with the audiometric test results of persons who avoided such exposure. Results of the study indicated that gun users demonstrated considerably more hearing impairment than did the control population. The sizable drop in hunters' hearing was heightened in the left ear (see Figure 7.2) because most shooters' left ears are oriented toward the muzzle of the gun. This result held for all ages compared. Most of the hunters reported that they never wore any form of hearing protection, and of those who did, half reported using it only occasionally.

The U.S. Public Health Service conducted a study that dramatically emphasized the need for ear protection while shooting. Researchers for PHS measured the hearing of police officers who fire between 60 and 5,000 rounds on the firing range each year and always wear ear protectors, then compared the data with norms for the officers' age groups. No noticeable trends could be found to demonstrate that one group's hearing was poorer than the other's for all age comparisons; thus indicating that ear protectors spared the policemen from hearing damage.

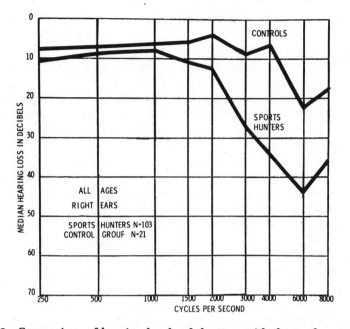

7.2 Comparison of hearing levels of shooters with those of control group that had limited exposure to excessive noise (from Taylor and Williams).

Since hunting and target shooting are becoming increasingly popular, ear protection must be emphasized as a necessary adjunct to the use of small arms. Displays of ear-protective devices in sporting goods stores have become prominent, and, in fact, safety equipment suppliers and sport shops are the two best sources for good-quality earplugs and earmuffs.

Imported toy cap pistols that use supercharged insert caps are a recent addition to toyshop shelves. These devices have the capability of providing a startlingly high instantaneous sound level; so frequent firing of such devices poses a serious threat to the ear. Although cap pistol reports have been found to peak as high as 161 dB, the duration of the entire shot is little more than 3 to 10 microseconds. The imported guns, however, provide both higher and lengthier sounds. Just before Christmas 1970 the Federal Trade Commission included certain toy caps and similar devices in a list of hazardous toys that pose threats to youngsters. In subsequent investigations, however, the FTC allowed the sale of paper caps, the familiar toy known to have been a part of almost every child's play history.

Most people have experienced the sharp, ringing sensation that begins immediately after a firecracker has exploded too close to the ear—a signal that such devices, although a whale of a lot of fun, are possibly dangerous in some aspects. Several factors may cause exposure to these sounds to result in varying types of hearing damage—if exposure is, in fact, sufficient to create an impairment. Although the sound generated is similar to that of gunfire and need not be treated separately, firecrackers hopefully will be set off at a reasonable distance from the ear, considerably lessening the danger. The hazard also is reduced because most fireworks are shot in an open area out-of-doors, thereby allowing the sound to be dissipated much more readily than it would be in an enclosed area where great reverberations would be set up. Fortunately, firecracker explosions are largely restricted to a few days in the summer.

Sadly, such toys as firecrackers often are used in pranks. To this end ladyfingers, 1½ inchers, torpedoes, cherry bombs, TNT bombs, or the like are ignited to shock or startle people. The story of one such prank, which caused shock to the hearing and balance mechanism, came from a lawyer who sought advice on ways to proceed with a legal case he was handling. Just as his client was leaving his college dormitory room a cherry bomb exploded a short distance down the hall where it had been taped onto a door. Apparently the shock wave was sufficiently great and the student's location just right, for he was rendered unconscious for six hours. After he regained consciousness the man was troubled by recurring periods of dizziness and headaches. Although the hearing damage noticed shortly after the accident slowly decreased until his hearing returned to normal, the dizzy spells still bothered him if he became even slightly fatigued—a severe handicap for a young man preparing for a medical career. Extremely sudden sounds potentially can cause troubles above and beyond the recognized hearing loss, but happily these situations do not occur often.

The damaging characteristics of continuous sounds are becoming quite well known, but damage-risk in impulse sounds has been considerably more difficult to determine. Criteria limits for impulse noise proposed by the Committee on Hearing and Bioacoustics and Biomechanics (CHABA) of the National Research Council have established that the maximum allowable peak pressure level is 164 dB. This maximum value is applied to the short-duration impulses—25 microseconds or less. (A microsecond is 1 millionth of a second). As noted earlier, with the increase in duration of exposure the allowable peak level must be reduced.

Repetition also must be considered. A sound that occurs in rapid-fire succession is considerably more damaging than it would be if it were only occasional. The CHABA guidelines apply to 100 impulses extended over periods between 4 minutes to several hours on the day of exposure. In cases of more than 100 exposures the limits are to be reduced by 5 dB for each 10-fold increase in frequency of impulses. For example, if a person fired a gun 100 times per day and if the sound of the gun were such that it fell just within the acceptable limits for shooting a gun 1,000 times a day, the individual would need to use a gun whose sound was 5 dB lower.

These CHABA limits are not just numbers pulled out of the air but are based on the best knowledge of the effect of impulse sound on the ear. They are intended to protect 95 percent of people exposed to impulse sounds.

With more knowledge the CHABA figures may be amended, but regardless of the normative data, impulse noise must be respected as a potential source of dramatic and traumatic reactions, as the college student's story indicates. Dr. W. D. Ward and Dr. Aram Glorig also have reported a case of quite severe one-sided permanent hearing disability that resulted from the explosion of a firecracker 18 inches from the ear. Further, a Danish survey reported that 72 percent of the patients treated in a state hearing center during a 3-year period had traumatic hearing losses that were traced to exposure to New Year's Eve fireworks. Noise trauma can change recreation into "wreck creation" if good judgment and propriety do not prevail.

THE SOUND OF MUSIC

A fine pastor who because of a birth injury had some brain damage manifest as *intention tremor* trembled severely whenever he attempted to extend his arms and hands in order to grasp an object. The gentleman had not allowed his disability to become a handicap. In fact, his hobby was magic, and he had become so accomplished in overcoming his tremor and at times putting it to good use that he had gained membership in the very exclusive International Federation of Magicians. During his act he told the audience to disregard the occasional quivers and tremors in his hands because "the trembling is the result of the fact that my folks rocked me a lot when I was a child—and they used such big ones."

The subject of this section will be the big rock—not the pastor's rock but the type of rock known to the Rolling Stones and their genre.

Exotically named rock groups such as the Beatles, The Who, Jefferson Airplane, Pink Floyd, and the Grateful Dead have been assembled and subsequently have risen to economic prominence in surprisingly short time. The subculture that has sprung up around rock music is mysterious to the generations of people raised on the older sounds of the big bands but not exposed to the greatly amplified, pulsing beat of contemporary music. The expressions of ecstasy quite apparent among the disciples of the rock culture defy linguistic description. Frank Zappa, leader of the Mothers of Invention, said in *Life* magazine that one of his greatest moments was hearing Bill Haley and the Comets play "Rock Around the Clock" in the film *Blackboard Jungle*. What he considered the teen-age national anthem was played so loudly that he could not resist the urge to jump up and down.

Rock music has had a noticeable impact on the music industry's economy. In recent years record sales have risen by 15 to 20 percent annually, and in 1969 the *Wall Street Journal* reported that rock music accounted for 60 percent or more of the total market. Promoter Bill Graham (not to be confused with the popular evangelist), who established the rock emporium Fillmore East, rolled in vast sums of money and gave rock music a great boost in the New York City area. He is reported to have grossed more than $100,000 each for many of his shows. Interestingly, the rock scene's instability is illustrated by a 1971 Scripps-Howard editorial, "Requiem for Rock," which discussed the demise of Fillmore East in New York and Fillmore West in San Francisco.

In recent years with the advent of powerful amplifiers and modifications in technique, music, a previously benign sound source, has generated sound levels of astounding proportions, and rock musicians seem to search continually for ways to increase the sound output even more. In the words of Jack Casady, bass player in the Jefferson Airplane, "Our eternal goal in life is to get louder."

This stated aim is being augmented with new developments in electronic technology, which has now produced the high gain amplifiers that promote ever-increasing sound levels. A stereo set listed in the latest catalog of a major electronics supply house has available a power output of 100 watts per channel, and one of their four-channel systems produces a total of 260 watts from all 4 channels combined. This power potential is considerably more than is necessary for most home use, but it pales into insignificance with the revelation that some rock musicians now use 1,000 watt amplifiers and combine units to produce systems rated at as much as 2,500 watts of sound power.

Great amounts of money are being used in setting up for the big sound. A musical instrument salesman in a southern city observed that when young persons, even high schoolers, contract for instruments and electronic gear sometimes amounting to over $20,000 he has little fear that the budding musicians will not pay off. With the increase in popularity of that type of musical equipment the salesman knows that the groups soon will be making it well enough to get the debt satisfied.

Live musical performances pose a situation that allows for excessive high-level sound, but the *British Medical Journal* also has reported that stereo amplifiers with earphones can provide music at levels so intense that hearing damage is possible. The article indicated that a few people expressed pain when listening to ámplified music through earphones. Scott Wood, a graduate student in the Department of Audiology and Speech Pathology at the University of Tennessee, attempted to verify that claim after a search of the available literature revealed no documented studies about the potentially available sound levels from stereo components. In order to investigate the maximum sound levels generated by stereo receiver-driven earphones and to compare these sound levels with damage-risk criteria established by the American Academy of Opthalmology and Otolaryngology (AAOO) he combined 10 popular stereo receivers and 4 popular earphone sets, chosen from local music outlets according to dealer estimates of consumer demand. A commercially prepared rock music tape was played through the receiver to the earphones after the receiver had been set for full volume. The output of each unit combination was measured by a specialized device that accumulates the time the sound is in each of 10 5-dB ranges. If the range of a sound is between 90 and 140 dB, this unit reports how long the signal hovered between 90 and 95, between 95 and 100 dB, and so on. These time values then could be calculated according to the percentage of time sound was present at each 5-dB interval. Wood chose to estimate that a stereo buff might listen to music through earphones as much as 10 hours per week; thus he used that period as his reference base for later calculations.

It was quite surprising to note that the instantaneous sound levels produced by the 40 receiver-earphone combinations ranged between 74 and 155 dBA. Even the least effective combination still yielded sound pressure between 105 and 110 dBA 48 percent of the time. A calculation was made in order to reduce the sound level ranges to a single number, the *equivalent continuous level*, which reflects the level to which varying sound pressure would be equivalent if the sound were at the same level all the time. When these calculations were made it was found that the softest combination of earphones and receiver was the same as listening to a continuous 97-dBA sound for 10 hours a week. The most powerful combination was found to have an equivalent continuous level of 136 dBA—a devastating potential for ear damage.

The AAOO guidelines have suggested that an equivalent continuous level of 90 dBA or greater is indicative of dangerous exposure. In Wood's study all of the receiver–earphone combinations were found to be well in excess of that level in potential sound output. In a subsequent study in which young persons listened with headsets to music, most appeared to hold the sound to a safe level. This is a pleasing result to report.

The popular demand for stereo components has been on the increase. According to High Fidelity magazine, new technology has made stereo receivers and headphones higher in quality and more modest in cost than were previous components; so stereo units have become widely used. Earphones apparently have become so popular that manufacturers have produced headsets that may be used with cartridge decks in automobiles, and some people use them even while operating a car. Then, with the results indicated above and the acoustic factors in present-day private automobiles, we may conjecture that the driver is rendered functionally deaf to certain warning sounds that can affect the safe operation of the motor vehicle.

Popular use of stereo earphones in the home is partially due to the sound effects one obtains while listening to music. The consumer may: (1) heighten the stereo effect; (2) play recordings as loudly as he wants, at any time, without disturbing others; (3) increase the dynamic range (sound quality); and (4) avoid background noise levels that could discolor the sound.

Some distraught parents have encouraged their children to use earphones as a means of reducing music levels throughout the house, but since the individual controls the sound level he can with commercially available stereo units produce sounds potentially hazardous to the ear. Consistent use of these electronic components in combination may lead a young person to the condition depicted in a newspaper cartoon when the physician during a physical examination is forced to shout to his long-haired patient, "I said you've been listening to too much rock music!"

The question, "Why do the young people want the sound to be so loud?" is at best very difficult to answer, but a number of possible reasons might be suggested.

1. *Conditioning.* In recent years young persons have been conditioned to the sound that emanates from rock combos. As the sound level increases, apparently more and louder music is desired; thus the sound levels continue the upward spiral.

2. *Anesthesia.* High-level music has an anesthetic quality. Dentists have used loud music through earphones in place of topical anesthetics, but this practice has been largely discontinued because of the deleterious effect of such sound stimuli on the ear. It appears that young people now seek solace or a sense of well-being through the loud, discotheque-type environment.

3. *Musicianship.* Loud music tends to cover mediocre musicianship. As sounds become increasingly intense one anticipates that the sounds will be distorted; so poor-quality musicianship goes largely unnoticed.

4. *Competition.* Some rock groups use the phrase "the loudest group in town" in order to compete with other groups for patrons.

These theories may not speak so well as the words of a Florida teen-ager who explained: "The sounds embalm you. They numb you. You don't want to hear others talk. You don't want to talk. You don't know what to say to each other anyway."

Because intense sound can be felt as a vibratory as well as an audible sensation, rock enthusiasts have coined the term "the vibes" to describe another sought-after effect of the music. In addition, the incessantly blinking bulbs of psychedelic lights tend to overload the visual system. As indicated earlier, there is rather convincing evidence that intense sounds have a far-reaching effect on the physiology of the human body. Such auditory stimulation coupled with the psychedelic lighting effects and vibratory sensations can surely be considered to deal severely with normal bodily function. That it is harmful is still to be proven, but there is no evidence that these stresses extend life and make one more healthy.

Of most immediate concern to persons interested in hearing conservation is the potentiality of damage to the delicate structures of the ear. Studies in many segments of the nation, including Cleveland, Houston, Gainesville, Knoxville, Denver, San Francisco, Philadelphia, New York, and Memphis, have been largely in agreement that the intense character of rock music poses a hazard to young ears.

Fortunately, for the sake of quality research not all studies agree, nor do people who have observed the rock music scene agree totally on hazards that intense music poses. It was already mentioned in another context that Dr. William Rintelmann and his colleagues discovered a surprisingly small effect of their acoustic product on the ears of rock musicians. It was most appropriate to use the musicians as subjects since they undoubtedly constitute the group with the single most extensive exposure to the sound, in terms of both length of exposure and intensity of music. Because the ears derive benefit when relieved from sound stimulation for even a few moments, Dr. Rintelmann conjectured that their exposure danger was somewhat lessened since interludes spaced the numbers. Parenthetically we might add that most discotheques use recorded music played at high gain during the intermissions to fill the sound void; therefore the rest factor may not be so great as one might hope. In their study Rintelmann and Borus tested the hearing of 42 rock musicians and found only 2 with a hearing impairment of any consequence. This small percentage (5 percent) led them to surmise that concern over the dire consequences to rock-and-roll fans was overstated.

Another voice among those who insist that the threat of rock music is not so great is that of Dr. Joseph Sataloff, outstanding Philadelphia ear specialist. In the Charlotte, North Carolina *News* he maintained that budding musicians who incessantly play rock music with high-powered equipment may be prone to some mild loss of hearing in the high frequencies, but he surmised, "Before it makes him deaf, it'll drive his parents crazy."

The final answer is still in doubt. Whether rock music is the hazard some have touted it to be remains an academic question, with subscribers to both the negative and affirmative sides. If this sound source ultimately is found to be a benign influence on the hearing health of its exponents those who have signaled warnings and made devastating predictions must apologize for having unnecessarily caused an overly great amount of concern. If, however, the predicted dangers of rock music are substantiated at some future time those who played down the threat must apologize to persons whose hearing has been permanently destroyed. The wisest course seems to be the conservative stance that warns against undue lengths and amounts of immersion in the rock music atmosphere until it is proven unequivocally that the reported dangers do not exist.

Several new audiometric techniques and approaches to the study of the ear may give valuable insight into the amount of danger rock music poses, and one technique is becoming more widely used in hearing test facilities around the world. The restricted range of frequencies traditionally used in hearing tests, between 125 Hz and 8,000 Hz, has been used for good reason, since most of the important sounds in our environment occur in that region. From a diagnostic and predictive standpoint, however, extra high-frequency test tones ranging between 10,000 Hz and 20,000 Hz may prove valuable in giving some indication of the status of ears in the upper reaches of human hearing.

In Denver, Marion Downs and her colleagues have used these tones to look for any discernible differences in hearing the tones among populations of noise-exposed and non-noise-exposed persons. For one study they used male high school students who were (1) on the rifle team, (2) rock musicians, or (3) engaged in neither activity. Hearing levels for test tones above 10,000 Hz were found to be consistently worse among the rock and roll group than among the control group (3). These differences exceeded 10 dB or more. Rifle team members were found to have poorer hearing, but the variations from the control group were not so great and did not occur until the higher tones were used (those above 16,000 Hz).

Perhaps the most important aspect of this study was that three-fourths of the rock musicians were shown to manifest hearing deficiencies strikingly greater than those found among

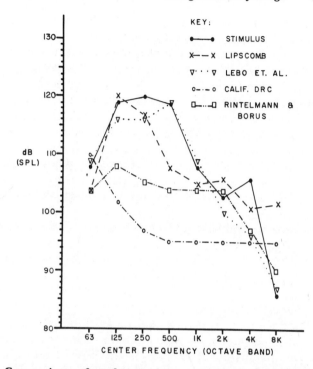

7.3 Comparison of peak sound-pressure levels in discotheques measured at three locations in the country. The reference level is given as the maximum sound level considered safe for the ear in California law (DRC). The solid line distinguishes the level of stimulation for guinea pigs in laboratory experiments.

the control group. Most of these differences were not apparent when conventional hearing testing was used; so we must suppose that great and useful information lies in the testing of the extra high-frequency response of the ear. This technique is not offered as a panacea but must be considered as an adjunctive approach to understanding the effect of loud sound on the ear structures.

The discussion until now has been concerned with high-intensity sound being generated by live rock music combos or other forms of amplified music. But how high is the sound level?

In what ways do the sounds of musical aggregations relate to established damage-risk criteria?

In Figure 7.3 comparative sound levels as measured by three observer groups are presented in relation to a popular damage-risk criterion. The points on the graph represent frequency ranges. Rather than reporting the total content of the sound, an acoustic environment can be broken electronically into several bands. Most often used as in Figure 7.3, are octave band measures which represent the fractional breakdown of the total sound environment. If the peak on the chart is at the lower frequency (left) side the sound is regarded as low-frequency loaded. The higher the marks on the chart, the greater the measured sound pressure.

The measures of Drs. Lebo and Oliphant in California and those made in Tennessee are quite similar. Any variation between the two can be attributed to the acoustics of the situation or the repertoires of the groups being measured. One set of figures was not so high (Rintelmann and Borus), which demonstrates that ranges in the levels used by bands vary so that no simplistic assumptions can be made about their effect.

Consideration of rock music characteristics led to the studies described at length in Chapter 3. Those results will not be repeated here other than to say that high-frequency hearing disorders were found in large numbers of young persons in the high school and college age ranges. We cannot establish that rock music was responsible for this condition, but it must be included in the list of possible causes because the use of rock music as a sound stimulus for experimental animals gave positive indications of the damage sound can cause in mammalian ears. Nor can we, of course, predict that humans will sustain the same amount of inner ear damage as did the guinea pigs, but we can reason that the music is sufficiently intense to warrant concern.

It is an established reality that some noise in the highly technologic society is inescapable, but dangerously great sound levels that can be reduced by simply turning a volume control on an amplifier should not be allowed. A newspaper reviewer discussing the concert of a popular English rock group asked if pain has become a form of entertainment. Citing the music hall's four well-placed speaker systems, which emitted immense sound with widely varying musical textures, including shouts and screams, he closed his critique by concluding that once the threshold of pain is passed, pain itself is no substitute for musical trippings.

Consideration of the impact of rock music on the ear cannot be complete without brief mention of its impact on other realms of life. Much of the information currently held is highly speculative and may yield to better and more accurate projections in some future time.

It is not uncommon to see rock music linked with quite unsavory pastimes and reactions. In *High Fidelity* magazine songwriter Gene Lees noted that his concern over the relationship between rock music and violence was initiated as a feeling of being bothered in some inner part of himself, which he described as a social sense. Extensive damage to several theaters during and after rock concerts led him into an attempt to determine a possible underlying association between the music and the destruction.

From a historical perspective, Lees mentioned several instances in which music forms had been quite effective in creating mass reactions for revolutionary causes for fierce nationalism. He observed that all such movements were not for the good and drew the plausible conclusion that the need for more police staffing of concert halls was directly related to an untoward trend in violent reaction to rock music stimulation.

He then introduced an even more devastating coupling between rock music and drug usage. Noting that exhortation to drug use was buried in many rock and folk-rock lyrics, Lees concludes his statement:

> I believe that rock music has given young people a virulent fever. Whereas jazz flows along with an exciting but ultimately satisfying and releasing 12/8 time feeling, rock music just stays there, its beat jumping up and down in the same place and producing in the end only pent-up energy or frustration.

Pour that stuff into the ears of an entire generation of young people, make it almost impossible for them to hear anything else, alienate them from their parents with lyrics leading them to the distrust of anyone over 30, and I would say you've invented a surefire formula for trouble.

And trouble we've got!

That rock music contains several dangerous aspects is virtually unnecessary to mention further, except that numerous others support Lees's contentions. Indeed, the great tragedy of his daughter's hallucinogenic leap into eternity prompted Art Linkletter to state to a congressional hearing that "secret messages" contained in rock music lyrics pose an attractive invitation to the drug culture. Others, including peddlers of rock music and recordings, admit the tie between the two cultures.

The untimely drug-induced deaths of several popular rock music performers stand as mute testimony to the hazard this music poses in addition to the considerably less ominous loss of some of the hearing sense. Of course, not all of these deaths result from drug ingestion. One young man was electrocuted before an audience of 1,200 when his equipment developed a short circuit, sending a fatal charge through his body as his fingers touched the strings of his electric guitar.

Rock festivals have introduced a fascinating dynamic into the whole picture. From an acoustician's standpoint the outdoor location allows for considerable dissipation of the sound, greatly reducing any ear hazards that may exist. The other problems these gala events create do not seem to be abated, however. The conjoint use of intense music and drugs can disturb the auditory physiologist because of the realization that many of the drugs in frequent use at rock festivals and other events of like nature are muscle-relaxing potions. Such drugs increase the danger to the ears, for they may greatly reduce the protective influence the tiny middle ear muscles may have.

One final area deserves brief mention. Billy Graham (not to be confused with the owner of Fillmore East) is said to have told some people at a rock festival in Hollywood, "You can get high on the Lord, too." Thus, height seems to be the goal, either through music sensibilities, drug intake, religious experiences, or a combination of some or all of them. This purpose has an idealistic value, but the price of the journey to these quasi-highs for some may be a hearing deficit that will plague them in later life, making them rue the earlier remark that they would "just get a hearing aid." For others the cost will be even more dear.

Since humans must live together, intense music enters into their relationships. One such case arose when a lawyer filed suit in chancery court seeking to enjoin his neighbor from playing stereo music loudly over outdoor speaker systems. In his suit the plaintiff complained that the music went on for days and weeks at a time while the defendant was away. The excuse? It was played while the house was vacant in an effort to keep burglars away.

Little can be said now that would not be repetitious. Some final comments are provided as one person's approach to understanding the loud music phenomenon.

Among all of the available high-intensity sound sources in the recreational environment rock music must be considered the most otohazardous in terms of amplitude of sound, broad spectrum of sound energy, impulsive character of the music with strong beating sensations, duration of individual exposure to the sound, number of persons exposed to the sound source, and the ugly side issues associated with rock music.

We may ask, as in an old graffiti: "Why did modern music have to come in our time?" Put another way: "Why can't you hear through the noise in your ear?" With the use of high-efficiency stereo earphones the musical group is sensed to be directly inside the listener's head, which perhaps leads to what one psychologist has described as rock music's deep spiritual aspect. According to this student of the mind it produces a "natural high." Following the implied and expressed philosophy of some members of the rock family to "live life as hard as we can," hard rock lends itself to various forms of abuse and perversions. It serves as a vehicle for revolution—the outward expression of an inward desire for change.

Since to many patrons of this vastly popular esthetic medium the music relates the symbolism for the violence around them, they become entrapped in the quest for power, of sorts. There is nothing innately wrong with seeking power; most are so inclined. Economic power can give a man the ability to do great good. Academic power can liberate the minds of great multitudes. Political power can mold peaceful unions between and within nations. The power that corrupts is the power over another human being. Unfortunately, heinous deeds have been and will continue to be perpetrated for that power.

With the lyrics, "Power to the people," one of the Hit Parade songs stated an idealistic precept. Current programs advance Black power, people power, White power, women's power, child power, love power, flower power, and so on. Any one of these goals loses its purity, however, when the ideal direction is bent by proponents who scramble for power over others.

Although their thrust appears to be in the direction of peace and peaceful things, the modern rock idiom and its expressionists have achieved an ultimate form of power over others. By employing vast technology and high volume the musicians exercise power over communication between persons. By their sheer volume they forbid freedom of speech in a music hall by making it physically impossible to converse, even with the mouth placed directly at the listener's ear. The wall of sound invades others' privacy as it allows a type of privacy for the musician who cannot be bothered during the performance.

RECREATIONAL VEHICLES

The call of the wild has not dimmed in modern times. In fact, greater affluence makes possible more recreational vehicles, which are descending on the mountain paths, trails, and back roads. In response to demands on sparsely inhabited federal and state land the Department of the Interior has moved, through its state arms, to relegate public land use to the most appropriate and conservation-minded purposes possible. Consideration is being given to hiking, horseback riding, motorcycling and jeep riding. Trails designated as hiking trails will be off limits to any other form of conveyance. Bridle trails will be used by hikers, horsemen, and others.

Motorcycles

The increasing popularity of off-the-road cycles has introduced another source of high-level sound exposure. Under the guise of increasing power, cyclists have been inclined to strip the muffler—an act that does little more than increase the noise, which the rider senses to signal great power. In 1972 the Motorcycle Industry Council, a group representative of most cycle manufacturers and dealers in the United States, agreed that they would restrict the allowable amount of tampering with the exhaust systems. In new models the muffler and engine are tuned units, and if a muffler is altered or removed the cycle's performance will be negatively affected and its warranty canceled. This action will serve well to limit the overall exhaust noise of motorcycles and hopefully will result in quieter wilderness roads and trails.

That motorcycle sport activities are enjoyable is attested to by the great numbers of professional people who are joining skilled youngsters on the trails. Few communities are void of physicians, lawyers, teachers, and other professionals who greatly appreciate their newfound recreational activity. A lady from Michigan traveled 752 miles on her cycle from her home to a southern city to attend the annual convention of Motor Maids, Inc., a nationwide organization of women cyclists. The 68-year-old woman continues to enjoy this activity after 42 years and indicates that her 81-year-old husband often rides her motorcycle, as well.

The hazard to the ears is no less from long exposure to motorcycling than from industrial activity. Greater use of recreational vehicles causes more persons to be subjected to sound outside the safe limits. On the racetrack high-powered racing motorcycles, found to generate intense noise, are creating a potential danger to the hearing of racers and fans.

New legislation in most states to require the use of crash helmets has provided some protection for cyclists' ears, since the helmet tends to suppress exhaust noise, but this unintentional benefit does not spare a person who is frightfully distressed by cycle noise. More will be said of this aspect of motorcycle noise in Chapter 8.

Snowmobiles

The invasion of an estimated 1.5 million snowbuggies into some sections of the country has brought with it a rash of complaints about noise, lack of safety, trespassing, and vandalism. These products of a fast-growing industry are powered by small, two-cycle engines that direct pulling thrust to a cleated track. On packed snow these ski-wheels achieve speeds of 50 miles per hour or more, and some of the racing models have been found to go over 90 mph.

Some states have rapidly enacted control legislation to promote safety by registration and licensure. At least 10 states have regulatory laws, and 5 others are in the process of bringing laws into being. Minnesota, where over 40 percent of the snowmobiles are manufactured, has registered more than 110,000 of the vehicles.

Quite evidently snowmobiles are fun, but they are noisy too. Sound levels measured at operators' ears have reached 130 dBA, which led Dr. Fred Bess of Central Michigan University to conclude that snowmobile riding must be added to the growing list of recreational activities that pose a threat to the health and well-being of the hearing mechanism. An executive of one company said in a telephone conversation, "I can assure you that snowmobiles will soon be quiet." Hopefully that assurance will become a reality before too many winters have passed.

Pleasure Aircraft

In recent years sound measuring equipment taken aloft has revealed the overly noisy condition of private aircraft cockpits. The smaller craft are generally more noisy because the pilot is in a tight enclosure separated from the engines by only a small distance. As the interior becomes larger and more plush, the sound levels tend to decrease, but no direct relationship exists between the plane's interior noise and its cost.

According to one estimate the average levels found in small

plane cockpits should be tolerated for no longer than 45 minutes per day or 3¾ hours per week. At that rate one could not go very far and so must either use ear protection or risk hearing damage. Again, the use of headgear may cover the ears and provide a small degree of protection from the sound.

Only 1 hour of exposure to small-plane noise between 89 and 91 dBA was sufficient to cause measurable shifts in pilots' hearing threshold. This shift, regarded as temporary, was found mostly in the lower frequencies because the low-pitched sounds prevailed in the engine noise. Shifts ranged between 5 and 10 dB, insufficient to cause considerable concern, at least for exposures no longer than 1 hour. With greater exposure time the pilots would be expected to demonstrate greater hearing threshold shifts. For the most part small-aircraft cockpit noises exceed established damage-risk criteria when considered for long periods of exposure.

Pleasure Boats

Because boating has been a part of the recreational scene for many years, it has hardly been noticed as a problem to hearing. In fact, only in rare situations does there seem to be any reason for concern. The exhaust in modern outboard motors has been redirected so that it is expelled under the surface of the water, and motor casings are sound-treated, greatly reducing noise.

The inside of closed boat cockpits of inboard boats can be rocked with vibratory sounds that emanate from the motor well. Sometimes these sounds exceed safe limits, and long-term exposure can be hazardous to hearing.

CONCLUSION

The nonoccupational environment undoubtedly is filled with sounds that may assault our hearing sense with sufficient strength to cause some ear damage. At worst these exposures supplement the exposure experienced at work and result in accentuated hearing deficit.

One might ask, though, "What is safe and what is excessive exposure?" In an attempt to answer, Dr. Alexander Cohen has

Table 7.1   Noise limits for nonoccupational noise exposure.

Limiting daily exposure times for nonoccupational noise conditions	Sound level (dBA)
Less than 2 minutes	115
Less than 4 minutes	110
Less than 8 minutes	105
15 minutes	100
½ hour	95
1 hour	90
2 hours	85
4 hours	80
8 hours	75
16-24 hours	70

listed a proposed set of limits for nonoccupational exposure to noise. Rather than keying on the 90 dBA figure used in the federal guidelines for occupational exposure for an 8-hour day, the list uses 75 dBA as its baseline. These figures, given in Table 7.1, demonstrate how the 5 dB rule is predicated on reducing the allowable exposure time by half each time the sound level increases 5 dB. From the reference of 75 dBA for an 8-hour stimulation period, the restriction is given for allowing exposure to an 80 dBA noise for only 4 hours. Note that the bottom value given is 70 dBA, which suggests that sounds below 70 dBA do not constitute dangerous levels to the ear.

Even if the nonoccupational exposure schedule were equal to the federal guidelines, combinations of the on-job and off-duty noise exposure obviously can be hazardous in numerous examples. Several hypothetical situations demonstrate this point. In the first case cited in Table 7.2, G. P. rides to and from work on his motorcycle, which adds an hour of high-level noise exposure that would not normally be taken into account in a sound survey of G. P.'s occupational sound environment. When combined with this occupational exposure according to present federal standards, the additional period of noise exposure is sufficient to cause his total exposure value index to exceed unity (1), thereby creating a condition that may ultimately become hazardous to his hearing status.

A similar situation obtains for R. B. He rides a noisy subway to and from work each day. The sound generated in the subways is sufficient to increase his daily noise exposure index to a level that is considered excessive.

The noise to which E. S. is subjected comes from a small stamping press that emits periodic impulse sounds peaking at

Table 7.2 Examples of the influence of nonoccupational noise exposure when the federal guidelines for occupational noise exposure have been satisfied.

Name	Exposure	Duration of Exposure	Level	Ratio (D/P)	Exposure Value
G. P.	On job	4 hr.	95 dBA	4/4	1.000
	On job	4 hr.	90 dBA	4/inf.	0.000
	Motorcycle	1 hr.	97 dBA	1/3	0.333
		Total			1.333
R. B.	On job	6 hr.	92 dBA	6/6	1.000
	Subway ride	2 hr.	92 dBA	2/6	0.333
		Total			1.333
E. S.	On job	8 hr.	137 dB peak	8/inf.	0.000
	100 rounds 0.45				
	magnum load pistol		144 dB peak	—	excessive*
		Total			1.000+
J. J.	On job	8 hr.	90 dBA	8/inf.	0.000
	Discotheque	2 hr.	110 dBA	2/0.5	4.000
		Total			4.000
S. R.	On job	2 hr.	100 dBA	2/3	0.667
	On job	6 hr.	90 dBA	6/inf.	0.000
	Overtime	2 hr.	100 dBA	2/3	0.667
		Total			1.334

*Federal guidelines designate a 140 dB peak limit for impact sound.

137 dB. According to the guidelines this exposure can be considered to be within tolerable limits. In the off hours, however, E. S. engaged in pistol target practice several evenings a week. The handgun he uses discharges with an impulse sound that peaks at 144 dB. This exposure is considered excessive and would be expected to cause ear damage.

J. J. frequents a different type of nonoccupational noise environment. He regularly attends dances at a discotheque that employs rock-and-roll combos. The group's sound output consistently reaches 110 dBA, a level that creates an otohazardous situation if exposure to it exceeds 30 minutes per day. The two-hour period J. J. spends in the discotheque exceeds the safe limits by a factor of four.

The federal guidelines do not consider the possibility of additional exposure to occupational noise during overtime. As shown in the example, S. R. works two additional hours on a regular basis. The noise level in his plant is highest during the first two hours of each shift; thus he doubles his exposure to excessive noise each time he picks up some overtime. The additional amount is sufficient to boost his daily noise exposure index beyond safe limits.

All these examples are drawn from common situations. They are not intended to comprise an exhaustive list of the many variables to be considered but, rather, have been described to point up the need for an awareness of the interaction between occupational and nonoccupational noise exposure. In short, hearing conservation, industrial or not, is a 24-hour problem. It is imperative that nonoccupational noise exposure be taken into account.

Several references already have been made to the detailed article on socioacusis by Dr. Cohen and his colleagues. Their conclusion to the article seems appropriate here.

> **1.** Noise conditions in recreation, in using public transportation, and in some communities close to transportation facilities and construction sites, when rated against noise limits offering more complete ear protection than those used in industry, suggest some risk of hearing loss

in those segments of the population receiving frequent or protracted exposures.

2. While daily exposures to a single source of nonoccupational noise may offer no distinct hazard to hearing, the combined exposures from many different sources each day may do so. Also, the prevalence and severity of hearing loss problems in industry may be increased by the inability of the worker to find an off-job environment or activities quiet enough to allow his ears to recover from the occupational insult.

3. Evidence for permanent losses in hearing from nonoccupational noise exposures is still quite limited. Apparent losses of this type are most prominent at the high frequencies and not sufficiently great in the range of the speech frequencies (500 Hz to 2,000 Hz) to warrant compensation. Goals for hearing protection against undue noise, however, should be geared toward preserving hearing for more than the minimum requirements of speech reception.

·8·

Concerto in Cacophony

All cities are mad: but the madness is gallant.
All cities are beautiful: but the beauty is grim.
Christopher Morley

In *The Wish*, Abraham Crowley lyrically described the city as the "great hive," a fitting description for the world's largest "people hive"—Tokyo, thought to be the noisiest on earth. At one busy intersection in the city a lighted sign that flashed the sound level there stated the acceptable level as 70 dB, but the actual level seldom dropped below 88 dB, comparable to the sound of a loud shout from close range. Sounds noted at this Tokyo street corner included traffic, bells, pneumatic drills, machines, pedestrians, power tools, animal noise, sirens, power generators, air conditioners, air compressors, construction equipment, and other common surface noise-generating things.

This condition is not peculiar to the gem city of the Orient; most American cities are beset with the same type of noise problems. One common area of concentrated commotion is the shopping area, where the hum and buzz of shoppers and their vehicles are augmented by go-cart concessions, carnivals, and canned music. Residential areas, though, are no longer a haven where one can relax in quiet. Seldom is a neighborhood free of lawn mower, power tool, or vehicle noises.

Recreational and resort areas have lost their quiet characteristics to speedboats on the lakes and trail bikes in the mountains. In some of the northern states the snow resort regions have been inundated with snowmobiles whose sound output exceeds 130 dB, a level near the auditory pain threshold. Also in and near snow resort areas the nighttime quiet is shattered by the roar of snowmaking machines replenishing the ski slopes. Bermuda firemen carry pocket buzzers to alert them to a fire call because fire department officials feared that increasing noise levels in the community would keep them from hearing the siren at the station, calling them to duty.

NOISE SURVEYS

One of the early community noise studies was conducted in New York City during 1929 and 1930. In that city a Noise Abatement Council estimated that city noise could be attributed to the following sources:

Traffic	36%
Transportation vehicles	16%
Radios	12%
Collection and delivery	9%
Whistles and bells	8%
Construction	7½%
Miscellaneous	7-10%

Later, in 1956, a similar project described some radical changes in the citizens' outlook toward the various noisemakers when it listed refuse collection as most irksome. One wag stated that somehow the collection agency managed to reclaim all of the city's garbage between the hours of 4 and 6 A.M. on Sunday. Following garbage collection in order as irksome noises were horn honking, truck and bus accleration, blaring radio and television sets, aircraft noise, unmuffled exhaust, street repair crews, sound trucks (now outlawed in many communities), riveting, and hotel doormen's taxi whistles.

As the population continues to increase in the heart of large cities, the number of noisemakers also rises in order to serve that growth in numbers of persons to be exposed to the noises. Estimates of noise sources vary with the community and cannot be easily assayed, but a researcher in Cleveland generalized that air and ground traffic contribute 80 percent of the noise in the community, about 7 percent derives from industry, 4 percent is the product of construction, and the remainder is a mixture of miscellaneous noises.

Dr. John Dougherty, staff member of the Harvard School of Public Health offers this precaution: "What's passed unnoticed is that many noise levels encountered in the community exceed the standards found in industry."

JET AIRCRAFT

Aircraft noise is a familiar part of the life of virtually every person in developed nations; thus few noise sources have encountered so much ire from the population as have airplanes. Interestingly, aircraft noise as a source of irritation has been known for many years. As early as 1917 a patent was granted for a device said to dispel airplanes by creating severe air turbulence. The inventor disdained aircraft noise enough to attempt to stop planes from ever flying.

Over a time span of 50 years aircraft speed has gone from a glide to more than the speed of sound. This increase in speed as well as in size has, in turn, increased the commercial value of this mode of transportation. In 1966 commercial airlines carried 110 million passengers in America—over twice the number carried in 1958. In addition, 90 percent of these persons traveled by jet. In 1968 world airplanes carried 261 million passengers 191 billion miles, and more than 6 billion tons of air freight were carried that year.

Global air traffic has more than tripled since 1959. Currently, over 180,000 active civil aircraft and 3,500 commercial jets are served by more than 11,000 airports; hence airport congestion has become a major factor of the growth and projected status of air travel in the future. In the past few years Chicago's O'Hare Airport has developed to the level of nearly 2,000 landings and takeoffs per day—about 1 per minute. This rate of activity can be extended to the staggering number of 700,000 per year.

Predictions are that the nation's airlines will transport as many as 3 to 4 billion passengers during this decade. At present the industry, a $500 billion factor in the American economy, and its many accessory components account for as much as 1 in every 6 dollars of the economy and provide work for 9 million men and women. Certainly it is a vital industry.

The aviation noise problem has grown partly as a result of a strange, albeit predictable, phenomenon of urban development. Most early airports were built away from heavy population concentrations, but in time housing developments have sprung up next to nearly every major terminal even as airports have expanded to accommodate larger and more numerous aircraft. The end result has been increasing numbers of people exposed to the sound of airplanes. Total abatement of aircraft noise does not seem to be within the realm of possibility; so some are beginning to argue for the reduction and eventual elimination of planes—a proposal that makes very little economic sense.

Morris Sloan, general manager of Kennedy International Airport, indicated that aircraft noise, not crowded air lanes or inadequate access roads, is the greatest problem this nation's airports confront. He stated from his administrative stance, " . . . making peace with your neighbors is more important than crowded skies and ground traffic tieups. . . . Until the airports start living in harmony with the community surrounding them, we cannot hope to expand or build new airports."

Aircraft noise also impeded the educational processes. In 1970 Airport Junior High School in Los Angeles closed because aircraft noise made teaching and learning physically impossible. The building, erected in 1955 to accommodate 1,600 students, had been rendered useless because of its placement on the flight plan for Los Angeles International Airport. Two years earlier, in the same region, Westchester Elementary School was abandoned for the same reason. These occurrences prompted the Los Angeles City Unified School District to file suit against the airport for nearly $96 million. In the suit the system claimed that the education of 46,000 school children in 31 schools was hampered by the recurrent noise of ascending and descending planes.

The school district's action raised the total amount of legal action against the flight facility to $2.3 billion. Prior to that suit a number of class suits had been leveled against L.A. International, the nation's second busiest airport. In addition to the 22 million people it serves each year, the airport handles 975 million pounds of air freight annually and provides jobs for 34,000 persons. These figures add to the enormity of the problem, for such a vital community function cannot be just snuffed out without terrible economic, social, and legal consequences.

Los Angeles International Airport is not the only American air terminal in this kind of trouble. At last count 40 of the nation's 140 major airports were defendants in similar lawsuits, whose claims totaled over $4 billion, a staggering sum—so staggering that the entire aircraft industry and governmental monitoring agencies are acutely aware that commercial aircraft noise abatement must receive the highest priority.

One important step is being taken in the form of research and development. Aircraft manufacturers are busily engaged in revamping aerodynamic designs and engine placement to provide an adjunct to quieter engines, and groups of engineers are striving to design an even quieter jet engine. Noncommercial interests are being served by research institutes that delve into the problems of aircraft noise. In this area the Federal Aviation Agency awarded to members of the University of Tennessee Space Institute a $345,000 grant to permit studies of methods for reducing exhaust noise from aircraft engines. In accepting the grant Dr. B. H. Goethert, Dean of the Space Institute, noted, "Noise pollution created by aircraft engines is one of the most serious problems facing future development of the air transportation industry in this country."

Dr. Goethert's point is all the more valid as one considers the expanding nature of air transportation. Most cities have air terminals that are presently inadequate for the great volume of travelers and shippers who want service. Expansion plans are on the drawing board for many air facilities, but expansion of existing plants is a near-impossibility because of the housing developments around most airports. Unless sizable amounts of additional land are obtained, expansion undoubtedly will be a very hotly contested issue. In the vernacular of one lawsuit against the Los Angeles terminal: "Residents won't stand being a garbage can for the noise, smog and other pollutions from the airport. Aircraft noise is a social cancer which must be removed."

There is general agreement that some form of compromise is in order. Exhaust noise of aircraft must and hopefully will be reduced; yet members of the aircraft industry maintain that people must achieve a greater tolerance of aircraft noise. Perhaps, this tolerance will come in part from knowing that everything is being done to abate the noise and that aircraft personnel are not simply ignoring the distressing aspects of the noise they make. The outcome of these deliberations will not be known for some time since the complications are so vast.

The use of jumbo jets may be a factor in reducing noise around airports. Each of these mammoth steel miracles has seating capacity to replace three planes. In some of the busier terminals the introduction of sizable numbers of the big planes ultimately will decrease the number of takeoffs and landings, but as demand continues to increase, the impact of this development is still greatly in doubt.

Aircraft noise has at least three aspects. Each presents a unique set of conditions and problems.

1. *Takeoff.* The greatest volume of sound occurs at takeoff when the powerful engines must develop sufficient thrust to push the heavy craft into the atmosphere at the steep rate of climb. During maximum takeoff thrust, the sound immediately behind the engines of a commercial jet transport is approximately 140 dB—the sound level generally regarded as sufficient to evoke a pain response. The sound quality is that of a roar and contains a heavy loading of low-pitched sound energy. As the distance from the departing plane is increased, the sound level decreases. From a distance of 100 feet the sound will have become approximately 120 dB; a thousand feet away the sound will be 100 dB. Since jet takeoffs occur in the open it is possible to apply the rule mentioned briefly in Chapter 1. Each time the distance is increased 10-fold, the sound level will decrease 20 dB. The figures given here reflect that rule.

2. *Landing.*   Quite a different situation exists during jet plane landings. The sound is not nearly so great and the perceived sound quality is markedly different. Rather than the low-frequency roar noted during takeoff, the arriving jet emits a shrill sound often described as piercing. While not so intense as takeoff noise, landing noise is still irksome because of its penetrating sound quality and because the human ear is quite acute in the frequency ranges of the heaviest concentration of the sound energy.

3. *Taxi.*   The shrill sound of the jet on the ground is often most dangerous to hearing health. The engines are not laboring so much as during takeoff and landing, but the distance between the plane and persons in and around the terminal is reduced. Reactions of persons awaiting an arriving jet plane are almost comical. In the marvelous honesty and openness of youth, children shriek and cup their hands over their ears. Others wince and grit their teeth (actually not a bad practice on this one occasion, for forced jaw movement may cause a reflex action by the protective middle ear muscles). Most interesting to watch, however, are those brave souls who feel it is less than a sign of strength to express chagrin or discomfort and so glare blankly at the plane, attempting not to let on that they would give almost anything for a good set of earmuffs like those the ground crew is wearing. The best action, incidentally, is to place the tip of the index finger of each hand over the small flap of skin in front of the ear canal and press the skin flap toward the open canal until the sound is reduced to a comfortable level; then one may remain true to the ancient and important adage: one should never put anything smaller than his elbow into his ear.

Comparison of the federal regulations for general industry with those governing the aircraft industry, both designed to promote noise control, reveals a wide discrepancy. Dr. Clifford Bragdon has noted, " ... industrial noise generated in the sky is allowed to be 38 dBA greater than industrial noise that occurs on the ground. We allow a double standard to persist, but our environment can ill afford to have any sacred cows."

Much is known about the noise around most major air terminals. Detailed sound studies have been completed and the data converted to perceived noise (PNdB) figures and organized

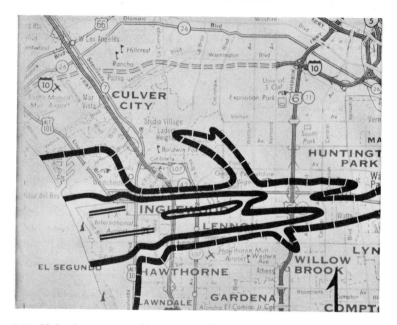

8.1 Noise isocontours drawn around an airport. Each line represents a sound level in PNdB. Lines closest to the terminal indicate the highest sound levels. (**From** *Sound and Vibration*)

into a set of isocontours drawn around the periphery of the airport property. Each contour line in the set of isocontours in Figure 8.1 represents a certain PNdB level as measured at the points on the map. The PNdB level reduces as the distance from the runways is increased. With studies such as this one it is possible to determine the number of persons who are inside the air traffic generated "annoying" range of sound, which normally begins at a level of 102 PNdB. (A 102 PNdB value corresponds roughly to an 89 dBA figure.)

It is important to note from the isocontour map in Figure 8.1 that the reduction of noise by 5 to 8 PNdB will result in a sizable narrowing of the high-value contours. Such shifts might affect the lives of a great number of persons whose homes are in the flight path. During their testimony before a U.S. House of Representatives subcommittee, representatives of the Air Transport

Association argued that the cost of sound-treating existing aircraft engines in order to reduce the noise just a few decibels would be inordinately great. On the surface this logic seems appropriate, but if a reduction of 6 dBA were effected by fitting aircraft with specially designed muffling material the isocontours around airports would be appreciably altered. This reduction would serve not only to take some residents of the surrounding community out of the irritated classification but also to diminish the amount of annoyance caused in homes where sound levels still were undesirable. Hundreds and perhaps thousands of persons could gain relief if appropriate abatement procedures were put into effect. Hopefully the logic of vested interests will not prevail.

One resident of an airport community reported on a television special that he had kept a count from June 1 to July 11 and found an average of 40 distinctly different aircraft gracing the area with their exhaust noise each hour. This figure amounted to 14,000 landings in 5 weeks. Apparently this man wound up counting airplanes instead of sheep in his futile efforts to get some sleep.

To reduce the sound of aircraft engines aerospace engineers are making several intelligent efforts including attempts at a new design that will be the quietest ever and alterations of operational procedures to steer the more noisy aircraft from heavy population concentrations. Communities are being better planned so that zones for residential use will be compatible with airport operations, and sound barriers are being built to reduce the amount of sideline noise broadcast to a community by ground-roving aircraft.

For an overly long time officials of aviation regulating agencies did not take a firm stand relative to allowable aircraft noise limits. In recent years, however, both local and federal authorities have defined their relative responsibilities. It is now understood that local governments can amend the federal aircraft noise standards only if the amendment meets federal approval. Some cities, such as Paris and London, have restricted the hours during which large aircraft can use their terminals, usually limiting service between 11 P.M. and 6 A.M.

One major problem in aircraft noise regulation has arisen because local authorities have no control over interstate matters and thus must wait on completion of the federal regulations. The first step was taken in 1969 when the Federal Aviation Agency determined that the upper limit of a plane during takeoff was to range between 93 and 108 EPNdB, depending on plane weight, number of engines, and location of the sound-measuring apparatus. These rules apply only to new planes, however. According to the FAA guidelines, measures for maximum noise during takeoff or landing are made at three stages of flight.

1. During the final approach the sound is to be recorded at a location 1 nautical mile from the leading edge of the runway on a line with the landing strip to be entered.

2. After takeoff the sound is measured at a point 3.5 nautical miles from the point where the takeoff roll began on an imaginary line down the center of the runway.

3. After the wheels have left the ground, sound can be assessed at a distance one-quarter of a mile to the side of the runway, the point where the sound is greatest in most situations. This measurement for turbojet engines is to be made approximately one-third of a mile to the side.

As an example, the limit for the large craft weighing over 600,000 pounds is 108 EPNdB. Smaller planes weighing between 75,000 and 600,000 pounds must meet a maximum noise limit of 102 EPNdB.

That these limits are satisfactory is entirely open to debate. The aircraft industry is concerned that its planes cannot consistently meet the guidelines, but residents of airport communities would like more stringent limitations on jet noise. A few months after the FAA regulations were made public, Allard K. Lowenstein, state representative from Nassau County in New York, near Kennedy International Airport, charged that the FAA had "not the slightest intention of doing anything to relieve the nightmare of noise." On making these remarks Lowenstein dramatized the problem by holding part of a press conference at a park near the end of a Kennedy runway. Quite often during their attempts to question the congressman reporters found their words and his responses drowned out by the noise of arriving jets passing only a few hundred feet overhead. In response to emphatic requests that current planes be required to have noise-reducing modifications, FAA officials indicated that such a rule was then under preparation. Those subjected to the man-made thunder that emanates from existing jets took little comfort from the thought that future craft would be quieter; they demanded that present aircraft be sound treated—not necessarily an unreasonable demand when it is considered that some of today's planes may still be in service a decade from now.

The cry was for retrofitting—that is, extensive reconstruction of the cowling of aircraft engines to reduce noise output. At this writing the FAA has not brought into active use any effective plan for retrofitting existing planes, partly because the program will be frightfully costly and the aircraft industry is lobbying forcefully against such changes. The FAA's preliminary plan, which would be the second step in control of aircraft noise, following the 1969 regulation on new planes, would require installation of sound-absorbing material around the plane engines. These planes were made as a result of a study initiated by NASA and backed up by a Rohr Corporation investigation that indicated that the technology presently exists to reduce the noise of the Boeing 707 and DC-8 by as much as 12 dB. This alteration would be costly, however—an estimated $665,000 per plane for the DC-8 and over $1 million per plane for the 707. These figures have led Secor D. Browne, chairman of the Civil Aeronautics Board, to estimate that retrofitting all of the 2,000 planes that would come under the plan would cost the airlines $1 billion. In so saying he expressed grave doubts that the plan ever would be promulgated.

On occasion, some sacrifices in safety procedures are made in order to satisfy the demand for quieter aircraft operation. FAA administrator John H. Shaffer admitted one such compromise when he observed that many airplane pilots consciously get around the noise measuring equipment, called "little black boxes," by cutting back the throttle at a point about 3½ miles from takeoff. After they pass the checkpoint they again accelerate the engines over residential areas in order to continue the ascent.

A much more sane approach to the problem is in some of the suggested operational procedures whereby glide angles on descent and ascent are altered to create somewhat less overall noise. These developments have been suggested with maximum attention to overall safety. Another idea initiated a short while ago at Kennedy International is the rotation of runway use. This FAA-devised program rotates landing and takeoff patterns to avoid routing planes over the same community areas for extended periods.

Noise suppressors—large, sound-absorbent tunnels—have been designed for the flight lines in order to reduce the sound of engine revs during ground repair and maintenance. Another set of ground-level devices includes sound fences constructed to prohibit the escape of high-volume sound during taxi and runup. Sometimes these fences are constructed of steel and may reach 40 feet high, as in Frankfurt, Germany. Others are constructed by mounding dirt into acoustic dikes around air travel facilities.

The farther away the noise abatement device is from the noise source, the poorer are the results. If possible it is always preferable to mute the source itself. Since source control of aircraft noise apparently is not going to take place soon, the use of effective sound treatment of houses near airports is being considered, but that, too, is an expensive proposition. A group of 25 houses remodeled to make them more livable in the presence of jet noise cost $300,000, in effect nearly doubling the original cost of the houses. Remodeling included the placement of thick tile on the roof, installation of fiber mats, sound treatment of the attic spaces, installation of felt-layered acoustic doors, utilization of double-pane windows, and vibration isolation of floors. Others estimate renovation costs at between $2,700 and $8,900 for each house and as high as $225,000 for a school.

The solution is not a simple one, but logical minds continue to point to muffling the noise source, the aircraft engine itself.

Hopefully this thinking will prevail before more legal action is taken against the industry.

VTOL AND STOL

In order to avoid exposing vast numbers of people to aircraft noise most cities have located their municipal airports well outside the city limits. Future airport developments probably will have to be built in remote regions—generally a desirable feature of planning but one that creates a logistic problem, as well. The traveler who has arrived at his destination likes to think that he is ready to take up his activities, but in some locations his trip has just begun. After having covered several thousand miles in a minimum of time by plane, one may encounter frustrating delays because ground transportation is becoming increasingly snarled. Passengers often are perturbed to find that the trip from the air terminal to the city doubles their travel time.

One solution to the provision of swift transportation to and from the airport is the use of vertical takeoff and landing craft (VTOL). These noisy devices, usually dubbed helicopters, have found increasing use in ferrying persons between airports or on short hauls to convention or business centers. The traveler who wants to make a short flight, though, sees little advantage in journeying downtown, boarding a helicopter to the airport, jumping a jet to his destination, then boarding another chopper for the last leg of his journey; hence the concept of the short takeoff and landing plane (STOL) has arisen. These interesting new developments in the armamentarium of aircraft industrialists are small, limited-capacity planes that are so overpowered that they can ascend to flight status from a very short runway. Both travel time solutions would require establishment of VTOL/STOL ports in the centers of large metropolitan cities.

Whereas the basic concept is admirable, a frightful noise problem still must be overcome. The tall buildings in central cities are sounding boards off which the roar of these planes can reverberate. The power generated by the engines requires great thrust in order to assure safe ascent; thus the noise output would be inordinately great for the size of planes used. City planners certainly will be challenged in choosing the most judicious and appropriate locations for these tiny metropolitan air terminals.

Ordinances against the use of such aircraft are beginning to appear on the books of some American cities, and in other locations citizens are issuing strong statements against any additional noise-producing aircraft. The following Letter to the Editor appeared in the *New York Times* in 1970.

The Federal Aviation Administration has awarded a $36,000 contract to American Airlines to study the feasibility of a STOLport . . . in the Hudson River between 23rd and 34th Streets. Rationalization for this study, as supplied by American Airlines, is that such a facility in Manhattan is the key element in any solution to the overcrowded air lanes linking Boston, New York and Washington.

However, there simply is no developed place in New York City, and even more surely, no place in Manhattan where the noise of several planes hourly flying at or near rooftop height, the extra pollution these planes would add and the extra congestion their passengers would generate in already congested streets would be anything but an added and most severe blight on a city which is struggling to rid itself of a surfeit of blights. The concept is completely counter to and would substantially offset private and public efforts to make New York a more gracious place to work and live.

Within the probably affected area are St. Vincent's, French, Polyclinic and Roosevelt Hospitals; Haaren and Charles Evans Hughes High Schools, the Fashion Institute, and the General Theological Seminary. The area contains also several grade schools, a large residential community in Greenwich Village, Chelsea and Clinton, the site of a city approved urban renewal project in the vicinity of 50th Street and 11th Avenue, and the side projected for low and moderate income housing in the underutilized industrial area west of Tenth Avenue, near 23rd Street.

To a greater or lesser extent, similar conditions prevail in any other developed section of New York. To inflict an airport, operating an extremely busy shuttle service on any such community would be a grievous and unforgivable assault on the quality of urban life.

Because the bulk of the aircraft noise problem has hit without adequate prior notice, the problem of abatement is far more difficult. How the development of VTOL/STOL ports progresses will signal the extent to which city planners have learned their lesson from the agonizing conflicts known to other forms of established air terminals. If they continue their plans to set up open facilities in crowded urban surroundings, they probably will be rushing headlong into a lot of flack. If, however, they carefully lay plans that include restrictions on noise from short-distance carriers and if the terminals are well situated with respect to the considerations for adding to the existing environment, the success of VTOL/STOL use can be assured.

HEARING LOSS

Although most of the concern about aircraft noise is related to its irritating quality, some disquieting data suggests that repeated exposure to low-altitude aircraft flyovers may result in measurable hearing shifts. Hearing tests were given to two small groups of residents near a busy airport—one composed of persons at home during most of a six-hour period when airport activity was greatest and one of people away during those hours. Each member of the noise-exposed group demonstrated measurable hearing loss for 2,000 and 4,000 Hz tones—loss that could not be discounted as a product of chance happenings. Members of the non-noise-exposed group showed no such hearing shift. These preliminary findings give no final indication that aircraft noise radiating into nearby residential areas causes hearing loss, but they do hint that such consequences might be proven in a large-scale, well-designed, and controlled study.

The complexity of the aircraft noise problem defies description. A hopeful trend, however, is evidenced by the move to develop quieter engines—the dream aircraft engine of the future. Perhaps, as Clifford Bragdon indicated, "community comfort" also will become a concern of the airlines, which have thus far placed most of their emphasis on "passenger comfort."

The aircraft noise problem will prevail for quite some time, since any abatement procedures, like those for industrial noise, must be evolutionary. Sometime in the future, hopefully within the next decade, wilderness hikers will be able to enjoy the rugged mountains without the recurrent banshee cry of jet flyovers—perhaps the most disconcerting and inappropriate sound outdoorsmen encounter.

SST

After having been bravely proclaimed by presidents of a past decade, the future of the supersonic transport (SST) fell into a state of limbo because of the boiling controversy that surrounded its development. At the outset the SST was envisioned as the ultimate technologic achievement of the aerospace industry. Specifications included speeds twice the speed of sound, smooth travel altitudes above air turbulence, economical travel costs, and the greatest array of safety features ever assembled into one aircraft. During the development stages critics of the supercraft began to voice opposition to the SST on grounds of noise, economics, air pollution, and national priorities.

In order to operate at maximum efficiency SSTs must exceed the speed of sound at an altitude of 35,000 feet or more; then they create what has been called the sonic boom. This thunderclap does not occur once when the speed of sound is exceeded but, rather, follows the plane, laying a carpet of sound along the ground. Thus one person hears the sonic boom where he is located, and another person a mile away hears the sound a fraction of a second later.

Early in the controversy over the sonic boom predicted for the commercial SST a man remarked, "Well, why don't they take off, go over the ocean, make the boom and then fly over land." This, of course, is not the situation at all. Besides, how does man consider it within his province to subject the ocean surface to sound he will not tolerate on land?

Invectives against the boom are numerous, but few approach the colorful quality of a comment from Dr. Garrett Hardin, University of California at Santa Barbara: "The sonic boom is something much worse than noise. Experiencing it is like living inside a drum beaten by an idiot at insane intervals." And a giant drum it would be, for the carpet of a boom can be as much as 50 miles wide, narrower as the plane sinks to lower altitudes, but more intense. In a presentation on the sonic boom, a lecturer showed a photograph of the United States map on which had been drawn boom carpets along the major air routes projected for future fleets of SSTs. Virtually no areas on the map were free of future sonic boom activity.

The sonic boom is not the only noise concern associated with the SST. The planes are certain to generate engine noise levels greater than those present craft produce. Because engines with exceptionally great thrust are necessary, the design and type of power plant will necessarily be different—and predictably noisier during takeoff.

Supporters of the SST development project assured citizens that the loud sonic boom the plane produces will never be allowed over land. Opponents of the project point out that sea life may be jeopardized if sonic booms occur repeatedly over the oceans. They argue further that overland flights eventually will be allowed at supersonic speeds to make the venture profitable for the airlines.

Aircraft-created sonic booms certainly are a most disruptive event in the average citizen's life—so much so that consistent exposure to the boom must be avoided. Somewhat a misnomer, the sonic boom would be better named the sonic boom-boom, since twin reports have been measured to peak at levels up to 130 dB per boom. A European who had just been subjected to the boom of the Concorde, French-English version of the SST, stated that at the first crack his chest seemed to be pressed quickly inward by an invisible giant hand. An instant later, on the second boom, he seemed to feel a small explosion in his chest, pressing it outward.

A 26-week, government-supported study conducted in 1965 attempted to evaluate the impact of sonic booms on a community by creating as many as eight sonic booms a day over greater Oklahoma City. This area, populated by approximately 750,000 persons, generated over 15,000 complaints, 9,600 of which were alleged damage claims. Complaints included startle reactions caused by rattling windows, fear responses, and interrupted sleep, rest, and conversation. The researchers' major conclusion was that a level of acceptability of sonic boom exposure never was established during the study. In brief, the citizens of Oklahoma City and the surrounding area never accepted or became accustomed to sonic booms.

In a similar study conducted in Chicago, 49 booms occurred over a 3-month period. Citizen damage claims numbered 3,156, including requests for funds to replace broken glass, repair cracked plaster, correct building structure damage, replace injured animals, and compensate for personal injury.

Additional evidence that sonic booms leave damage and destruction in their wake is found in the air force records of claims payments. Between 1956 and 1968 the air force paid claims totaling nearly $1.5 million, which included settlements for injury to startled and panicked domestic animals, such as hogs, rabbits, pheasants, turkeys, mink, cattle, horses, and chickens. In addition, poultrymen have been compensated when they were able to document reductions in egg productivity among their hens.

W. F. McCormack, Claims Division, U.S. Air Force, has acknowledged that sonic booms "may cause glass damage and may aggravate preexisting plaster damage." Of much greater consequence, however, are the human correlates, such as irritation, shock, loss of sleep, and physiological reaction, which do not lend themselves to easy quantification and analysis.

Some have speculated that the boom places people in jeopardy in several ways. Older structures are held to be subject to partial or complete collapse as a result of the shock wave a supersonic aircraft creates in flying at low altitude faster than the speed of sound. It must be emphasized that such an event is unlikely and that much of the concern for ancient European buildings was considered unwarranted. Still, in 1967 when a French farmhouse suddenly collapsed and three occupants died, the survivors reported that the rafters had given way moments after they had heard a loud clap attributed to a sonic boom. In other similar events sonic booms have been suggested as probable causes for 11 deaths in France since 1963.

Another tragedy that possibly can be precipitated by sonic booms according to one aerospace scientist is the creation of gigantic avalanches. A well-placed shout can start an avalanche; so the significant overpressure of a sonic boom also appears to have great potential as a snow roller.

The end result of overland supersonic flights on busy schedules would be a form of chaos for those who live beneath the flight path; all for the purpose of enabling a relatively small group of persons to go from one end of the country to the other in approximately two hours less time. The price for saving a few hours in flight is too high in human and animal discomfort to ever permit overland movement of these aircraft at supersonic speeds. It has been estimated that every SST allowed to travel across the continent at the cruising speed for which it was designed would disturb 20 million persons. The question must be asked: Is it worth the travail?

Another severe problem area American SST development engineers face is that of sideline noise—the sound the aircraft engines generate on the ground and at takeoff. Original estimates were that the powerful engines would cause noise equivalent to the simultaneous takeoff noise of 50 subsonic airplanes. If true, such an estimate would indicate that these proposed planes would have created sound similar to an Apollo space launch.

Revised estimates, reported by no little coincidence during the final legislative debates on the fate of the Boeing SST prototypes, stated that engine redesign had reduced the estimated takeoff level from 127 EPNdB to 108 EPNdB. This result is encouraging in that the level was reduced to about that of present planes, but for a plane of future decades, this improvement was not enough. People would have nothing of a plane that would bring them back into the noisy 1960s when the crafts were taking off in the 1980s. It was pointed out that the SST would be quieter at a distance of one mile from the runway because of its steeper ascent. This information was countered with the observation that during the low-level aspects of the flight more persons would be subjected to high-level noise because the plane could broadcast sound to the community from a greater height, covering more people.

The story of the rise and fall of America's first SST is frought with controversy, overstatement, half-truths, frustration, and confusion. This expensive venture first encountered significant opposition in the 91st Congress when the House of Representatives by a very narrow margin approved a $290 million appropriation to Boeing for continuing development of two SST prototypes. Later the Senate failed to go along with the House and rejected the appeal for funds. In a subsequent joint committee meeting it was suggested that most of the funding request be reinstated. This agreement passed in the House; the Senate, though, again turned thumbs down on the project for a full year of funding but did agree to continue funding for three months until the 92nd Session met and decided the project's ultimate fate.

Through all the infighting and debate Senator William Proxmire steadfastly opposed the use of federal money to underwrite a commercial project that he said commercial interests would not support. Advocate for the federal government's active involvement in the program was William M. Magruder, an impressively persuasive man who served as acting SST director for the Department of Transportation.

Arguments against were balanced by those for the project when it was pointed out that close to $1 billion was already committed and that it would cost about half the requested figure to close out the program. Secretary of Transportation John Volpe proved to be a staunch supporter of this program, which had President Nixon's blessing. Perhaps the weight of influence was wielded too heavily, for at mid-March 1971 Congress tolled the Boeing project's death knell, and the Boeing Company found itself housing two very lame duck prototypes. The action caused termination of several thousand jobs in the Seattle area. Walter Swan, SST project director, mentioned in a private conversation the day after he signed job termination notices, "Well, the

American people won a victory, but they don't know what they won."

One feeble attempt to resurrect the project was made later but was rapidly nipped by a statement attributed to the president of the Boeing Company, indicating that much more funding would be needed to reclaim the SST project. Throughout the controversy some had maintained that because of a dwindling potential commercial attractiveness the Boeing Company had become quite disenchanted with the SST as then envisioned. The high official's action did nothing to dispel that suspicion.

In a battle such as this one no victory can be claimed. Only the most insensitive defender of the environment would rejoice over the loss of several thousand jobs in an area already economically depressed by other cutbacks in the aerospace industry. However, one may take heart in the possibility that congressional defeat of the SST project signaled a reordering of national priorities that will result in better life quality for more persons. Fortunately, a program of job reorientation for the unemployed aircraft workers tended to overcome some of the economic shock, and the spirit and resilience of Seattle's citizens withstood the crisis. As Tom Wicker of the *New York Times* indicated, perhaps it is now time to broaden the base of the aerospace industry into other realms of transportation so vital to future generations.

A final point should be made about the future of the SST. There is no reason to believe that the death of the Boeing project necessarily terminates any future hope of supersonic commercial flight. One operational aircraft already exists in the free world (the French-British Concorde), and the Russian version is presently in use. These planes will tell much about whether commercial SSTs truly have a future. Perhaps major breakthroughs will cause the sonic boom to be dissipated, thereby rendering viable such a mode of transportation.

Throughout the debate some have been undaunted defenders of the concept on which the SST program was based. Others, such as Secretary Volpe, have seemed to soften their stands. In a news conference in 1972, approximately 15 months after the demise of the Boeing program, Volpe stated that the product of the joint effort of France and Great Britian, the Concorde, was "noisy and dirty," and he expressed doubt that the SST would ever fly over the United States or even be allowed to land at coastal cities.

Numerous other countries have given serious consideration to banning supersonic overflights; so the plane ultimately may have no routes save over water, which would necessitate sizable detours and would cut into the major selling feature, time conservation.

Little is known of the Russian SST, but the French-English Concorde has been found wanting in several categories. It is projected to be a very expensive device to operate—particularly undesirable from an economic standpoint because the seating capacity is small. Also, the fully loaded Concorde has a limited range, making it incapable of crossing the Atlantic Ocean. One student on noting this limitation asked if Air France, the only airline to commit itself to the purchase of any of the planes, would supply paddles to the passengers in order to finish the trip from Paris to New York.

TRAFFIC NOISE

In *Retirement*, William Cowper described "Cities humming with a restless crowd." The seething, boiling urban areas meet that description well, and the contribution traffic makes to the illusion is incalculable. Historically, few noise sources have caused more comment than has traffic noise. Although these sounds have been a major source of citizen complaints, the citizen had little control over the steady encroachment of vehicular noise until a New York court's epic judgment in 1968. The decision handed down then required that the state pay damages for traffic noise to a citizen if part of his property was taken in order to construct a highway.

Of course, a single court decision won't provide a meaningful solution to such a complex problem as traffic noise. In modern life, cars, buses, cycles, and trucks have become an integral part of our transportation system; in fact, vehicles and highway construction account for approximately one-seventh of the Gross National Product, and one in five members of the national work force is employed in the manufacture of products related to the automobile industry. In March 1972 there were 88,840,541 registered automobiles, 189,085 buses, 17,789,280 trucks, and 1,616,997 public-owned vehicles. This amounts to a grand total of 108,435,903 vehicles competing for a piece of the road. Because of these sizable social and economic factors the traffic noise problem cannot possibly be abated by dictating the removal of vehicles or by severely restricting vehicular traffic.

Vehicles are sources of noise in several ways. Engine exhaust creates sound that is only partly controlled by a muffler. As speed increases, tires create sound that on some road surfaces can be noisier than the engine. Depending on the maintenance and general condition of the vehicle, rattles and squeaks may add to the total sound output.

Not only do single vehicles generate a considerable amount of racket but the problem is compounded by the large number of transportation units in use. Multiple-lane thoroughfares increase the volume of traffic, and each year the number of cars increases by 8 to 10 million, so that by the year 2000 it is projected that as many as 240 million cars will be in use if no modifications in travel styles and habits are made. These staggering figures dictate that traffic noise factors receive serious consideration as plans are made for future modes of transportation. Of course, continued energy crises such as the one experienced during the fall of 1973 and winter of 1974 may alter these projected trends in vehicle usage.

At present in urban areas rush-hour traffic produces a concerto in cacophony that ascends to the distressing level of 90 dBA or more. The automobile and its family of vehicles have not always enjoyed the acceptance and accord evident today. In early times these handicrafts of the devil were regarded with extreme suspicion, and anyone who had the gall to own one was considered to be an object of town gossip.

In England around the early 1830s steam-powered buggies were subjected to the Red Flag Law, which required that a man on foot precede each vehicle, waving a red warning banner to signal the buggy's approach. The intent of the law was twofold: first, to reduce the danger of startling horses pulling other carriages; second, to make traversal of the countryside slow enough to dissuade many from obtaining the contraptions, since they were necessarily slow when operated in compliance with the law. Surprisingly, the law was in effect for over 60 years and was finally repealed in 1896.

Various forms of mass transportation have served cities for many years. In fact, some of the original equipment quite apparently is still in operation on some of the transit lines, causing a tremendous stir in the central city. In Chicago such a problem prompted a leading audiologist to remark: "Every time you go downtown on the elevated, you endanger your hearing." For persons familiar with the elevated, no further comment is necessary. That city is actively engaged in an ongoing program to reduce community noise; so these concepts hopefully will rest only in the minds of oldtimers within the next generation. In San Francisco the Municipal Authority's suggestion that the diesel-powered buses be dropped in favor of electrically operated vehicles came after an 18-month study in which a leading bus manufacturer attempted unsuccessfully to design an environmental improvement kit to cut down on the noise and other pollution these vehicles caused.

Subways in some cities are being totally redesigned to accommodate rubber tires on pavement instead of rail cars. Not all subways can be reshaped at once, but certain little acts of consideration can be offered with a minimum of expense. One letter to the editor in a large city newspaper complained that "Trains which bypass stations blow their whistle on their way through. In stations located underground the reverberation of the whistle can cause discomfort or damage to the eardrums of passengers on the platform. Why cannot trains be equipped with a muffled signal for use in the subterranean stations?"

Another writer complained: "Yet one more example of the remarkable insensitivity of the Metropolitan Transportation Authority is the shrill, rasping sound systems that have been installed in many subway cars so that stations may be announced. In addition to being virtually deafened by the screeching of subway trains as they turn corners and come to stops, we must also endure the screeching of announcements."

Although it is somewhat less important to all but those

relatively few subjected to the noises, recreational traffic should be briefly mentioned here. Boats on water recreation areas can be heard for some distance, especially if the craft is large or is a high-speed racing rig. Snowmobiles already have been mentioned in some detail.

Perhaps one of the most maligned of all community noise sources is the motorcycle. In times past cyclists have gutted or removed their mufflers in order to increase the effective power of their bikes or to vicariously sample the vehicle's power through the auditory sense. Another habit that has not endeared cyclists to the nonmotorcycling public is the incessant revving of the motor when the cycle is stopped. A person subjected to the various stressing agents in a job and in the traffic battles to and from it rightly expects to enjoy some quiet. Hence, when the teen-age whiz kids spin up and down the street all the pent-up anger and hostility accumulated during the day is vented toward the motorcycles. On one occasion a neighbor carrying a baseball bat ran into the street after a particularly noisy cycle had passed several times. When the cycle spun by one more time, he shoved the bat into the spokes. Although he lost a bat, he gleefully related that most of the spokes in the rear wheel were stripped free. Certainly that immature action is no way to combat the unnerving influence motorcycles, trail bikes, and minibikes can have on the neighborhood.

Most vehicles have a muffler designed to reduce engine noise, but sometimes the muffler is grossly inadequate to suppress noise or, specifically in motorcycles, the exhaust system is modified. One young man who participated in the university freshman hearing test program detailed in Chapter 3 was found to have a 75 dB hearing impairment at both ears for the 6,000 Hz test tone. When he indicated a belief that frequent motorcycle activities had caused the loss he was asked to bring the cycle to the laboratory parking lot adjacent for sound level measurements of the engine. The cycle was found to be generating a sound level of 114 dBA, an especially astounding figure in that the measures were taken with the cycle only partially revved because the young man was concerned that he might harm his new motor by advancing the accelerator too far. This level is the highest allowed under the Federal Occupational Safety and Health Act, and the guidelines state that exposure to a sound level of such magnitude should be avoided for periods in excess of 15 minutes daily.

Another problem in outlying districts of towns and cities is the location of car racetracks in close proximity to houses. Construction of such facilities is becoming increasingly difficult because neighbors obtain court injunctions until the racetrack promoter can show unequivocally that noise and dust from the arena will not disturb the residents, who insist on a form of squatter's rights.

The mystique of the city continues to baffle this small-town boy. Thoreau described city life as "millions of people being lonesome together"; yet the multiplicity of noisy vehicles continues to pry into each citydweller's life, doubtless increasing any proclivity to develop jangled nerves.

One of the greatest traffic noise offenses is the interruption of sleep and relaxation. On city streets the sound generated by a tractor-trailer truck has been measured to peak at 96 dBA. Large diesel dump trucks in low accleration cause a 114 dB rumble, which is comparable to the roar of a jet at takeoff from a distance of approximately 500 feet. An old car amidst its own rattles and squeaks can broadcast as much as 98 dBA of sound, even though it is going no faster than 35 mph. It is nearly impossible to unwind if one is repeatedly beset with such sounds as these.

Multiply these sounds hundreds and thousands of times in each city, and the magnitude of the traffic noise problem comes into perspective. Some persons who live in the city near a high-speed interstate tend to run their bedroom window air conditioners constantly at night in order to cover up the intermittent noise and produce a somewhat better sleep environment.

There are several means of combating traffic noise. In some states maximum permissible sound levels for vehicles have been legally established, and others have such laws in process. Ultimately the Environmental Protection Agency will establish a national vehicular noise emission standard to which each state and locality must subscribe, thereby maintaining a consistent level from one state to the next and from one city to the next for the benefit of interstate travel. Although the logic behind this idea is strong, considerable resistance to it is welling up from communities that have set more stringent guidelines than those projected by the federal government. Enforcers of the strict vehicle noise law in Boulder, Colorado, claim it is working well. For that reason, the city manager of that community sent a letter to large numbers of persons around the country, seeking assistance in the battle against establishing a blanket vehicle noise law at the federal level. The outcome of this activity is still in doubt in that the EPA has taken no final action. One significant step was taken in 1973 with the publication of truck noise regulations by the EPA.

Other tacks being taken to reduce traffic noise include attempts to redesign tires to reduce sound, efforts to develop quieter automobiles and trucks, and stricter enforcement of the muffler laws in city codes. For the future, however, the impact of traffic noise can best be modified with establishment of efficient, low-cost rapid transportation, reduction in numbers of trucks through more efficient cartage techniques, and lessening of numbers of private automobiles on city streets. Then, and only then, will community noise drop to an acceptable level.

Horn-honking has been a part of vehicle operation since the first oo-oo-oo-ga was sounded by means of a squeeze bulb tooter mounted atop the hood or fender of a tin Lizzie. Some drivers have never matured away from inordinately great reliance on this device. Many years ago I took a cherished trip to another city with a favorite pastor. The church spiritual leader honked incessantly each time a stop light changed to green if the car in front did not dash into the intersection within a fraction of a second. Kind thoughts and respect for that man were tarnished in this teen-aged mind.

One New Yorker wrote, " . . . a source of noise which I, having recently returned to New York, find the most jarring and annoying of all—the angry, insistent honking of horns." She noted that an ordinance against horn use was effectively enforced in other cities around the world, and she questioned why this type of traffic noise was tolerated in her town.

A classic example in enforcement of the horn control ordinance is the city of Memphis. Law enforcement officers issue up to 1,000 citations annually for unnecessary use of the signaling device along with other automotive noise offense. This type of adherence to the letter of the law has earned Memphis the title in some publications of "America's quietest city."

All aspects of the noise problem must be seen in proper interrelationships, however. Robert Alex Baron, author of the angry book, *The Tyranny of Noise*, points out that many municipalities have adopted the model antinoise code recommended by the National Institute of Municipal Law Officers, written to prohibit "unnecessary and unreasonable" noise. Nonetheless, Baron maintains, these laws are nothing but a license to pollute. He points out that while a barking dog or honking car horn may be deemed unreasonable, builders are free to go on banging with unmuffled jackhammers, air compressors, cranes, bulldozers, and transit cement mixers simply because daytime construction work is exempted from the code.

A short while ago a member of the staff for filming a Public Broadcasting System documentary on noise called to relate a strange, incongruous tale. She told of the photographer for the documentary being arrested after blowing his horn at a traffic officer. According to the story, he was held up at an intersection for what he judged an inordinately long time while the policeman directed vehicles going the other direction. He decided to sound a little toot to gain the officer's attention in order to be allowed to pass—apparently the wrong thing to do, for the policeman came to the car and began a verbal exchange that apparently was none too kind. The only charge the officer placed against the photographer was violation of the noise ordinance. The embarrassed photographer paid the fine, which unfortunately was not deemed appropriate for coverage in the filming budget.

In a fascinating study two psychologists discovered that horn honking could be related to status level in that most drivers honk angrily more often at old, low-status cars than at shiny new, high-status cars. On the basis of these findings they concluded that the honker fears that the honkee will have a greater chance to exercise sanctions if his status is higher, or a high-status car may unnerve the frustrated driver, completely inhibiting his urge to honk.

The researchers used three cars to study Californians' driving habits: a shiny new Chrysler Imperial, a rusty 1954 Ford station wagon, and a grimy 1961 Rambler. Test drivers were asked to stop in a narrow intersection after the stop light had signaled "go" and to stay there until the car behind had honked twice or until 15 seconds had elapsed, whichever came first. They found that 84 percent of the trailing drivers honked at the old models and about half of the drivers honked twice; but only about 50 percent of the cars behind the new, high-status car honked once, and less than 20 percent sounded the second beep. In an interesting sidelight to the study the experimenters noted that men did not honk more often than did women but were somewhat quicker to do so.

Well-meaning, spiritually oriented persons are inviting trouble in the use of bumper stickers that read: "Honk if you love Jesus" or "Honk for Jesus." Unfortunately, a heaven-directed horn blast sounds exactly like the angry toot of a frustrated driver; so perhaps members of the Christian community will find other, quieter means of expressing their faith. It is interesting to ponder the situation in which the Memphis motorist pleads, "But officer, I was just honking for Jesus."

NOISE AND VEHICLE SAFETY

In the epilogue to *My Host the World*, George Santayana wrote: "The cry was for vacant freedom and indeterminate progress: Vorwärts! Avanti! Onward! Full speed ahead!; without asking whether directly before you was a bottomless pit." To an alarming degree progress can be described in this way. Improvements and changes are made for the moment without sufficient thought about long-term factors. Each of the countless examples of this quirk and dilemma offers the same theme: the good comes with some bad.

Claim agents are abundantly aware of the hazards citizens face as they move about in their daily cycles. Doubtless every agent could cite many examples of claims filed against their firms by persons who denied hearing some audible warning sound until catastrophe was imminent. Often such claims have been made not by the person involved but by his or her survivors. There are good reasons to believe that a large part of the time audible warning signals are unheard because their signal of impending danger reaches the ears of persons enclosed in a vehicle at insufficient volume to cause awareness of the signal.

One of the most irrefutable reasons for failure to abide by an order or suggestion is "I didn't hear you." In the parent–child relationship it is a child's frequently used excuse for having failed to carry out a command. The considerate and compassionate parent is hard put to justify punishment because the child may well not have perceived the nature of the instructions. Often, however, the tendency is to dismiss the "didn't hear" plea with a harsh observation that the orders should have been heard. Further, few excuses are more common or overworked; so one becomes hardened to the possibility that the message really was unheard rather than unheeded.

The various physiological disruptions laid to noise may work singly or in combination to decrease one's vigilance, creating an accident situation. For instance, pupillary dilation in response to high-level noise exposure may create an artificial change in color perception, which may create some accident risk in activities that require accurate visual perception. Untoward reactions in the vestibular system during intense sound stimulation may create in the individual an unsteadiness sufficient to place him in jeopardy—particularly if he is a steeplejack!

In England two researchers stated that drivers can become "drunk" without alcohol because of the low-frequency sound encountered while driving a vehicle at relatively high speeds. They indicated that such sounds can blur vision, affect the balance sense, slow reaction times in an emergency, and impede the driver's ability to follow and track other vehicles. The source of these problems is called infrasound—sound that is so low in pitch that the human ear does not recognize it as sound. The researchers attributed "many inexplicable highway crashes" to the effect of long-term exposure to these sounds. In conjunction with these observations NASA has found that high-intensity infrasound causes headaches, noticeable vibratory sensations in the chest and abdominal regions, gagging and nausea, as well as blurred vision. Further, the space scientists related that for a period of 24 hours after being subjected to intense infrasound the subjects continued to be unduly fatigued.

Many years ago in Italy Dr. Tullio noticed that he could cause a pigeon to veer off course in flight by presenting to the bird an intense, low-frequency sound. His discovery has not been widely known, but apparently it has importance in consideration of the effect of infrasound on driving skills. In fact, the British scientists cited earlier measured a 10 percent reduction in driver reaction time when the vehicle operator was moving at 60 mph in a small sport sedan. This lag in reactivity was credited to infrasound stimulation. Some of the drivers reported a feeling of euphoria, which on the highways can be a deadly high. Apparently not all persons are subject to these sensations and reactions in that tolerance for infrasound stimulation effect varies widely.

With a little bit of imagination one could list great numbers of ways in which a noisy environment can pose a threat to the health and safety of its inhabitants. Sufficient here is one detailed account of a very interesting paradox that is becoming widely recognized.

The automobile industry has been striving during the past few years to develop a product that provides a smoother and quieter ride. With the effective use of undercoating, special suspension systems, carpeting, acoustic treatment of the top liner, padding and isolation of especially noisy areas, the modern automobile is considerably less noisy to the occupant. An acoustic barrier is afforded the rider, insulating him from disturbing and distracting outside noises—including audible warning signals.

Recorded sound measures demonstrate that car interiors are considerably less noisy in popular models and makes of automobiles. Dr. Clifford Bragdon has observed, however, that there appears to be very little correlation between the car's price and its quietness. Figure 8.2 lists several cars, foreign and domestic. In the spring of 1972 students of a class in environmental noise conducted a limited survey of the newest models of cars and compared them acoustically to the same models of preceding years. They drove the cars on a straight, smooth stretch of interstate at 60 mph in order to take sound readings at the ear of the driver, then compared the readings to those reported in Dr. Bragdon's book. In the figure the comparisons are indicated by horizontal lines connecting the two symbols. In all the 1972 models the sound inside was lower, ranging between a 4.5 dB and 10 dB improvement. Interestingly, the car that demonstrated the greatest noise reduction was still one of the noisiest because of collateral improvements in the other models.

The acoustic barricade that has been designed into cars is a

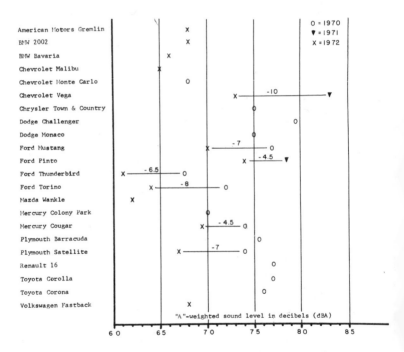

8.2   Sound levels in automobiles as measured at the driver's ear. Lines connect measures taken on the same model in consecutive years.

welcome development, but it does present a paradoxical situation. The sound treatment that insulates car occupants from
unwanted outside noise also baffles them from warning signals.

An automobile traveling at acceptable speeds is bound to
have some internal noise, which generally increases with the
speed. Some typical sound levels are as follows.

Inside Sound Levels

A. Not moving, motor off—50 dBA
B. Not moving, motor idling—70 dBA
C. 30 mph—72 dBA
D. 60 mph—78 dBA
E. 70 mph—81 dBA

These figures vary with models and types of cars, but they serve
as an appropriate example of midrange sound levels in cars
currently on the road. Although the sound levels are not excessively high they are likely to cause one to raise his voice in order
to be easily heard by others in the car. With respect to outside
noise a general observation is that the shell of the car reduces
(attenuates) the sound by a factor of approximately 20 dB.

Other conditions in the car add to the overall sound environment.

Special Conditions—at 60 mph

A. Moving, windows closed—78 dBA
B. Wing window open—81 dBA
C. Both side windows open—81 dBA
D. Windows closed, radio on (audible)—81 dBA
E. Radio on (loud)—90 dBA

Further, internal sound levels rise with the use of heater fans, air
conditioners, conversation, mechanical malfunction (e.g., bearing whine), and so on.

Certainly, acoustical treatment of the automobile interior is
desirable, but insufficient attention has been paid to ways of
providing the driver with adequate awareness of warning sig-

nals. As a group the deaf have a quite remarkable driving safety record, largely because visually they are extremely vigilant. A deaf driver knows that he cannot rely on hearing a warning signal, thus he pays exceptionally close attention to the task of driving. The driver with hearing is not so alert to the unheard dangers he may encounter. He continues in the belief that he can and will hear a siren, whistle, or horn in the event of an emergency. That unfortunately is often not the case as supported by the observation in a National Aircraft Noise Abatement Council publication that many accidents can be attributed to drivers' lack of awareness of an emergency vehicle's siren. The situation was summed up in the speculation that " . . . more lives are lost because of speeding fire apparatus, police cars, and ambulances than are saved by this practice."

A tragic accident that occurred in a southeastern city left a young policeman paralyzed below the neck. He was speeding to an emergency call, and when his car topped a rise it collided with another car that had pulled into his path. There is good reason to believe that the acoustical conditions were such that the other driver could not hear the approaching siren until a collision was unavoidable.

Each accident laid at least partially to noise has its own peculiar twists that defy the simplistic notion that a single solution is possible. When the funeral train carrying the assassinated Bobby Kennedy slammed into a car at a crossing, killing two people and injuring several others, secret service and news media helicopters hovering in the area were thought to have created a noise level sufficient to obliterate the train whistle, in effect making the driver of the ill-fated car "deaf" to the approaching train. In a recent court case the family of a man killed at a Memphis train crossing was awarded $85,000 when they convinced the court that there was little evidence that the driver ever heard the approaching train. Two nearly identical accidents occurred within a three-month period in Knoxville, Tennessee. In one a tanker-truck driver was injured when his truck was broadsided by a freight train; in the other a man was hospitalized when a train struck his car at a crossing. In both instances the drivers maintained that they did not see the train and that no warning signals were given. The train engineers stated that both the bell and whistle of the engine were at full volume on approaching the crossing. Again the audible warning signals seemed to fail.

Of course, not all such claims are valid. A lawyer who asked for help in a case explained that a "26 year-old teen-ager" on his motorcycle had lost a race to the crossing by 27 feet and had been killed when he hit the engine. The attorney wondered about the possibility that the man did not hear the train whistle, but there was not much evidence that such an appeal would have any success.

These few examples are offered to emphasize that situations can and do arise wherein claims can and will be made on the basis of inability to hear a warning signal. Many of these claims probably are valid. How do warning signals become lost and rendered ineffective? At this time, a precise answer is not fully possible, but some theoretical factors appear to have bearing on the question.

1. *Warning signal sound levels.* Safety equipment for emergency and transportation vehicles offers a wide range of sound levels. The following list is representative of some of the common devices.

Warning Signal Sound Levels

A.   Car horn—90-95 dBA (3 feet)
B.   Police siren—100 dBA (100 feet)
C.   Train whistle—90-100 dBA (100 feet)
D.   Train bell—90-100 dBA (50 feet)

These figures cannot be taken to be absolute, for acoustic conditions in the area and the sound each unit produces will alter the sound level of all warning signals. Since the shell of the car reduces the outside noise by approximately 20 dB, each warning signal sound level can be reduced by that amount. The distance from the sound source also must be considered. The general rule is that in an open field sound is reduced by 6 dB each time the distance from the sound source is doubled. Thus a police siren on an open stretch of road will be rated as 94 dB from a distance of 200 feet. Remember, though, that 200 feet is still a very short distance when a vehicle is traveling at a high rate of speed—a fact the National Safety Council advertises often in stressing the distances required for complete stops from various speeds.

2. *Signal to noise.* In discussing signal-to-noise (S/N) ratios in Chapter 1 the relationship between a desired sound and background noise was described. The S/N concept has considerable bearing on inability to hear warning signals. Those audible sounds that one wants to hear or that are important to be heard may become lost in the background of interfering noise. This masking of one sound by another is one aspect of the audible warning signal problem. Generally speaking, the better the S/N ratio, the more clearly audible the desired sound will be.

In automobiles the car shell's attenuation of outside sound and the ongoing interior background noise combine to create sound levels that make warning signals difficult to receive. A car traveling at 30 mph may generate an interior sound level of 72 dBA—a level that frequently occurs when windows are closed and other sound-producing devices such as radios and heaters

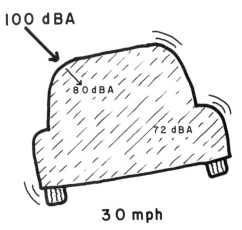

8.3 A schematic illustration of the signal-to-noise conditions in a car traveling at 30 mph.

are not operating. As shown in Figure 8.3, a warning signal impinging on the car's shell at 100 dBA will enter the car as an 80 dB sound, allowing a normally hearing driver to easily pick up the signal.

A more difficult condition is shown in Figure 8.4. The same car moving at 60 mph generates an interior sound level of 78 dBA. Since the warning signal still enters the car at a level greater than the background noise, the driver may hear it, but not so readily, and he may not be startled into realizing the signal is a harbinger of danger. In addition, the driver will become aware of the signal only when the distance between his car and the warning device is quite small.

Figure 8.5 shows a final example. Here the warning signal enters the car but is immersed in the ambient (background) noise of the car and will be nearly impossible to hear. In this condition the driver has little chance of averting a crisis situation if he is to depend on his hearing for guidance.

3. *The situation.*   This set of conditions is not altogether new, but many factors now cause more concern. More vehicles are on the roads now than ever have been before; hence the space between vehicles is reduced, even though more roads are being

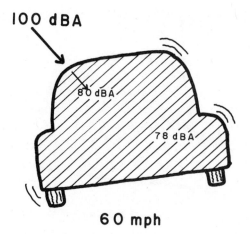

8.4   Signal-to-noise ratio in a car at 60 mph.

built. Speeds of traveling vehicles are moving upward. Additional acoustical treatment of new car interiors reduces the ability of alerting signals to perform their function. Driver vigilance may be diminishing because of fatigue from long spells of driving. Driver reaction time may be dimmed by high-volume low sounds.

4. *Additional factors.*   The foregoing discussion of warning signals has been based on normally hearing drivers or deaf drivers with little or no functional hearing. In the middle range are large numbers of drivers who have some hearing difficulty even though they may not be aware of it. In the past few years high-frequency hearing loss in younger persons has been seen to increase, as was pointed out in Chapter 3. This population and the many persons with age-related hearing deterioration constitute a sizable segment of the driving public whose diminished ability to hear certain tones might preclude adequate responsiveness to a siren, especially in the less desirable signal-to-noise situations.

A second additional factor, and a serious one for the few persons involved, is the advent of stereo headphone jacks in automobile cartridge tape players. This factor was discussed

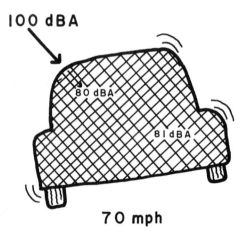

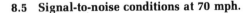

8.5   Signal-to-noise conditions at 70 mph.

earlier and is mentioned here only as a reminder of the problem headphone misuse can create.

In recent times, audible warning signals are encountering the greatest resistance in their history. Previously heeded, they are becoming just a part of the background noise; so few persons take conscious note. For safety's sake, modifications in the use of warning devices must be made, or Santayana's words will ring even more true.

CONSTRUCTION NOISE

Historically, the rattles, bangs, squeaks, and clangor of construction activity heralded progress and desirable developments. In the hope for a better city, residents tended to sacrifice comfort temporarily for a promise of better tomorrows. This attitude has been true from very early times when the pyramids were tolerated as a sign of the greatness of civilization. New designs, advanced technology, and abundant resources have fostered a new race—the race to the heavens. Scarcely is one building proclaimed the "world's tallest" until another, even higher one appears on the drawing boards.

In all of this the construction industry has developed a very indifferent attitude toward the comfort of residents near the jobs. It had little need for public relations in the past, and construction people clearly have almost no inclination in this direction. In all probability, however, the builder's need for good public relations will increase, for citizens are no longer passively tolerating construction noise but are garnering support for their side and demanding increasingly stricter codes and laws to govern the amount of racket radiated from a building site. This tendency is not going to diminish, thus, the construction industry is due for some reordering of attitudes and actions.

The intolerable nature of subway construction noise in New York City spurred Robert Alex Baron to leave his theater profession to become a full-time activist for noise control. He formed Citizens for a Quieter City, a group dedicated to bringing the need for quiet to the attention of city government. To an extent, this purpose has been fulfilled in that city officials have responded positively to some of the organization's demands. The inevitable frustrations that come from the victories of vested interests are there, but citizen organizations to promote noise control are becoming more numerous and their clout inevitably will be greater. May their tribe increase!

The ear-damaging aspects and irritating qualities of construction noise have been discussed earlier, but it should be considered a contributor to community noise as well. A newspaper account of one of New York's largest construction projects described the noise in the lead paragraph. ". . . The area reverberated yesterday with the staccato sound of air compressors, punctuated by the splash of a huge steel 'clamshell' bucket dredging the sand-compacted river bottom."

And so it goes, the big sound of the city—construction noise. Exhaust noise of the engine that powers a giant crane hovers between 102 and 104 dBA. The holler of a bulldozer mauling the remains of an old building reaches 106 dBA and never falls below 90 dBA.

In a man-on-the-street interview a construction zone resident was heard to say: "Well, we've just been suffering just terribly from it. You can't hardly hear yourself think in any of our own apartments." When the interviewer asked, "Do you notice you're staying up longer and enjoying it less?" a man replied, "Yes, I have. I try to hide out in the Ginger Man, which is a saloon on the next block, and it's so noisy you can't even drink in peace. And that's really getting too much."

Finally, in response to the question of what happens to her husband when he returns from the quiet office a woman said: "Well, usually he would come right home. But now, because he knows the noise is here, he'll stay out and have a few drinks instead of coming right home. I try to understand that and, you know . . . we don't . . . we don't talk to each other. We figure we can cut down on the noise that way."

These examples prove that building bridges for cars and trucks does not foster building bridges between people. Bandleader Doc Severinsen observed, "Sometimes I think the noise made by hard hats is a deliberate attempt to give the rest of us soft heads."

GARBAGE COLLECTION

Bob Brumfield, columnist for a large Ohio newspaper, has assailed the activities that surround the accumulation of waste and trash as the most hideous of soundmakers.

> Air pollution isn't what's going to get us. Noise pollution is going to do us in.
> If it doesn't actually kill us, it's going to drive us so bananas it won't make any difference whether we're alive or not.
> The biggest single source of noise in the world is not the jet aircraft engine. It is the Cincinnati garbage men and their incredible whining trucks.
> You can hear the garbage men coming for miles. It's like the approach of Theodoric the Ostrogoth. Instead of beating on their shields, however, the garbage men strike terror into the hearts of the citizenry by beating on the tops of garbage cans.

Not all garbage cans have to be noisy, however. James Bottsford, engineer for Bethlehem Steel, has used a good dose of common sense and his engineering background to design and build long-lasting metal garbage cans that do not emit the familiar clatter on handling. The renovations in design are remarkably simple but immensely effective. The outside of each can is banded with two or three sound-damping strips of steel. The can bottom is treated with an undercoating material, and six rubber bumpers are affixed to the bottom rim. To eliminate handle noise a rubber bumper is placed on the center of the handle, and rubber guards are pressed into the hinge. The can top is crisscrossed with metal stripping so that each lid resembles a hot-cross bun. The results are garbage cans that produce virtually no bothersome noise when dropped and banged about. It is most convincing to watch Bottsford drop flashlight batteries into an untreated can with a horrible clang and then to hear the dull thud of a like battery pitched into the modified can.

Around the laboratory, Bottsford's idea has been incorporated into a few of the trash receptacles by banding them with two-inch masking tape and running tape lines along the bottom. Although this modification certainly does not work so well as the manufactured can, existing metal refuse containers respond well to this type of treatment.

INDUSTRIAL NOISE

Industry apparently can do no right with respect to noise. Not only is it a place where high noise levels threaten workmen's hearing health but it also can be a significant contributor to community noise levels in circumscribed areas. Many cities now have a boundary noise code, which establishes the maximum amount of sound a plant may spew into the surrounding area. To enforce these codes the noise is measured along several points of the company boundary line. If the sound exceeds established levels, the company must reduce the noise. Normally these levels are adjusted according to the type of neighborhood where the plant is located, becoming more stringent as one moves from an area zoned for industry or business into areas that border on regions zoned residential. Unfortunately, boundary noise codes are seldom enforced on a routine basis, and too few citizens realize that the rules exist and so assume that they can only attempt to tolerate noisy industry.

LAWNMOWERS

If 100 people were asked to list 10 noisy contributors to the community sound conditions, lawnmower noise would appear on virtually every list. Most people have been subjected to the seemingly insomniac neighbor who at 6 A.M. on Sunday can find nothing to do but mow his lawn. Of course, other times of the week are not much better, for the use of lawnmowers has no fully acceptable time as far as neighbors are concerned. A civic club attempted to combat this problem by selling several adjustable mufflers that would fit most lawnmower engines. At last report the club had sold one muffler.

Perhaps this form of indifference to one's fellow residents caused a frenzied man, according to a newswire story, to enter garages, start the lawnmowers, and leave them running all over the neighborhood. Crazy? Maybe he was trying to say something.

COMMUNITY RESPONSE

The term *socioacusis* has been used to describe the condition of an individual who has sustained a permanent hearing loss as a result of nonoccupational noise exposure. It connotes social implications in community noise, and it poses several questions.

1. What is the role of environmental noise as one of the dehumanizing influences in inner-city life?

2. Is there a relationship between noise levels and the apparent social upheavals in heavily populated urban areas?

3. A large proportion of young people who were activisits in the recent peace movement were from large cities. To what extent did the high ambient noise levels in their environment create in them a drive to change their world?

4. How does noise relate to other factors in the crowding problems of overpopulated areas?

5. If noise abatement were effectively initiated across the country, what would be the possible effects on the social climate of the population?

6. What are the leading noise irritants in various areas of the country?

The social implications of environmental noise have been subjected to insufficient concentrated study. Hopefully these questions and many more will be the target of scientific investigation during the upcoming decade.

BACKGROUND MUSIC

During a scientific meeting I shared an elevator ride with the director of a large botanical garden. As is often the case, the conversation got around to noise. As he darted away for a conference he said over his shoulder, pointing to the loudspeaker in the elevator ceiling, "See if you can't do something to still that ____ racket!"

One correspondent has asserted that music piped in to stores, restaurants, offices, and other places is the work of the Mafia. His theory is that the musical stimulation distracts people so that they tend to loosen their grasp on the purse strings.

These reactions and overreactions to what has been heralded as a great innovation indicate once more how weary humans are becoming of incessant sound around them.

Little is being done to minimize the spread of the loud-speakers everywhere, which is especially understandable in reading the promotional material of a prime purveyor of atmosphere. The following assertions were found in a pamphlet *Practical Management Ideas*.

> The power of music to influence people has long been known. ____ harnessed this power over 30 years ago to make it a management tool. Since then, ____ has broadened its sphere of activity to include research in vigilance and human factors research, medical and dental studies, noise control, the interaction of color and music on emotions, the use of music in education and of course, the effects of scientifically arranged and recorded music on worker productivity and efficiency, among others.
>
> ____ research efforts are being conducted in government, university, medical and industrial applications. Professional guidance is provided by the ____ Board of Scientific Advisors which consists of distinguished professionals in the field of education, industrial engineering, medicine, psychology and human factors.
>
> Under the guidance of the Board, ____ aims to make dramatic contributions to the business community through new discoveries in the scientific applications of music.

CONCLUSION

Most of the discussion of community noise has been specifically related to problems in the urban environment. Rural areas are becoming more densely populated; so the noise of the city is moving into suburbia and the countryside. Persons who have sold their property in the city in hope of having a quiet abode in an outlying district have received a terrible surprise as they have discovered, much to their dismay, that country lots do not necessarily come with a lifetime guarantee of solitude and quiet.

Humans apparently have much less opportunity to rest from sound, which may have some bearing on the propensity to develop hearing losses in the wake of exposure. Community noise, which seldom drops to levels one might describe as quiet, is a major contributor to man's acoustic dilemma.

Several guidelines and suggestions for control of rising sound levels in the environment are outlined briefly here.

1. Community planning should be augmented with advice from competent acoustical engineers and architects.

2. Traffic patterns should be modified according to the noise levels generated by vehicles that frequent the various regions of the community.

3. Efficient and well-engineered mass transit systems must be developed.

4. Appropriate and enforceable noise codes should be established.

5. Control of construction and industrial noise should be encouraged.

6. A program of community education on noise should be initiated. One such program is cited in Appendix I, which contains a number of radio spot announcements intended to alert and inform.

With the adoption of intelligent community planning, including consideration of community noise sources, future city development can occur with a minimum of the dehumanizing influence of noise. Otherwise, as a cartoon pointed out, a large billboard will greet new arrivals to a community with the message: "Welcome to our city.*"

---

*(may be hazardous to your health)

·9·

The Castle Crumbles

It takes a heap o' livin' in a house t' make it home.
Edgar A. Guest

In 1882 Oscar Wilde wrote, "America is the noisiest country that ever existed. One is waked up in the morning not by the singing of the nightingale but by the steel worker. It is surprising that the sound practical sense of the Americans does not reduce this intolerable noise. All art is based on exclusive and delicate sensibilities, and such continual turmoil must ultimately be destructive to the musical facilities."

This early invective against the uncontrolled racket in Wilde's world is applicable now in the home, the one place that has largely escaped attention as a location of excessive noise. Supposedly, the home is one's castle in which to seek refuge from most of the annoying aspects of life. Beyond that reliable bastion peace and quiet can be sought with a high probability of success. At least, that once was so.

In the words of J. G. Holland, "The sweetest type of heaven is home." With high aspirations for finding a place where they can engage in R and R, men and women return to their homes to find that they, too, have developed into grinding treadmills of noises that are a part of the mechanized world. The by-product of a home equipped with time- and laborsaving appliances and features is the loss of the restful sound environment to the noise of increasing numbers of modern devices.

Whether the home is a place of repose from work or the

189

place of work, noises from within clearly have a distracting effect. The housekeeper may be more fatigued at the end of the day because of immersion in various forms of clatter and whirrs throughout the waking hours. The independent merchant who attempts to house an office in the home comes to realize that quieter locations exist.

Some chose the home as a place to create, but artists and writers may find that a studio located elsewhere is more conducive to the pursuit of their interests and expressions. In an interview in *Intellectual Digest* the poet Jean Valentine remarked that she needs to get away from her "own clutter" to do real writing. She rarely finds the necessary silence in her own apartment.

Let us observe the various noises in the home by taking an acoustic stroll through the house.

THE KITCHEN

Generally regarded to be the hub room of the house, the kitchen contains a large assortment of noise-producing gadgets. Fortunately, not all appliances are noisy. For example, the newer refrigerators are dramatically more quiet than were their predecessors, but the frost-free varieties may have higher noise levels because of the constant use of fans. These models are as much as 10 dB more noisy than the frosty type.

In a typical kitchen one might find meat sizzling in a pan on the stove—not a disagreeable sound, but one that adds as much as 10 dB to the sound level of the room. When a blender is operating it produces a sound level of about 90 dB which completely covers up the sound of frying meat. In an already noisy kitchen the blender still can add as much as 20 dB to the overall noise level, and this amount can be increased even more if the blender is part of a unit built into the counter. When the blender motor is firmly attached to the worktop a *sounding board effect* can be noted. This acoustical phenomenon results in vibrations being transmitted directly to the wood tabletop and thus more effectively to the air, ultimately reaching the ear with more force. The sounding board effect can be demonstrated by placing a vibrating electric razor or other similar device on a table. The increase in buzzing sound is easily perceived.

In some homes the clothes washer and dryer are conveniently located in or near the kitchen. When operating, these devices can also add as much as 20 dB to the concert of noisemakers.

An exhaust fan, furnace fan, or window air conditioner can add another 10 dB or more each; so we may safely estimate that when several of these devices are operating simultaneously the sound in the kitchen can reach or exceed 100 dB for some periods. This level is not only shattering to the nerves but also creates a mild threat to the hearing.

Few persons, however, are exposed to kitchen noises for periods long enough to cause great concern for their hearing. Most appliances individually have noise output levels that range from about 75 dBA to 85 dBA, and a level of 85 dBA can be tolerated for as long as 2 hours a day if no additional exposure to high-level sound occurs (see Table 7.1). It is certainly possible that the sounds of kitchen activity might push a working person's exposure index over the danger mark, however, just as on- and off-job noise exposures (Chapter 7) can be considered together.

There is no question that the appliances mentioned here are desirable additions to the household; that they are too noisy is an established fact. Future devices of this nature will be designed to be quieter if the consumer continues to demand quieter units.

LIVING AND RECREATION AREAS

In the living room outside noises are abundant, since this room often is located on the street side of the house in order to allow bedrooms to be oriented toward the quieter areas. Because of its position the living room is susceptible to the rising and falling outdoor noises, such as those generated by traffic and lawn mowers. With air conditioning the living room sound level may become high enough to interfere with attempts at conversation.

Of greatest consequence in the living quarters are the sounds that entertainment centers broadcast into the room and bordering areas. Home stereo components are fully capable of producing musical peaks in the 120 dBA range, and television is distracting from both the auditory and the visual standpoints. Interpersonal communications are severely strained in living and family rooms when the wireless wisdom wreckers are blaring, although it seems to be a sign of the times, since sales for these home entertainment units continues to break records. There are currently 450 million radios, 130 million televisions, and 83 million phonographs in use throughout the country. For a nation that numbers something over 200 million people that means 1½ such appliances for each ear.

Dissension in the home often revolves around the use of the entertainment devices. Arguments spring up over which television show will be watched. Parents berate their children for playing phonographs or radios too loudly. A family member who wants to read must vacate the area and find silence and solace in a remote corner of the house. Intended as sources of entertainment and gaiety, too often the musicmakers become problems, not only from the standpoint of sound levels but also, more importantly, because a disagreeable atmosphere is created.

The entire home is subjected periodically to the roar of a vacuum cleaner, but most frequently this appliance is operated in the living room over carpets and furniture. Because vacuum cleaner suction must be created by a powerful motor-driven fan, considerable sound is emitted as the dust is sucked in. Some cleaners have been found to create sound that nears 90 dBA at the operator's ear, and when they are placed on a wood floor the *sounding board* effect creates more noise. Although one manufacturer marketed a quiet vacuum cleaner that did not sell well, it must be considered that the device was just ahead of its time. That unit now would probably be a popular item.

BATHROOM

The most reverberant room in the house is the bathroom. Bordered on all sides by mirrors, tiles, or slick surfaces, the room magnifies any sound that occurs in the little chamber—the reason many bathroom baritones enjoy singing during their showers, where the acoustical characteristics give the voice an added lift and a deceptively increased volume. In this small space, however, noisy appliances such as a shaver or an electric toothbrush may mildly irritate some people and interfere with communicative ability. Add the sounds of a heater or an exhaust fan, and the bathroom becomes an acoustically live room.

BEDROOM

The one area of the house that should be geared to a quiet and restful atmosphere is the bedroom; yet somewhat high sound levels have become commonplace here as well. Window air conditioners, water coursing through the pipes, radios or phonographs played in adjoining rooms—all interfere with sleep.

The unwanted sounds from inside or outside the house are becoming so bothersome that many people are purchasing acoustical sleep-inducing machines—devices made to produce a sound of a desirable quality loud enough to cover up environmental noise. Some models now available allow a selection of various sounds, such as waterfalls, bubbling brooks, sounds of the surf, and rushing mountain streams. The Wall Street Journal is not given to devoting space to areas of the economic scene that are of little consequence; thus, when a lengthy article on acoustic sleep aids appeared in it, the industry appeared to have come of age. A Manhattan apartment resident quoted in the article said, "The first thing I do when I go to bed at night is turn on the fan." This attempt to assure a steady ambient noise situation—"If it costs me a dollar a night in electricity and I freeze to death, it's still worth it"—was necessary because her next door neighbors' incessant playing of a particular record was beginning to wear thin. For citydwellers forced to sleep during the daylight hours such items as the Sleep-Mate are considered helpful. According to one user, "It makes just enough sound to drown out the traffic noise."

Because these gadgets have become so popular the Department of Housing and Urban Development contracted with an acoustical consulting firm to assess the positive and negative aspects of what they termed "added sound." Their interest was related to a consideration of the devices for use in churches, hospitals, schools, and apartments as well as in homes. Specifically, HUD's concern was the aircraft noise and the interference caused by flyovers. The head of the acoustical firm observed: "If you're going to have aircraft overflights, or any persistent noise for that matter, you can achieve a comfort situation by making a background noise level continuous and uniform."

The firm installed numerous systems in buildings at a cost per building of as much as $25,000. They maintained that "Introducing a non-unpleasant noise into buildings is like dumping rose water into the air conditioning at Madison Square Garden when the elephants are on. It doesn't make the elephants smell any better, but it gives you a somewhat pleasanter environment."

The use of masking noise is coming into use in quiet buildings, too. Banks are beginning to investigate the feasibility of using some acceptable noise that raises the overall level in order to allow persons at adjacent desks to converse somewhat privately with their respective customers.

The bedroom application remains the most popular one, however. A store that retails the Sleep Sound device ($19.50) describes its sound as a constant hum, like "a breeze in the trees," which has a "pacifying effect." A two-speed model ($25) in the line covers up more intense sounds. A major catalog supply company offers a Sleep-Mate (about $15) whose sound is described as a "soothing SWOOSH." Among several exotic (and expensive) versions is the Sleepatone ($120), which produces three sounds—falling rain on a wood-shingled roof, the rustle of the wind, and the ocean surf.

Somewhat different but still in the scheme of reducing outside noise interference is an egg-shaped easy chair lined with six loudspeakers that envelop the head. This $600 gimmick not only provides comfortable seating but also screens its occupant from any outside sound short of an atomic explosion. The chair is claimed to be better than stereo headsets because " . . . your whole body is exposed to the music."

A Melbourne, Australia, engineer who designed a noisemaking device supports its use. "The technique has so many uses. You can combat traffic noises, voices *and even silence*. The beauty of it is that one hardly senses the sound present in the room."

Not all specialists, however, are convinced that acoustic sleep aids signal a quieter future. Dr. Samuel Rosen of Mt. Sinai Hospital in New York says that using the sound machines is like taking aspirin to fight a brain tumor or codeine for tight shoes. That sizable portions of the population are forced to make noise in order to sleep is, in effect, a sad commentary on this generation.

Whether sleep is attempted with or without such sleep aids, many still consider recurring environmental noise to distinctly affect sleep itself. Sleep observation, modification, and deprivation studies have noted some ways in which noise-riddled sleep may affect personal and community status. Animals sleep in order to allow the body to recuperate from the rigors of the day. During human adult sleep periods the dream stage occurs up to five or six times each night. This stage, which accounts for about 25 percent of sleep time, is found to be vastly important in preparing for the next day's activities. Studies in which persons have been deprived of this sleep stage have revealed psychological changes and a generalized state of excitement and nervousness. Also, indications are that acute psychotic reactions can be precipitated by recurring interruption of the dream stage. Sleep disturbance caused by noise can have some dramatic effects that are neither fully understood nor predictable with the present state of knowledge.

Many sounds can interrupt the vital sleep stage and cause a person to shift to another, less deep level of rest. Canada's Dr. Theissen has noted that traffic noise no greater than 55 dBA can evoke an alteration in sleep level. Dr. Jansen at the Max Planck Institute in Germany confirmed these findings. In America, aircraft flyovers of 60 dBA were found sufficient to cause a sleeping subject to shift one full step away from the deep sleep stage. On occasion the subject was found to be completely awakened by the noise. One study of a large number of subjects indicated that 60 dBA noise awoke all but 10 percent of those sleeping.

The solutions seem to be varied. Some persons are using ear-plugs at night—not a fully acceptable solution since the plugs may become uncomfortable when the weight of the head is resting on one, forcing it to gouge into the ear canal. In addition, important warning signals or sounds might go unheeded. Others frequently or chronically use sleeping pills—a practice whose dangers are obvious. Some find that the use of masking devices to obliterate environmental sound is the best approach to their sleep problems. Others at great expense attempt acousti-cal treatment of their sleeping quarters. This method is some-times successful but never so effective as quieting the noise sources themselves. In disgust some people have relocated, often taking a sizable financial loss in the exchange because they can no longer stand the noise.

HUD has established standards for the noise inside sleeping areas of buildings. Facilities are approved: (1) if the sound does not exceed 55 dBA for a total of 60 minutes during any 24-hour period; (2) if no more than 30 minutes of 45 dBA level sound occurs between 11 P.M. and 7 A.M.; (3) the 45 dBA level lasts no longer than a total of 8 hours during a 24-hour period. Few regions of large cities conform totally with these regulations.

FAN AND MOTOR NOISE

Heating units, fans, and air conditioners usually set the ambient levels in homes and other occupied buildings. When all other noise-producing items are silenced, the lowest sound level ob-tainable is that of the steady whir of air-moving equipment, which in sleep activities often serves the same purpose as the store-bought noisemakers. Typical air conditioning and heating units create a vibration that sets up a continuous hum over a relatively large area. The sound radiates from the central unit itself, and sound is also carried through the duct work into regions of the building quite far removed from the heart of the system.

Three figures illustrate the impact air-moving equipment

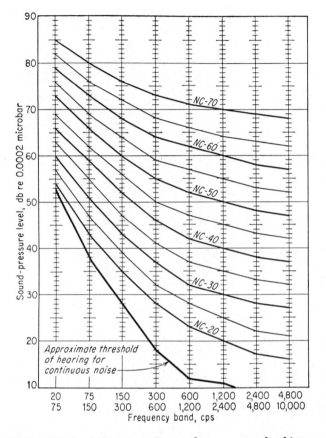

9.1   Noise criteria (NC) curves. For each curve, standard interpretations help one to place noise levels in perspective.

can have on the sound environment. Figure 9.1 shows a series of curves on a chart. These noise criteria curves plotted as octave bands have specific values with respect to the types of activity possible in the presence of various amounts of sound. For example, an NC of 55 indicates that this noise level makes telephone use difficult. An NC curve of 40 is a popular criterion for an office. The sleep criterion curve is NC-20. To determine which criterion curve is appropriate for a certain sound environment,

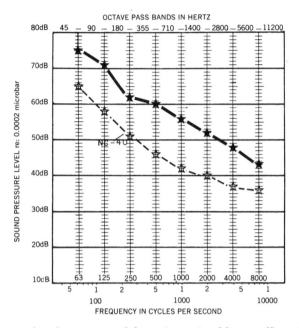

9.2   Octave-band measures of the noise emitted by an office air conditioner as compared to NC-40.

sound levels are measured using octave-band measuring equipment. Readings for each test frequency are marked on the chart, and the highest point determines the NC curve that best describes the acoustic conditions in that setting. In Figure 9.2 measured noise of a central air-conditioning unit in an office is compared with the NC-40 curve. Note that this curve, a criterion for a quiet office, is exceeded. A window air conditioner's effect on the sound environment of a bedroom is given in Figure 9.3. Certainly, the sound the unit emits is excessive with respect to the criterion for appropriate sleeping conditions (NC-20).

HOME CONSTRUCTION

One problem with indoor noise relates not to the use of specific devices in a given room but to the annoyance that sound causes another person located elsewhere in the building. In 1958 a study of the Federal Council for Science and Technology cited seven major causes of noise in homes and apartment buildings:

1. Heating and cooling plants, plumbing and domestic appliances.
2. Poor acoustical design.
3. Light frame construction, thin walls, and hollow doors.
4. Poor workmanship—holes, cracks, and inadequate equipment installations.
5. High-rise buildings—greater concentration of people.
6. Rising costs of sound-insulated construction, resulting in building cost cuts.
7. Inadequate codes and standards of construction pertaining to building acoustics.

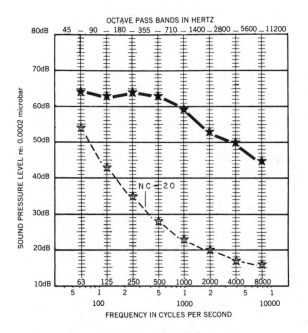

9.3   Sound output of a bedroom air conditioner compared to NC-20, the criterion level held to be applicable for sleeping.

Noise in houses continues to be a serious problem, but the consensus is that apartment living is even more fraught with irritating crosscurrents of sound. In one account of apartment walls and their seeming acoustic transparency, a woman, having had her differences with a man, withheld her bedtime favors for a long while but finally gave in. The event was celebrated by the cry from two apartments down the hall, "Atta boy, Harry!"

One seldom sees a house or apartment advertised as "quiet" or "sound isolated." Recently a developer who was designing a large, high-class resort condominium, beautifully architectured and augmented by unique and eye-appealing landscaping, asked about the best type of sound isolation between units. He explained that these two- and three-room hideaways would sell for $50,000 and more; hence he did not want the quality downgraded by crosstalk between apartments. Since they were planning to go first class all the way with the various components of the apartments they were most interested in providing more than adequate sound isolation and planned to use that feature as one of their main selling points. It was most gratifying to find that a builder was interested in the acoustics of his product in addition to its convenience and appearance. When asked if he would have thought of acoustics if he were building these units 15 years ago, his answer was, "No, it probably would never have entered my mind"—a good example of how public education can serve the cause of quiet.

In a general sense, cheap construction can be given as a major cause of the failure of living quarters to provide adequate sound control. Most small houses are founded on a cement slab floor, which is then covered with vinyl or asphalt tile. These tiles provide a very smooth and hard surface from which sound is reflected with virtually no absorption. Thin walls and ceilings of plasterboard or paneling again set up a reverberant surface that either reflects or transmits the sound with very little reduction.

Poor quality of workmanship in the plumbing and inappropriate pipe layout is another cause of undue noise in houses and apartments. When the electrical wiring is done, outlets are placed at adjacent points of a common wall between rooms, allowing a good path for the sound from one room to find its way into the adjoining area.

Some house and apartment layouts are not well conceived from an acoustical standpoint. The master bedroom may be located next to the family room, and sometimes a double fireplace may be built into the wall that separates the two rooms. This feature is not bad if the fireplace is constructed with double flues, but often sound carryover between rooms is augmented by a single flue between the fireplaces. How well do mom and dad sleep while the kids are having a dance party? The answer is obvious.

Other layout oversights are passthrough counter walls between the kitchen and other rooms so that the kitchen noise easily reaches areas where others are attempting conversation. Also, closets for adjoining bedrooms are commonly located in the same wall, giving each bedroom half the length of the wall for closets. This means, of course, that a person rummaging in his closet will be easily heard by the person attempting to sleep in the adjacent bedroom.

Each person can take a tour of his home and find numerous areas where layout does not facilitate good acoustic control. The structure is built, though, and cannot be destroyed and started over; thus the obvious task ahead is to do what one can to work with what he has. Chapter 11 contains a number of suggestions to assist in garnering ideas for modifications of the living quarters in order to create a more sound-free environment.

Unfortunately, the most glaring of all causes of transmitted sounds between rooms or between apartment units is sloppy workmanship. A consultant for a major acoustic firm pointed out that prefabricated units are particularly bad in this respect. He has noted that these structures are put together for the first time on the building site, and that measurement and cutting errors committed at the factory must be rectified on the lot. Often large gaps and leaks between walls, floors, and ceilings bring about an acoustic disaster. These flaws can be covered up by a clever carpenter, but the sound will find an easier path.

Commercial buildings may provide better sound isolation. Heavier construction is fostered by the increased need for security, and sound treatment is a desirable by-product. Hotels are supposed to be made for sleeping; thus it is an unthinking designer who does not do all he can to prevent the sounds of a party in one room from disturbing sleep in another.

Office buildings have an abundance of typewriters, duplicating machinery, computer equipment, and other office mechanisms known to create a good deal of noise; so these units usually are designed with sound isolation in mind. Duplicators send out clicks and bumps that reach as high as 85 dBA, and a high-speed programmed typewriter was measured to generate sound over 90 dBA; so continuing care must be taken to provide both sound transmission control and reduction of sound reverberation.

Schools recently have been designed with open classrooms where dividing walls go only partway to the ceiling. From an aesthetic and symbolic stance these innovations are desirable, but the acoustics in some of these situations have caused designers to abandon the earlier concept and put glass partitions from the top of the existing wall to the ceiling. Wood and metal shops in schools need special treatment to keep sound from radiating into classroom areas. New rooms are known to have occasionally high-level sound. With the increasing interest in music, school bands are getting larger but their practice rooms aren't. One band director recently initiated a project to tack fiber egg cartons on the ceiling and walls of the room, which had the effect of cutting the reverberant quality of the room, making it a more desirable location for him. He was told that the fire inspector would have a fit, though. Sound levels as high as 114 dBA have been measured in band practice rooms.

While in the Graduate School at the University of Tennessee Roger Compton recorded practice sessions at several high schools and played the recording through the sound analyzing equipment described in the discussion of Scott Wood's study (Chap. 7). For two of the eight high schools studied, the sound was sufficiently intense to surpass the damage-risk criteria (DRC) for hearing loss. For all band directors the sound exceeded DRC figures because they are exposed more often for a greater total exposure. A hearing test revealed that some instructors were beginning to show a high-frequency hearing loss that could not be attributed to aging. Interestingly, the oldest director, who had been on the job for many years, had nearly perfect hearing.

Solutions to the noise problem in dwellings and other buildings can be given as three basic qualities:

1. The use of good common sense in designing the structures.
2. Advance planning for sound control.
3. Expert advice with respect to the acoustic ramifications of building design.

A SHIFT IN FOCUS

A greater degree of attention obviously has been given to the problem of generalized noise in urban surroundings, but only to the extent of recognizing that a problem exists. Now city planners and builders apparently are concentrating their efforts in the direction of doing something to abate the noise problems.

The problem of house and apartment noise transmission between rooms can be solved if two major failure points are overcome: (1) ignorance and indifference of builders and planners, and (2) cost of sound treatment. The first factor is being combated by the general education efforts of people concerned with the effects of continuous noise exposure. The second factor must be solved by the consumer's willingness to take his share of the responsibility as manifested in slightly higher costs. It is estimated that good sound treatment of a house or apartment should add no more than 5 percent to the cost of the structure. In terms of one's health and enjoyment that is a reasonable and wise investment.

The greatest area of difficulty continues to be flimsy construction materials and inadequate supervision of workmen. Older buildings in many cities continue to serve well because they were built with thick walls and some form of insulation, but most importantly they were shaped by craftsmen who took pride in their trades. According to Ted Schultz, acoustical engineer for an outstanding acoustical consulting firm: "No breakthrough in materials or methods will be of any use unless there is good on-site supervision. Inadequate supervision almost always kills you. Carpenters nearly always ignore the problem." This strong statement comes from one who knows that even small cracks around doors, at the bases of partitions or around window frames can have a disastrous effect on the sound qualities of a building.

OUTSIDE AND BASEMENT NOISE

The home is seldom void of various power tools, such as saws, drills, and wood lathes, each of which can generate considerable racket that should be kept acoustically separate from the other residents of the structure. Generally such tools are used in the basement because of the mess they create; so sound isolation is somewhat adequate.

Outdoor tools bring with them a combination of problems. For many years ol' Jeb had earned his living by cutting and splitting fireplace logs. He was a powerful man and for years had maintained his average of preparing two cords of wood a day. When he heard about the power chain saws on the popular market he figured that device would speed up his productivity, but two days after he obtained the saw he took it back to the store and demanded his money back. When asked why he was not satisfied he said that he still was only getting two cords of wood put up each day and he was more tired at night. Attempting to save the sale, the clerk made a few minor adjustments here and there and started the motor of the saw. Ol' Jeb shouted, "What's that noise!!??" Often people in a neighborhood, startled by the sound of a chain saw, echo the question Jeb raised. These devices approach sound levels of 120 dBA at the operator's ear and broadcast the noise over a wide area.

POSTLUDE

We do not intend in this chapter to be picky and cite as irritating every sound source within a home. Most persons endure such noise exposure and appear to be completely unruffled by it, but others are quite irritated and angered that their hopes for a quiet place are dashed by the continuing proliferation of noisy appliances and gadgets. Future developments in these items will surely include noise control—or the devices will ultimately be taken off the market and replaced with ones that meet sound standards. The outlook is good because increasing awareness of some of the problems has caused the words "noise" and "acoustics" to finally become a part of the working vocabulary of design engineers, architects, and builders.

·10·

FROM INQUIRING MINDS

I keep six honest serving-men
(They taught me all I know):
Their names are What, And Why and When
And How and Where and Who.
Rudyard Kipling

As the activities of the Noise Study Laboratory have become
known, the volume of mail and telephone calls received has
been considerable. Inquiries and comments have come from
nearly every state as well as from over 30 foreign countries.

The laboratory's philosophy has been to attempt answers to
each letter in the belief that efforts to pose questions or to request
assistance should be honored. As Hans Morgenthau stated:
"Man will not live without answers to his questions." The replies were not always answers in the complete sense, but they
were geared to lead the correspondent to reliable and accessible
information. Often, references were made to appropriate trade
journals or reference works deemed of interest to the inquiring
minds who thought enough of the subject of noise to seek further
information.

The tone of the letters to the laboratory varied. Many simply
asked for copies of articles or pamphlets to be used in speeches,
school reports, or science fair projects; some posed good questions that deserved an informative response. Some comments
have been informative to the laboratory staff, and occasional
offers of assistance have been made—and accepted. The mail

has not been completely without angry notes, but with few exceptions they have been intelligent and reflected the writer's strong view. The local FBI office suggested that we turn over to an FBI investigator a letter from New Jersey addressed to Dr. David Lipscomb, Mad Scientist, Knoxville, Tennessee. Perhaps the most upsetting thing about that piece of correspondence was that it was delivered—with no more than that address! The letter, a vile denunciation of all who attempted to uncover the mysteries of life, health, and sickness by means of laboratory experimentation, was so abusive that the law enforcement agency wanted it on file "in case something happened to one of the members of the laboratory staff." They could have offered a more comforting reason!

As might be expected, many letters expressed misconceptions born of misinformation or lack of information. Some of those letters and our responses are cited in this chapter, not to poke fun at the writer but, rather, to disseminate correct information because we fear many people hold the incorrect notions stated in the letters.

GENERAL CORRESPONDENCE

Normally, anonymous correspondence is disregarded because replies are not possible. One such piece from Chattanooga came in a plain envelope and contained a statement on glare and light pollution. The dittoed letter stated: "We read about air pollution, water pollution, noise pollution, and waste pollution. But we read nothing about *glare and light pollution.*" The paper then established a case for the consideration of yet another determinant of decreased quality of life. Such mail helps the laboratory staff retain a sense of perspective. Since noise is the object of intensive study in the laboratory it is often possible to lose sight of the many other problems in the environment.

During the summer of 1969 Ralph Nader visited the laboratory en route to Oak Ridge, where he was to deliver an address the next day. A news story about the visit, carried on national news wires, initiated a satisfying and helpful exchange with a man in Sacramento, California.

Dear Doctor,

Noise is certainly going to have to be contained the same as birth control and pollution of the air we breathe.

I would naturally like to do my part and one particular area is the loud, noisy TV and radio commercials which exceed the decibels far beyond that of your own volume control setting. It is my pet peeve and it seems there is no one to lend assistance. Could you or Mr. Nader lend some assistance or afford and send addresses where I might air my complaint against noise.

Sincerely,

J. S.

Sacramento, California

An encouraging aspect of this letter was the man's willingness to do something about the problem, and subsequent correspondence showed that he translated his willingness into action in another realm. Researchers are greatly frustrated when problem areas are identified and solutions suggested, and then nothing is done by way of follow-up. A glaring example is the results of a survey in which investigators asked citizens to what extent they would be willing to assist in the combating and cleanup of various types of pollution in their city. The conclusion—that the average family was willing to put $2.30 annually toward the fight against pollution—makes it truly heartening to find that someone has offered to do something about environmental problems. Here is part of our reply to the Californian.

Dear Mr. S.

Your concern with the sound level of the TV commercials is understandable. Several years ago, the FCC ordered limits on the degree by which the engineer can "ride" the volume on any portion of a broadcast. Since time has passed, the broadcast industry in certain locations may be inching the volume of commercials higher, hoping that the increase may not be noticed.

In our area, I have not observed a significant problem, but this is generally a regional matter. If possible, I would suggest that you document your findings (date, channel, time, sponsor, etc.) and send a formal complaint to the FCC. They have regulations on the book and, if pressed, will enforce them in your area.

Perhaps your best way of gaining additional support in your locale is to write a letter to the editor and request that others also complain to the FCC. Believe me, if the agency receives a large number of complaints from your community, they will act upon them.

Good luck in your campaign to reduce this bothersome and inconsiderate activity.

Sincerely,

D.M.L.

About a year later, after testifying before the U.S. House of Representatives Subcommittee on Health and the Environment, we received another letter from the same man.

Dear Prof.

The noise level has risen one decibel in this city over the past year. At this rate we will all be deaf by year 2000. That means such articles as yours and other warnings will go unheeded.

The State Assembly has a bill before it limiting the noise of motorcycles and I'm sure of its passage. However, much more has to be done if we are to maintain our sanity. . . .

Sincerely,

J. S.

Sacramento, California

He concluded the note with a request for information.

The laboratory has been established to meet a threefold challenge: (1) increase the knowledge of the effect of noise on the ear and body; (2) offer training to students who want to conduct research into various aspects of noise; and (3) provide general information to the public on the effects of noise, especially translating the results of noise research into informative articles and papers. One such paper was sent to the man in Sacramento in response to his request.

STUDENT AND TEACHER INQUIRIES

Noise is being discussed in public school science classes; so we have received a large number of questions relating to various projects.

A junior high science teacher in St. Louis who hoped to do more than show pictures to his pupils wrote the following letter.

Dear Dr. Lipscomb,

I will be entering my third year of teaching this September, and I am interested in new approaches to teaching biology. I am especially interested in the type of approach that takes problems that have some national or international meaning to the students, and even if nothing new is discovered, I at least expose the students to laboratory procedures.

Therefore, I was especially interested in the short news article that I heard over a local CBS radio station here in St. Louis about your experiment of hearing losses in guinea pigs when exposed to go-go music at discotheques.

I would very much like to ask you a couple of questions concerning your project, as this is something that I would like a class of mine to do. Firstly, how practical is it to determine cell damage? In other words, what are the major procedures for examination? The junior high that I am at is very well equipped with laboratory instruments. We have almost the best types of microscopes, glassware, stains, and anything else that a complete lab would need. I would like your opinion as to what additional equipment is necessary in the planning of a study like this. Secondly, the 90 hours of loud music over a period of 3 months average to be about 1 hour per day. Is that rate all right, or are longer but fewer "sessions" better?? Is it correct to assume that any loud noise (music, horns, etc.) at approximately 120 decibels for a long period of time is dangerous?? Of course I can see that by announcing that go-go music is dangerous has a definite meaning to a certain group of kids. And listing motorcycles in your article also brings up an appropriate and meaningful point to kids of this age. So, I just wanted to let you know that I am very interested in your work and your findings, and would appreciate it very much if you could send me any information concerning your basic techniques that I have either left out or seem to have missed completely.

Sincerely,

W. L.

St. Louis, Missouri

This was a difficult letter to answer, for the laboratory techniques used in the study he mentioned (see Chapter 3) are quite outside the scope of a junior high laboratory. Rather than discourage the young teacher, we replied to his inquiry in this way.

Dear Mr. L.

It was certainly encouraging to read your letter. I think that the ninth grade pupils at _____ Junior High School can consider themselves fortunate to have an instructor who is so interested in stimulating their young minds by the use of contemporary approaches.

I am not sure that the approach used in this study is one which is amenable to a ninth grade curriculum. However, I feel that you would be the best judge of this. Perhaps the most meaningful information that I can provide you would be through referring you to an excellent text by Engström, Ades, and Andersson entitled *Structural Pattern of the Organ of Corti*. This book is published by Williams and Wilkins and provides the nucleus for my procedures in our lab.

The equipment necessary in addition to the sound stimulating equipment would be some device which would measure the sound intensity and, hopefully, a method of graphically recording the sound pressure levels. In addition to this equipment, it would be absolutely essential to have phase contrast objectives on the microscope. The material in the inner ear has such little contrast that observing it without the advantage of phase contrast microscopy is very difficult. I am not sure that the ninth grade curriculum would include the handling of such highly dangerous substances as osmic acid (osmium tetroxide). This is the fixative which is most appropriate to use with the experimental animals. I do feel, however, that with a little bit of practice the removal of the organ of Corti from the cochlear region can be accomplished by a person such as yourself who has a fair amount of dissection experience.

I would be most interested in knowing the results of your experiment if you plan to follow through with it. You did ask whether one hour a day would be appropriate. I am afraid I can't fully answer that. Although it's an average figure, we purposely varied the presentation so that it would somewhat approximate the exposure that a young person would obtain during the course of a three-month period.

At the Central Institute for the Deaf in St. Louis, I am sure you will be able to obtain a great deal of guidance and help. This institution is one of the outstanding research facilities in our country.

Thank you for your inquiry. I wish you much success in this exciting endeavor.

Best wishes,
D.M.L.

The notes received from younger schoolchildren are always fun to consider, but space does not allow for more than a few representative ones, such as the following letter of inquiry from a girl.

Dear Sir,

Have you done any studies on the "noise pollution" if so will you send me something on your results? I am doing a report on noise pollution. My address is at the top of the page.

> Thank You
> Yours truly,
> P. W.
> Canton, Ohio

We honored her request by sending a number of lay-oriented papers that outline, in general, some aspects of the noise problem.

Two boys in Texas also asked for assistance.

Dear Dr. Lipscomb,

I am doing research on sound pollution. I have written to the Dept. of Health, Ed., and Welfare for information. The Dept. sent me your name and address recommending you to be able to give me some information on this. At first I was going to get a busy street corner but they said this had been tried to no avail. So instead I will tape some of today's rock and roll music. If you can give me any information on this it will be appreciated.

> Thank you,
> T. P.
> &
> D. F.
> Jayton, Texas

Their rather sketchy outline of a proposed project was difficult to assess; so our reply was largely information on example projects the boys might carry out.

Dear Gentlemen:

I am pleased to enclose some information you might find helpful in your project. As is usually the case, students have an equipment limitation; thus they must reduce the scope of their study.

In your letter, you mentioned that you would tape some of today's rock and roll music, but you failed to indicate what you intended to do with it. Perhaps some of the experiments discussed in the articles which are enclosed will assist you in developing a design.

Good luck in your efforts.

Sincerely,
D.M.L.

Very few of the inquirers have followed up by sharing the relative success of their project, but one of these boys sent a postcard by return mail with a rare thank-you and a brief additional note.

Dear Sir:

Thank you for the information you sent me on noise pollution. I neglected to tell you that I was going to use the tape of rock & roll music on a guinea pig.

Sincerely,
T. P.
Jayton, Texas

One of the most intelligent series of letters requesting information came from a girl in Seneca, Missouri.

Dear Sir:

I am a senior at _____ High School and enrolled in chemistry. For a Science Fair project I plan to experiment with either mice or guinea pigs on the subject of "Rock 'n' Roll" being hard on the ears. I am very interested in the way sound affects people as well as animals.

I first became familiar with your work from an article in the *Joplin Globe* newspaper giving details of your experiment on 88½ hours of exposure over a 3-month period. I, too, plan to carry this out to some extent with photographs of the ear, etc.

I would appreciate it if you would send me some possible information on this subject for my thesis. Any kind of material could be of real help. I realize you are busy, but this will be used for a worthwhile and interesting project.

Thank you.

Sincerely yours,
A. A.
Seneca, Mo.

We replied as follows.

Dear Miss A.

I am pleased that you are interested in engaging in a study of the effects of noise upon the ear structure for your science fair project. I am sure you will find the study both interesting and informative.

You mentioned that you would be interested in evaluating the effect of the noise upon the ear of the animal. I am afraid that it would be quite difficult for you to duplicate the study which was reported from our laboratory because of the type and quality of the equipment necessary. The picture of the ear cells which is enclosed with this letter shows the cells magnified several thousand times. This is accomplished through the use of a very special microscope (phase contrast), and I am not sure that such equipment would be available to you in your school.

There is no reason, however, that you cannot go ahead and conduct a good study. Perhaps you could take sound level measurements of certain noisy environments. On the other hand, you might find a change in the demeanor or the personality aspects of an animal in response to noise as compared to an animal that has not been subjected to a noise environment.

You might find a magazine entitled Noise and Vibration of interest and help to you in this project. This magazine has a lot of pretty technical information, but you can skip that part and find the ideas that are being presented and, therefore, learn a great deal about the scope of this problem.

Again I wish you good luck in your venture. If I can be of further help to you, please do not hesitate to call upon me.

Sincerely,

D.M.L.

Miss A. took the last paragraph to heart and did ask for more information.

Dear Dr. Lipscomb:

I would like to thank you for the prompt and valuable information that you sent to me for my science fair project. project.

However, later consideration and thought from my instructor seems to point to some difficulties on this project. But then, a project would not be interesting if nothing went wrong. After some thought we decided to do a similar experiment with bats. We thought it would be very interesting to see if a certain degree of sound would interfere with their flight. Our plans were to take a small shack and fix a maze of fine wires, turn the bats loose blindfolded so we could observe them and turn loose a certain frequency of sound, increasing it. However there were certain problems to this, too. Feeding them during winter months and in captivity seemed to be the main one.

Since a study with sound was my interest, I feel some project in this area will be accomplished. However, now a definite project is not worked out. If you could give me some suggestion, my instructor, Mr. _____ , and I would be very grateful.

Thank you again so very much for sharing your valuable time for some thought on my project.

Very truly yours,

A. A.

Seneca, Mo.

The following letter was the attempt to respond to her questions.

Dear A.

You asked for ideas on what you might do for your project. There are a multitude of things which could be done which you would find to be very interesting. For one thing, you might take two experimental animals, perhaps guinea pigs, which came from the same litter and keep one in a relatively sound-free environment and expose the other to high-level rock music for a several-week period. I think you would note that when you put those two animals back together, the one which has been exposed to the sound would be noticeably more jumpy, nervous and irritable.

One of the areas of study which we have found to be very fruitful has been to study the incidence of hearing loss as a result of noise exposure. I am enclosing an incidence statistical card which we have used in some of our study here. You will note that on the front side of the card there is an opportunity for an individual to relate whether or not he has had any exposure to noise. On the flip side of the card are the spaces for the hearing test results and remarks and analytic information. You might consider conducting hearing tests on a fairly large number of students in your school, using a cutoff criterion point of about 15 dB, and find out what number of students have some high-frequency hearing loss.

A related study which would not take quite as much time would be to conduct hearing tests on students who are going into a dance and then after a certain amount of time say, three hours, retest the hearing of these young people and analyze the differences in their hearing as a result of being exposed to the high intensity dance music noise.

I hope that these suggestions have set your inquisitive mind at work once again and that from these ideas you can generate a useful and worthwhile science fair project.

Best wishes to you and good luck in your project.

Sincerely,

D.M.L.

Another series of letters that culminated in a successful entry into a science fair was initiated by a young man in Iowa.

Dear Dr. Lipscomb:

I am a freshman in a high school and for my science fair project I want to do a study on the effects of rock music on the hearing of hamsters. I understand you have conducted experiments on the effects of loud music on the hearing of guinea pigs. Can you give me some information on the way you conducted this experiment, the equipment needed, and over what period of time it was done? I would appreciate your advice and any material you could send me on methods and procedure and expected results. Let me know if there is any cost involved for the material.

> Sincerely,
> P. S.
> Knoxville, Iowa

The response to this request was a rather standard one, which was sent along with some reading materials plus a suggestion.

Dear Mr. S.

I admire your interest in the subject you have proposed for your science fair project. Enclosed you will find some articles dealing with the methods used in our studies here. Unfortunately, the study I have completed used a great deal of expensive equipment which you may not have available to you.

Perhaps your approach could be one more inclined to note changes in the response to sound by animals. For example, you could condition an animal to respond in some way to a 4,000 cycle sound, expose him to a total of 40 to 50 hours of rock music played at a high level, and note what changes (if any) occurred in his response to the 4,000 cycle tone.

Good luck with your project. I know that you will enjoy working in this very interesting area of study.

> Best wishes,
> D.M.L.

A few weeks later, on a Sunday afternoon, the telephone

rang. An excited young Iowan had called long distance to relate that he had just won in his division of the regional science fair. He was already trying to come up with ways of improving his display for the state competition. The following letter offered additional suggestions.

Dear Paul:

I was delighted to receive your call Sunday. Congratulations on your achievement. Having just judged a similar Science Fair, I can appreciate the quality of work you must have done to win your division. Now, I wish you good luck in the upcoming state contest.

Enclosed you will find several items which may help you make final preparations for the show. Of special interest is the article which lists the number and percentage of cells damaged in three animals. You will note that the greater damage is found in the apical (upper) regions of the cochlea. The high-frequency region, however, is in the basal end. The assumption that we can make is that noise causes damage in all regions of the cochlea, especially in the apical area. When there is sufficient damage to cause a high-frequency hearing loss, there has been greater destruction of sensory cells in the apical areas but our hearing test procedures are unable to identify the damage.

In addition, I am enclosing some photomicrographs which you may like to include in your display.

If possible, I would like to hear how things go at the state science fair. If you have a picture of the display, I'd be pleased to see it.

I mentioned the report which is being prepared for presentation to the state legislative council. As soon as we get the report duplicated and bound, I will send you a copy. I would appreciate receiving information on the discotheque ordinance you mentioned on the phone. Perhaps I could allude to it in my testimony.

I'll be pulling for you as you prepare for the big event.

Your friend in research,

D.M.L.

In response to the request for information on an ordinance in a neighboring town, the young scientist wrote the following.

Dear Dr. Lipscomb:

Enclosed is a copy of the ordinance for the control of sound level that the city of Oskaloosa, Iowa, hopes to get passed. They passed the ordinance under their board of health. They have found that this would not be considered legal. Now they hope to get the city council to pass the ordinance. This information was given to me by the city attorney, Mr. _____.

I have also enclosed the picture of my exhibit that came out in our local paper.

Easter Monday, I spent a very interesting 2½ hours talking with Dr. Scott Reger at the University of Iowa, Iowa City. He gave me some posters and loaned me a book to use.

I have received a copy of the report you submitted to the Legislative Council Committee of the State of Tennessee and the photos. Thank you very much for all the help you have given me. I will let you know how I make out at the state science fair. This has been a very interesting project.

Sincerely,
P. S.
Knoxville, Iowa

One final note summed up the inspiring exchange.

Dear Dr. Lipscomb:

It might please you to know that I received a superior rating at the Hawkeye Science Fair on April 10th and 11th.

I hope you have received the proposed city ordinance and the newspaper clipping I sent to you.

Thank you very much for all the information you have sent me. I feel that I have gained much knowledge from it as well as helping me receive the superior rating on my project.

Sincerely,
P. S.
Knoxville, Iowa

To watch young minds grasp some of the concepts set forth in this book is a most rewarding experience. To be sure, few of the inquirers have succeeded to the level of the young man just mentioned, but sponsoring the activities in science fairs is fully justified.

FROM MUSICIANS

Musicians' utter dependence on their hearing has caused no little concern for research has shown certain forms of music to be hazardous to hearing health. Although one study of orchestral music indicated little need for concern about damage to the ears when compared to rock music, the questions still came.

Dear Sir,

I read with great interest the article in The New York Times concerning your findings in the deterioration of ear cells when one listens to much loud music. It raised a question between my brother and me: What is the decibel level in a symphony orchestra during a very loud passage, from the player's seat? As a violinist, it seems quite loud, although not as piercing as rock music.

I am quite intrigued by the question, and if you could possibly spare the time, I would greatly appreciate a reply.

Thank you.

Sincerely,
D. S.
Albertson, New York

A reply was attempted.

Dear Miss S.:

In response to your question, I am afraid I cannot give you an unqualified answer. Any musical aggregation, orchestras included, will produce sounds which exceed the damage level for the ear. The three factors which interrelate include duration of the loud sound, the type of sound ("impulse vs. steady") and type of sound environment ("acoustic treatment of the room").

I feel that the incessant loud sound of the present-day modern music is considerably more hazardous than the occasional loud passages of a symphony. The ear can stand a good deal of loud sound if the sound does not come with rapid repetition.

According to my understanding of the results of studies done in Los Angeles by Dr. Lebo who is cited in the article of *The New York Times* on page E7 of the Sunday, August 25 edition, rock music possesses a good deal more damaging quality of sound than do the other types of music, orchestras included.

I hope your question is satisfied. If not, perhaps you would find it helpful to inquire of Dr. Lebo whose work, I feel, more closely relates to the area of your concern.

> Sincerely,
> D.M.L.

A similar question came from a British Fulbright Exchange Scholar.

Dear Dr. Lipscomb,

I am a composer myself and I should like to read any literature you may have published on this subject. You mention 120 decibels for discotheque music for example—what about classical music? Do the students play Beethoven at 120?

> R. A.
> Brunswick, Maine

This correspondent also was referred to the source of those studies that concerned the sound levels in concert halls. In addition, the following was noted.

Dear Mr. A.:

I am afraid I cannot give an unqualified answer to your inquiry since I have not taken sound level measurements in the symphony concerts. I do feel, however, that the sound level during the playing of classical music for the most part is not as potentially damaging because the extremely loud passages of classical music generally occur rather infrequently. Modern rock music, on the other hand, is a very repetitiously loud sound.

Another variable which I think contrasts the two types of music has to do with the type of location in which the music is played. Most concert halls are large and the sound has an opportunity to disperse. On the other hand, the dance establishments are relatively small (especially for the sound volume employed) and therefore sound reverberates from the walls and provides a multiple stimulation for the individual.

> Best wishes,
> D.M.L.

One final example of inquiries about music comes from someone who coined an interesting term.

> Dear Mr. Lipscomb
> Please send me any information you might have on music pollution. Any information will be appreciated.
>> Thank you,
>> B. R.
>> Brooklyn, New York

Some probably resent the use of "music pollution" as an entity, but surely sizable numbers of people consider certain forms of music pollutants.

ANGRY LETTERS

No list of correspondence is complete without some of the less desirable letters. Naturally everyone wants to be universally held in high esteem, but that is only a dream, and it takes little time to realize that the work some hail others despise. Fortunately the laboratory has not received an overabundance of these letters, but there have been a few.

A lady in Washington, D.C., sent a clipping of a very brief news item that said only that the Laboratory "exposed one ear of a guinea pig to go-go music for 90 hours and discovered (what-else?) that the cells in the exposed ear had deteriorated." Her terse note stated the following.

Dear Dr. Lipscomb:
   What a silly experiment!! With all the problems in the world that need solving, can't you think of any more intelligent approach than this.
                    Very truly yours,
                    L. H.
                    Washington, D.C.

We could not send many materials to this lady, since her remarks came at a very early stage in the series of studies on the effects of rock music. We decided that a brief reply would be best.

Dear Mrs. H.:
   I appreciate your sending the clipping of the article as it appeared in the _____. Upon reading the article, I quite agree that their facetious treatment of our work leads to the interpretation that you made.
   I am taking the liberty of sending a copy of the full article. I hope that after reading it you will judge me somewhat less harshly.
   Thank you for your frank and stimulating response to our work here.
                    Sincerely,
                    D.M.L.

From New Jersey we received an intolerant note written on a 3 x 5 card.

   So how rediculous (sic) can you get—experimenting on animals when the facts regarding humans have already been proven as detrimental!!! Or was it just for the pleasure of torturing the animals?? How rediculous (sic) can you possibly get!!!!!
                    C. L.
                    Roselle Park, New Jersey

Resisting the temptation to point out the obvious misspelling of ridiculous, we attempted to relieve the writer of the fear that the laboratory was operating a 15th-century torture chamber.

Dear Miss L.:

I was distressed to receive your obviously angry reaction to the article which you read regarding our work here at The University of Tennessee on the effect of high intensity noise upon the ear structures. While your observation certainly is true that there is a quality of the sound which is detrimental knowingly to humans, the parameters have not been established. It was for that purpose that our studies have been undertaken and will be continuing.

I was quite surprised and disturbed to find that with relatively little stimulation there had already been a sizable amount of cell destruction in our experimental animals. You may be assured, however, that there will be no unnecessary "torture" of these or any other experimental animals with which we will be working.

Thank you for your frank, albeit disturbing note.

Respectfully yours,

D.M.L.

A letter of protest was addressed to the University of Tennessee Board of Governors and was later received at the laboratory with a note from the legal counsel, asking for suggestions for his reply. The letter came from a person in England whose personal view is that animal experimentation is not justifiable for any reason.

Sirs:

Recently I watched a disturbing programme on British television where, *inter alia*, your Prof. Lipscomb experimented with rats by subjecting them to sessions of modern pop music, with the result, as I recall it, that the hearing mechanism in the rats was destroyed. I gathered the object of your experiments was to prove that the sheer volume and discordance of what today passes for music can and does cause deafness.

To my mind this is tantamount to holding someone's head under water to establish whether or not he can still breathe! and about as pointless. Surely if researchers concerned themselves with simple arithmetic in its application to tone and volume of sound, such unnecessary torture would be avoided.

Mankind was given dominion over the Animal Kingdom—or so the Bible would have us believe. Such power carries with it a moral responsibility towards the defenseless creatures in our care.

Your views would interest me. I would also be interested to know who decides upon the suitability of a project for research, and why this particular programme was considered of sufficient interest to qualify.

J. M.
Worcestershire, United Kingdom

In a lengthly and very carefully worded response we explained that medical understanding and techniques had emanated to a great extent from systematic experimentation. The lady was also assured that the animals were receiving the very best care and never experienced any pain or discomfort. Parenthetically, we should add here that the Public Health Service, a branch of the federal Department of Health, Education and Welfare, has undertaken a rigorous program of assuring that the laboratory animals are kept in the most ideal conditions. It is paradoxical to observe that these animals often are housed in considerably better conditions than are a large percentage of the human beings in this country.

The British lady was told that her living beyond the 40th year was probably attributable to the significant medical breakthroughs determined by means of animal experimentation. Almost by return mail she replied that she had never seen a doctor nor been in a hospital, although she was past 70. It was quite obvious that her objections were not shaken in the least.

Not all correspondents are angry with the laboratory staff.

The following note is an example of letters in which pet peeves and frustrations are vented. It happened that this letter came from a local citizen at a time when a proposed noise code was being debated. It was subsequently used to strengthen the position of the code.

> Dear Sir:
>   I am sending you a copy of a letter written to Mr. _____ City Law Director—also Health Dept. Mr. _____:
>   I am writing to make a complaint on the Asphalt Co., on ———. The noise from those trucks is so loud that they shake my house when they go by. You cannot talk on the phone when they go by because you can't hear. Also they travel by night a lot and the noise wakes me from my sleep. It is affecting my *health* and I intend to get up a petition if something isn't done right away—I will take it to Court. The *smell* is bad enough—the *noise* is *worse*–
>
>   E. I.
>   Knoxville, Tennessee
> P.S. Dr. Lipscomb, if possible run a test on this.

The lady was assured that the city council was presently working on a code that would place restrictions on the noise made by large trucks. The hope was expressed that she would soon find relief from her irritating problem.

REQUESTS FOR HELP

Many letters to the laboratory are pleas for various forms of assistance in trying to combat noise problems in the writers' lives. Perhaps more letters have come from distraught parents concerned about their teen-agers' hearing than from those concerned with any other subject.

> Dear Professor Lipscomb,
>   I read of your work in our newspaper. I have made many calls to find out how to measure my son's amplifier in our home and at what point on the volume is it harmful to his

ears. No one can give me an answer. This is a large Fender Amp. Can you help me?

Thank you for your work. You may have saved my son's hearing.

> M. B.
> Wayne, Pennsylvania

Since distance so often makes it impossible to assist persons directly, an indirect course of action was necessary.

Dear Mr. B.:

Your basic question is one which is very difficult to answer. The volume of sound generated by your son's Fender amplifier can be considerable. You will need to seek a person in your area who has a "sound level meter" and can take appropriate measures of the output of the amplifier in various volume settings. You might find such a person in the physics department of a nearby college or university. Otherwise, many safety engineers in manufacturing plants are capable of taking such measures.

I would suggest that 100 dB (decibels) would be the maximum allowable peak readings permissible. Levels of 85 to 95 dB are much more safe for the ears. If you can accomplish this reduction in sound level you will, in all likelihood, protect your son's ears. Of course, there is the distinct possibility that some ear damage has already occurred, but it is important that you embark on a hearing conservation program.

Thank you for your interest. I wish you luck in getting the amplifier throttled.

> Best wishes,
> D.M.L.

Other parents are concerned about their youngsters' incessant radio listening.

Dear Dr. Lipscomb,

I heard a report read on the radio about a survey you made on guinea pigs and go-go music. Could I get a copy of your results. I've taken notes enough to tell it, but I want to show it to my son. He is 17 and thinks he should listen to _____ , a most go-go station. I will appreciate any type of material you can send.

Thank you.

L. W.

McDonough, Georgia

The reply observed that the choice of radio or phonograph music in a home seems to be a problem area in every generation. We sent information to the mother not because it would arm her in a war of words with her son but, rather, so that she might help him to see some of the dangers in listening to intense music. When during talks we project slides showing ear damage young people really pay attention. There appears to be a type of smokers' philosophy. Tell a smoker that a high percentage of cigarette users die of lung cancer, and he will shrug and say that he'll be in the group that doesn't. Tell a young person that a large percentage of people suffer ear damage from listening to rock music, and he will go on in the belief that it won't happen to him. But show him the photographs of ear sensory cell damage after intense rock music exposure, and he begins to believe that there is something to the warnings he has heard.

On an entirely different subject, a lady who lives in a resort area wrote the following.

Dear Dr. Lipscomb,

I read of your "Noise" problem in the Savannah paper and since we are beset with the "glunking" of drag lines the "whamming" of pile drivers and the constant whirring of golf course equipment here in this rapidly growing community, I thought you might give me advice on our latest noisemaker. The electric heat pump! Our neighbor has just put one in, not 20 feet away, and we are desperate! What are the mechanics of sound and how can we combat this? One says sound travels as smoke. I thought it more like a pebble thrown in a pond. One person has built a double 6 foot high wall with only partial benefit ($450 cost). His idea was that brick would absorb sound!

Any suggestions that you can give would be most grate-
fully accepted.

Thanking you, I am
> Most sincerely,
> M. B.
> Hilton Head Island
> South Carolina

The question was one for an acoustical engineer and
couldn't be handled from a distance of 500 miles; so we replied
as follows.

Dear Mrs. B.:

Well, you just hit me with a new one. I have been ac-
quainted with the problem in some neighborhoods which is
brought about by air conditioning units, barking dogs,
motorcycles, and other noise sources, but an electric heat
pump is new.

I'm afraid that you are asking information which I cannot
give easily. For your interest, I will enclose a paper which I
recently gave to a group of persons who were concerned
with ways to reduce woodworking plant noise. In that
paper, there is a discussion of some of the rules to follow
when beginning a program of noise reduction in plants. The
reason your inquiry is impossible to answer relates to the
differing ways to control noises as a function of the types of
sound they create. If the sound is high pitched, one type of
treatment is required. If the noise is low pitched, yet another
technique is called for.

It seems that you have more of a legal problem than any
thing else. I know of a group of neighbors in Aiken, S.C.,
who won a suit recently, forcing a utility company to silence
one of its transformer stations which has been placed in the
neighborhood.

The most practical solution would be to silence the heat
pump itself. Your other neighbor has already found that he
cannot barricade against the encroachment of the sound.

Sorry not to be more help, but there is too little for me to go on. I hope that you can find some assistance in your city ordinances regarding noise in residential districts.

Best wishes,

D.M.L.

Not all who write are brief and to the point. A recent typed, four-page, single-spaced letter broached a large number of subjects, including the speculation that the noise crisis is a Communist plot. The source of this man's major concern was snow machines at a winter resort area. These devices are operated during the night hours to prepare the ski slopes for the next day's activities. Apparently the machines have caused a huge problem in this man's life, for he issues forth a stunning invective against most forms of noise-generating devices. Interestingly, the first page of his letter was typed on the back of a replica of an advertisement for the Gatling Gun.

For many good reasons anonymous letters cannot be heeded, but the impassioned plea set forth in the following letter is worthy of note.

Mr. Lipscomb,

I have been informed that you have something to do with noise in excess of what a person should be subjected to. So I would like to ask for your help if possible.

I am employed at the Main Post Office. I've been working for the Post Office for the last four years.

The problem is that the Post Office bought a machine called the L.S.M. about two years ago and installed it in the middle of the workroom floor. The machine is some 40' to 55' long and produces a tremendous noise that is unbearable to the ear. The workroom is very big, but it does not help decrease the noise. The people working on the L.S.M. have to use ear plugs for their own safety. And on a few occasions more than five or six employees have gone to their doctors and have returned with reports that the machine's noise was dangerous to their health. The biggest problem doesn't lie in the one machine's noise alone, but the Post Office is going to put another one just like it beside it.

Then we will have two machines with a most unbearable noise for any human-being to *have* to cope with. An employee cannot do a day's work without getting a headache. There should be something done, but they will not. I made a suggestion that they close the L.S.M. in a room, but their excuse was that it would cost too much money. So, they refused it, figuring that the money was more important than the welfare of their employees. They even had to move the phone to a place where they could hear.

If you can do anything, it would be greatly appreciated because very soon the noise is going to be twice as bad as it is now. Please help, or if you cannot I wish you would inform someone of the problem that could do some good.

> Please Help,
> An Employee

That letter sat hauntingly on top of the desk for several weeks while an appropriate course of action was pondered. One day the management asked us to take measurements at the local post office; now sound levels are being reduced, and the worker's request finally was served.

WORD ERRORS

Surprisingly few misconceptions are reflected in the letters. A few problem areas seemed to repeat, hence the following example. A New Yorker wrote the following.

> Dear Mr. Lipscomb,
> Because I am concerned about excessive noise levels I am searching for ways and means to protect the *eardrums* effectively. I would be most grateful to you if you could send me any information pertaining to this matter.
> Thank you.
>
> > Respectfully,
> > M. F.
> > Queens Village, New York

A popular notion still is that the eardrums are the victims of high-intensity sound exposure. In reality the eardrum probably is safer than any other part of the ear except when an explosive sound occurs near the ear. It is the inner ear that needs (and deserves) the protection.

Another common misstatement appears in the following inquiry.

Dear Sir:
I am doing research on mice and how high-*frequency* sounds affect their hearing. I read an article in *Science World* on how you did experiments on guinea pigs and how rock music made most guinea pigs' ears collapse. This experiment interested me very much and I would appreciate any information you could give me.
Sincerely yours,
T. M.
Loyall, Kentucky

One portion of the reply contained an attempt to correct the misuse of *frequency*.

Dear T.:
Thank you for your letter. I am pleased that you are interested in the topic of the effect of noise upon the ear. You mentioned that you are interested in studying how high-frequency sounds affect the hearing of your experimental animals. I believe you are referring to the effect of high-*intensity* sounds upon the ears of these animals. We are finding that frequency has much less relationship to the effect upon the ear structures than does the intensity of the sound.
Best wishes,
D.M.L.

Sound-measuring devices often are referred to by many names, but the most unusual one so far was in an intelligent request from a high school student.

Dear Mr. Lipscomb,

I am presently a senior at _____ High School. I am considering doing a project on sound pollution, for my Environmental Studies class. Say the amount of decibels produced at the local dances and the effects it has on your hearing. I was wondering if this is a feasible project. Also, where could I get a *decimeter*? Would it be costly? I would greatly appreciate any and all information you can give me on the subject.

M. R.

Oak Ridge, Tennessee

The young man must be given credit for a good try, since he combined *decibel* and *meter* to come up with *decimeter*. A decimeter, however, is a mode of metric measurement (3.937 inches) rather than a sound-measuring device. These items are variously called sound level meters or sound meters. The letter brought up another interesting concept, too, in requesting suggestions on ways to determine the amplitude of sounds if sound-measuring equipment is not available. We offered several suggestions.

Dear Mr. R.:

Your question about the feasibility of the measurement of rock music is a complicated one to answer. Unfortunately, the equipment necessary to take accurate and meaningful measures is very expensive and is not easy to use.

Would it be possible for you to follow some other course of action? For example, you could use several noisemakers, e.g. a Halloween horn, various bells, a drum, etc. and note whether persons could hear them in the music hall. If so, how far away did they get and still hear the sound? You could then demonstrate to the class in the room the noisemakers and let them judge for themselves how loud the music environment was.

This is only one idea, but it gets around having such cumbersome and expensive equipment. Good luck.

Best wishes,

D.M.L.

INCORRECT NOTIONS

Varying forms of misunderstandings or overstatements are received in the mail. The following two are perhaps the most interesting so far. In the first example a lady in Vancouver, Canada, expresses a sincere concern.

> Dear Dr. Lipscomb:
> Am very interested in your findings re this rock music or whatever it's called—ruining hearing.
> May I have a few lines telling of your article on it.
> You see I missed the paper that had it in, I have not an American stamp to enclose for an answer.
> You see I notice these children that have radio station _____ on with this crazy music seem to be like addicts the way they have it on all the time. I feel it also affects their brains and is making mental cripples out of the children as well as putting them deaf.
> I notice after they listen to it they can't get down to their study or piano lessons. They seem to be stirred up or something.
> > Sincerely,
> > A. W.
> > Vancouver, British Columbia
> P.S. I really believe the rock and roll music is causing mental troubles in the young and ruining their brains so they can't think or sit still or even converse properly.

A reply was sent with some information in hope that her concerns about music-induced brain trauma would be somewhat abated. We suggested that she not judge the modern-day music too harshly, for it may be a symptom rather than a cause.

A housewife in California presented a most unusual idea.

> Dear Dr. Lipscomb,
> The area in which I live was once a very beautiful rural orchard area, but over the last ten years most of these have been replaced with highways and housing, unfortunately

many of the houses were built before the highways and so there has been a great hue and cry over this fact for years; people who once owned quiet retreats are now exposed to constant noise and not only that but their property values have dropped accordingly until this whole thing has grown out of all proportion, with many petitions being circulated complaining about it and asking local governments to put up dense plantings along freeways and even demanding resurfacing of roads to reduce noise. All of this I have watched going on these last few years, and I might add that although these measures have been taken in lots of areas still it is only a drop in the bucket in reducing the noise factor.

I have been thinking how clever mankind has become in many ways—i.e., sending men to the moon and back—yet the things that need attention on this earth go unsolved, I wonder [in this nonscientific] brain of mine why a device could not be made that could divert sound waves away from homes which border freeways. To elaborate a little more I feel that if a TV antenna placed on my roof can bring sound and pictures into my living room, why couldn't some sort of device like a TV antenna be used to divert sound away from one's garden or home; does this idea sound entirely unreasonable to you?

I have tried to find out if anyone has even got a patent on any kind of device which could be set up in one's garden to divert noise, do you know of any such thing and are you working on this kind of a problem? It certainly would be a blessed boon to thousands of people if such a device could be marketed and bought reasonably on the market, I would be first in line.

Yours truly,
B. D.
Los Altos, California

This lady certainly was very serious, but unfortunately we had to tell her that in no way could such a device be fashioned—at least with the present state of the art of noise control.

Dear Mrs. D.:

Thank you for your letter in which you expressed a hope for a device which would protect your home from the encroachment of outside noises. Unfortunately, the laws of physics do not allow the development of any such devices as you described. Envision a pebble dropped into a still pond, then think of a means whereby all of the ripples could be stopped immediately. The same problem is true with sound. It radiates in all directions, and the only way to keep sounds from entering your home is to insulate against them or to abate the sound source itself. The latter program seems to hold the greatest promise.

I appreciate your interest in the problems caused by noise. As more persons share your concern, more will be done to cause manufacturers to design and produce quieter items. Hopefully, that day is not far off.

Sincerely,
D.M.L.

GOOD QUESTIONS

Inquiring minds often pose excellent questions that demonstrate considerable insight into a problem area. Such questions are contained in a few letters to the laboratory. The laboratory staff has carried out many research projects, but those concerned with rock music have most often reached the mass media; so most of the questions relate to that subject.

Two letters offered comments on reasons the results of studies came out as published. The first was from a lady in Baltimore.

Dear Dr. Lipscomb,

I read in the paper about your experiment with the guinea pig and rock music.

The article also stated that the musicians suffered very little ear damage.

Have you considered the fact that the musicians are behind the amplifiers and do not get the full intensity of the sound?

You more than likely have considered this, but I thought I would write and ask just in case.

Hope I've helped.

Sincerely,

E. C.

Baltimore, Maryland

The reply was intended to answer her question as well as to correct her source's misquote of the study interpretations.

Dear Mrs. C.:

I am afraid that the news article to which you referred has given me credit for a statement which I have never made. It is my firm belief that rock musicians are most susceptible to ear damage from the intense sounds they generate.

Actually, in the acoustically live halls where most rock dances are held, there is little difference in the intensity of sound between the front and the back of the speakers through which the sound comes. Therefore, it probably makes little difference as to the location of the musicians during a performance. The factor which overrides their location in the hall is that they are exposed to this sound for a great number of their waking hours.

Thank you for taking the time to write. The question you pose is a valid one.

Sincerely,

D.M.L.

A second letter on experimental procedure came from a woman overseas with her husband in the military.

Dear Doctor Lipscomb,

With due respect for your education and your effort to discourage abuse of one's hearing, may I make the following observation?

I'm only a housewife with middle-class formal education, but if this thought would occur to me it will undoubtedly enter others' minds.

Your "research" appears invalid if you seriously intend to compare the human ear to that of guinea pig because of the difference in size of the creatures involved. Humans are much larger than guinea pigs and their tissues are proportionally stronger. Why aren't you using larger animals for your experiments?

I have six children who are just becoming interested in rock, or "no-think," music, and my argument for turning down the volume is just simply out of respect for the other people who live in our home, who may not care for "rock."

The article entitled "Stone-Deaf from Rock" which appeared in our Wednesday, August 21st issue of *Stars and Stripes* is what prompted this letter. Your point is well taken but your method of proving it is not, and is even uncomplimentary to your apparent ethics.

Sincerely,

P. H.

A.P.O. New York

The exact intent of the last sentence is not known, but here is the reply.

Dear Mrs. H.:

Thank you for your letter of August 21, 1968. The fact that you took time to write and point out what you felt to be a problem with our study was most impressive to me.

If we were talking about items of consumption such as food, water, or volume of air intake, your observation would be absolutely true. However, with respect to the structure of the ear and with respect to the nature of sound, the response of the guinea pig ear can be considered to be nearly identical to that of the human ear. In fact, the top researchers in the field of audition employ the guinea pig routinely because its ear is so similar to that of the human.

Perhaps another analogy would hold. Regardless of the size of the animal or the object, if a room is 110° F., the response to that temperature is not dependent upon the size of the object or the animal. In like manner, the sound environment is responded to in almost identical fashion regardless of the size or the makeup of the animal.

I am taking the liberty of enclosing a reprint of the original article which carries the information. It gives a good deal more of an idea of what we have done here than the article in *Stars and Stripes.*

Once again, I appreciate your taking time to write, and I wish you and your husband good luck and a safe tour of duty.

Sincerely yours,
D.M.L.

A high school guidance counselor expressed concern about the sound level of school dances and wanted a means whereby he could control the sound.

Dear Sir:

The article in a paper of last summer reported some of your findings concerning injurious effects of go-go bands or rock and roll bands. For some time I have hoped that someone would help me find a solution to this malady. Students love it and hope to keep its volume full power.

I have encouraged high school students to hire bands of less volume but to no avail.

What would be a good rule to set the sponsors, students, and bands aright. It would need to be simple so that all would understand. I am afraid that many bands would not understand scientific language concerning same.

Cordially yours,
C. E.
Oxford, Indiana

To this inquiry and to others like it we sent the following ideas.

Dear Mr. E.:

The problem you state is not an easy one to solve. The psychology which is prevalent in the young people who expose themselves to various hazards is "it won't happen to me." Despite the warnings we might issue, they seem satisfied to rely on the above reasoning.

Currently, there is some activity at the legislative level to consider high-intensity music as a threat to the auditory well-being of young people. Eventually, this might lead to federal control of some type. You are, I'm sure, aware of the immense problems of enforcing such a code.

To date, I have not hit upon a satisfactory way of discouraging the employment of loud bands when the students have the total say in their selection. If possible, administrative guidelines may be brought to bear to force the band to attenuate its amplifiers.

I would suggest that a sound pressure level of 95 to 100 dB (decibels) on the A scale of a sound level meter would be the maximum allowable at a distance 10 to 15 feet from the front of the bandstand. These measures can be readily made if the equipment is available. Perhaps a sound engineer is available in your community and would be willing to take such measures.

Enclosed is a copy of an article which outlines the problem. If the students are made aware of the potential danger and its consequences, they may extend an effort to reduce the sound level at the dances.

If you have further questions relative to this subject, please do not hesitate to call upon me. I'm sorry that there is no patent approach I can suggest.

Best wishes,
D.M.L.

A letter (in Spanish) from Caracas, Venezuela, posed a number of questions commonly asked about rock music. A student translated the letter so that it could be answered more intelligently:

Esteemed Dr. Lipscomb:

I am directing myself to you with the object of soliciting from you some more elaborated information with respect to the investigations carried out under your direction in relation to the "yeh-yeh" music and the destructive effects that are produced to hearing.

Also, I would like to ask you certain things. Do you believe that it is the high volume that causes these auditory destructions or the shouting and noise characteristic of this music? Being a fan of this music—that is to say, listening to it frequently—would it cause complete or partial deafness with time, or produce certain disequilibriums (problems) in some parts of the cerebral cortex? And as a curious question, I will formulate (to you) the following: When one suffers of cold or upper respiratory infections, would this be an unsuitable time for listening to the rock music, owing to the irritation of adjacent zones or those relating to audition.

Wishing you the best of fortune in your investigation.

A. P.

Caracas, Venezuela

We hope that the questions were translated correctly and that the inquirer was able to locate a translator for this reply.

Dear Mr. P.:

Perhaps the best way to respond to your interesting letter is to attempt to answer each question in order.

1. A copy of an article I recently published is enclosed in this letter. It will give some useful information for you.

2. I am not sure whether the type of music contributes to ear damage. I am inclined to believe that the sound level (volume) of the sound is by far the most important feature to be considered.

3. Exposure to loud noise, regardless of type, will not result in total loss of hearing. The accumulative effect of such sound exposure over time will result in reduced ability to hear, especially in the high-frequency regions.

4. There is no evidence of cortical deterioration in adults as a result of high-intensity sound exposure.

5. When one has a cold, his hearing mechanism is generally not as efficient; therefore the loud sound would likely have less damaging effect upon the ear than when the ear is unoccluded. In brief, having a cold would provide a degree of protection from the loud sound.

I hope that these brief answers will be helpful to you. If you have further questions, or wish me to elaborate on one or more of the above points, please feel free to call upon me. Thank you for your interest.

Best wishes,

D.M.L.

Numerous medically related questions come in, but since the laboratory staff is not trained in medicine the questions must be deferred. A grandmother expressed one area of concern.

Dear Sir,

Can you tell me if hair spray used frequently can also do damage to the ear?

My daughter and granddaughter use a couple cans of hair spray a week, and I heard that you can develop ear trouble from it. She says she holds her hands over her ears and granddaughter's when she sprays, but I heard it still gets in your ear when you take your hand away. I would be very grateful if you could give me that information.

Sincerely,

J. L.

Dayton, Ohio

The following brief answer was given.

Dear Mrs. L.:

The question you asked is a medical one and I am ill-prepared to attempt an answer. Perhaps you would be best advised to consult a dermatologist as to whether hair spray will cause skin irritation in the region of the ear. That would be the only way I could conceive of the spray's creating an abnormal hearing condition.

Sincerely,

D.M.L.

The continuing concern about hearing aids was noted in some correspondence.

Dear Dr. Lipscomb:

I noted with interest your comment that music played to a guinea pig led to the destruction of cells in the ear.

Let me ask if you could infer that hearing aids used over a long period of time could cause this same loss? I have worn hearing aids for several years, and have for a year and a half what a neurologist diagnoses as labyrinthitis. In your study have you any idea as to the cause or cure of labyrinthitis. I have been bothered with it about fifteen months. I am having difficulty controlling the vertigo. Any suggestions?

With kindest regards, I am

Sincerely,

J. H.

Benton, Arkansas

A reply was attempted.

Dear Mr. H.:

You asked if one could infer that ear damage could result from the use of a hearing aid. I am afraid that the information you gave in your letter would allow me only to speak in very general terms. In the past, I have noted a very few cases in which a very high-powered hearing aid was employed that there was some *gradual* deterioration of hearing over a long period of time. I do not wish to have you infer at all from this that the wearing of a hearing aid is going to damage or destroy hearing at all. That is diametrically opposed to the purpose of a hearing aid in the first place. The best way in which to advise you would be for you to periodically have your hearing checked and see if there is any change in an attempt to establish whether or not the hearing is being affected by the aid.

On your question of labyrinthitis, I must refer you to a medical person, since the questions you asked are strictly medical and I am not a medical doctor.

Thank you again for your interest and for your letter.

Sincerely,

D.M.L.

A member of the South Carolina Association for the Deaf asked a similar question.

> Dear Dr. Lipscomb:
>
> I read with great interest of your article in the newspaper about the Rock'n' Roll music which is hard on the hearing.
>
> Dr. Lipscomb, I always suspect that the hearing aids worn by so many people will not improve their hearing but will damage their hearing faster as they grow older.
>
> But—we have no way to prove them. Perhaps your audio clinical services can try these experiments and find out the truths about the hearing aids business.
>
> We will appreciate your reporting this to us.
>
> > Sincerely,
> >
> > R. R.
> >
> > Spartanburg, South Carolina

This is a controversial area, for some feel very strongly that hearing aids are nothing but detrimental. An attempt was made to suggest the other side of the argument.

> Dear Mr. R:
>
> Thank you for your letter of September 3, 1968. I have been interested that a number of persons have asked the same question that you have.
>
> I am afraid that in certain *isolated* instances the use of a very high-powered hearing aid will tend to reduce one's hearing acuity. This has been found to be true in my experience, however, only in those situations where the individual has a very severe hearing loss and the hearing aid necessary to provide any useful acoustic stimulus has to be extremely powerful.
>
> One must make the choice (especially in the case of the young child) of whether the risk of some additional loss of hearing is worth the use of greatly amplified acoustic stimuli.
>
> I am afraid that the research evidence so far does not support your contention that hearing aids destroy or dam-

age hearing. In fact, our findings have been quite to the contrary. A member of my staff, Mr. Jack Ferrell, is presently engaged in some most exciting research in which he is finding a number of very useful factors in the use of a hearing aid.

I hope that you will not be too harsh on the hearing aid industry. They have made great strides in recent years in the development of new and better instruments for the hard of hearing. The philosophy at our Center has been that a hearing aid, while not restoring normal hearing, certainly is something to be considered in all cases of moderate to severe hearing impairments.

Sincerely yours,
D.M.L.

Apparently that response did not satisfy the man, for a short time later we received the following letter.

Dear Dr. Lipscomb:

I have your letter of September 6, 1968. We still suspect that the hearing aids actually will damage the hearing as some of my friends after wearing the hearing aids so long suspect the experience of hearing loss. They had to buy more powerful hearing aids.

We ask that your clinic make more surveys of those who have worn their hearing aids for more than 10 years to find more evidences of hearing losses. We do not want to be too harsh on the hearing aid industry but to warn those not to amplify their hearing aids if they want to continue better hearing for the rest of their lives.

Now any one can buy a good hearing aid at the cost of a new color television set. This high price is ridiculous, and many of our friends prefer to live without them.

R. R.
Spartanburg, South Carolina

The next letter was saved for last because it hinges on the future.

Dear Dr. Lipscomb:

I am writing a proposed article on world environmental problems and am seeking answers or opinions to my questions of various categories from government and scientific sources for possible publications.

I have two questions pertaining to noise pollution.

1. If our large city noise rates continue to escalate, what will life be like 30 years from now?

2. Do you foresee in the near future any federal controls over unnecessary (or excessive) noise pollution, such as jet aircraft, factories, etc.?

Any other information you may wish to contribute that will be of benefit to the public will be greatly appreciated and acknowledged. Thank you very much.

Most sincerely,

L. C.

Highland, California

That was one of the most intelligent letters the laboratory received. It was with pleasure that a positive response could be offered.

Dear L.:

The questions you pose are both relevant and tough. I am not sure that my answers will be fully accurate, but here goes.

1. Life in 30 years if city noise rates continue to escalate. First, I might state that the upward spiral in urban noise must be reversed or we will encounter noise levels within the next decade which will be damaging to the ears. Actually, I feel that the urban sound environment will be less noisy and cluttered in 30 years than it is today. In the past few years, we have found an increasing concern (such as yours) about the noise problem, and many are turning their efforts to the reduction and abatement of unnecessary

noise. This prediction is based upon the increased interest in state and local governments in regulating noisy sources. As our technology continues to expand and develop, I am confident that the design engineers will be more cognizant of the noise generating potential of the device they are developing and will make sure that the noise factor is considered.

2. Federal controls in the future. I probably have partially answered this question in the previous paragraph. Not only do I foresee federal action in this area, it has already come about. Nearly two years ago, the Walsh-Healy Federal Contracts Act was amended to set guidelines for the allowable noise exposure for workers in plants whose income is derived from government contracts of $10,000 or more. This act has already affected over 70,000 plants. The states are now broadening the impact to include regulations for all plants whether they have government contracts or not.

The latest Congress voted a law which banned the proposed supersonic aircraft from ever traversing the nation at speeds faster than the speed of sound.

Vehicular noise standards are currently under review in the Department of Transportation.

So, I feel that the answer to your question is a resounding yes! The real question to be debated is the relative responsibility of the state, local, and federal regulating agencies and legislative bodies.

Best wishes,
D.M.L.

·11·

Reducing the Volume

Anything for the quiet life.
Thomas Heywood

The ancient Greek dramatic poet Euripides advised the "good
and the wise lead quiet lives." His advice has become modern
man's challenge, much more easily said than done because of
the numerous confounding barriers to the reduction of sound
levels.

As the population of civilized nations continues to grow, so
does the use of various technologic marvels that generate noise.
Man's ever-increasing thirst for technologic breakthroughs has
led to an abundance of gadgets heretofore unknown to the
human race. Further, as individual affluence increases, more
persons are capable of acquiring mechanized items. Thus it is
not enough to simply make slight reductions in the overall
sound level of each item. If, for example, next year's automobiles
were all 3 dB quieter than this year's model, the vehicular sound
environment would not be automatically lessened 3 dB. Since
the number of cars sold each year usually is greater than the
amount for previous year, more of the sound-making vehicles will be on streets. In addition, the older cars will have
developed more noises because of wear and tear; so the traffic
noise level will hardly be diminished by an across-the-board 3
dB reduction in sound output, even though such a reduction
amounts to halving the energy of the sound the car radiates.

Clearly, dramatic reductions in the sound levels of

machines, tools, appliances, and vehicles will be necessary before noticeable relief from environmental and occupational noise can be realized. This rather grim outlook has led some to observe that man is hurtling headlong into a rendezvous with auditory disaster, although some naturally would state the case a good deal less strongly because they hold that the evidence still is equivocal. Long-term studies ultimately will determine whether the anticipated potentially devastating side effects of excessive noise exposure and the resulting reaction of men to noise are viable, but to date scant evidence exists either way, for man has never before been forced to endure an acoustic environment composed of such high-level sounds as in this age, and his ultimate response to the sound levels thus is not fully predictable. However, some interesting related data on aging and other effects of noise has been obtained from a study of the Mabaans, a remote, primitive Sudanese tribe. At the outset, it must be noted that rigorous controls could not be exerted over many of the variables in this study. Although the study cannot be used to predict unequivocally that civilized man would have met the same medical test that the remote tribesmen did, the story of the Mabaans indicates that Euripides' "quiet life" may be good for the general health.

It has been thought that one could sustain long-term exposure to steady-state sound at 85 dBA with little or no threat to hearing, but this one investigation and a few others of a similar nature tend to indicate otherwise. An analysis of the hearing capability of primitive tribesmen led to the observation that persons in developed countries appear to sustain a greater degree of hearing impairment than do aboriginal peoples.

Most people have a favorite quiet place—a place where they can go to relax or to meditate, a place to regroup thoughts and feelings in order to brace for upcoming challenges. Perhaps the place is in the woods, a meadow, the mountains, or even an inner room set apart from other busy areas. Since noise is a by-product of modern civilization it is appropriate to study precivilization cultures in order to gain an understanding of quiet.

Surprisingly few such cultures remain in the world. The

homeland of one, the Mabaans, in Central Africa near the Equator is primarily bush near the swamps of the White Nile. To visit the area one must travel only in the dry season, and then by truck or jeep over a narrow dirt trail. Before 1956 the area was untouched by outsiders.

In 1960 a group from Columbia Medical School organized an expedition to study the hearing of these tribesmen, whose exposure to loud sound was very limited. The group of researchers included an audiologist who tested hearing and several physicians who examined the Mabaan people for general physical health.

The Mabaans are a very primitive tribal group considered to have developed to about the late Stone Age level of achievement. Dr. Samuel Rosen, one of the physicians on the expedition, described them as being peaceful and quiet. They live in small bamboo huts with thatched roofs and use spears for hunting as well as other primitive tools and weapons. Although considered to be pre-Nilotic their development lagged considerably, probably because of their remote location.

The people are described as shy and retiring, lean and well nourished. Medical examiners reported that they had very good posture, with very little obesity at any age, probably because of their monotonous diet of occasional fowl, some fish, sour-tasting bread, and citrus fruits. There was no evidence of vitamin or protein deficiencies, although animal protein was seldom available.

Coronary thrombosis, ulcers, nervous colitis, acute appendictis, and asthma were virtually nonexistent, but one of the most astounding medical findings was the complete absence of high blood pressure. Blood pressure variations between young and elderly Mabaans were very small, whereas in America the blood pressure normally rises significantly after age 40. Interestingly, the male tribesman's blood pressure was lower than that of the female. In America the reverse is true until after age 45.

Seldom does the environmental sound level rise above that of soft conversation, the Mabaan's means of communication. Tribesmen reportedly converse at very soft levels at distances as great as 100 feet. Hard, reverberating surfaces are lacking; so the tribe's "industrial noise" of smashing palm fronds with a club at about 75 decibels is considered to be one of the few high-level noises in the environment. Unlike many of the African tribes the Mabaans do not use drums; their percussion musical instruments are hollow logs struck with sticks.

An interesting parallel with other, more civilized parts of the world is that the loudest sound to which tribesmen are exposed is the singing and dancing of their young people. During the harvest celebration singing and shouting is as great as 100 dB, but the infrequent occurrence of this sound renders it of no consequence with respect to the natives' hearing health.

Since remarkably little noise exists in this setting it was expected that Mabaan tribesmen's ears would remain intact better than those of people in more advanced cultures. Hearing tests confirmed this theory even more markedly than had been anticipated. Little loss of hearing with advancing age was discovered in tests of 541 persons ranging in age from 10 years to over 90 years.

In distinct contrast to test results in the United States, Mabaan men had better hearing than did women in the later years. Mabaans between 70 and 79 were able to hear a test tone in the high-pitched range at an average of 35 dB better than Americans of the same age group are capable of hearing. In fact, the 80-year-old Mabaan has hearing comparable to that of a 30-year-old American, according to the study group reports.

The study group concluded that the lower noise environment accounted in part for the Mabaans' better hearing and better functioning circulatory systems. Just as it is not possible to generalize directly from animal research to human reaction, it is not fully possible to make generalizations from the Mabaans to civilized people—a mistake that the researchers did make in stating unequivocally that the noise environment is a major determinant of the vast differences in hearing and body physiology. It must be remembered, however, that no controls are available—that is, no tribal subgroups who had been exposed to various environmental contaminants, including higher noise levels.

In a follow-up study one year later the researchers sought out former tribesmen who had moved to Khartoum, Sudan. They discovered that the urbanized Mabaans there were prone to high blood pressure and coronary thrombosis, which strengthened their feeling that the quiet and uncomplicated environment played a vital role in the Mabaans' excellent health. Further study and follow-up are needed, however, to be sure that these observations were not isolated reactions to a very severe culture shock experienced in going from the very primitive life-style to modern living.

Hearing test results provided a very interesting comparison between the primitive ears of the Mabaans and the hearing of people in three civilized cities—Cairo, Dusseldorf, and New York. Of the young tribesmen, 94 percent heard a high-frequency tone of 18,000 Hz, whereas slightly fewer (88 percent) of the city residents heard the same sound. A 22,000 Hz tone was heard by 15 percent of the young tribesmen and by only 6 percent of the citydwellers. Even an extremely high tone of 24,000 Hz, whose frequency is usually considered to be outside the normal hearing range of human ears, could be heard by 6 percent of the primitive young people. Only 1 percent of the city youths heard that sound.

As comparisons were made between older groups, the gaps in hearing abilities widened, with the tribesmen showing the better hearing. Twice as many 40-year-old Mabaans could hear a 16,000 Hz tone as could civilized persons of their same age. Mabaans between 40 and 50 years required an average of 22 dB less volume for a 14,000 Hz tone. Tribesmen in the 60–69-year bracket responded to a 12,000 Hz tone 3 times as often (99 percent as compared to 32 percent). Elder primitive people were even more markedly superior in their ability to hear high-pitched tones in that 53 percent heard a 14,000 Hz sound as compared to 2 percent of the citydwelling oldsters.

Dr. Rosen theorized that constant use of the ear among persons in industrialized nations tended to wear out the ear at an earlier age. This "rug wear" principle must be held in perspective by remembering that several other influences may have played a role as important, or perhaps even more important. The slower pace, lower degree of stress, and cultural and hereditary factors also must be kept in mind.

The Mabaan story gives some credence to speculation that

the increasing noise in the human environment has played a part in reducing the health and well-being of urbanites. The example was given here in order to lend additional emphasis to the need for reducing environmental sound. It is, of course, impossible to cite the exact extent to which noise was the culprit in these findings, but the lesson of the Mabaan tribe should not be ignored. Although the results of the investigations must necessarily be interpreted with caution, strong evidence indicates that the aging processes as well as the occurrence of internal disorders might be at least augmented by the presence of high environmental noise.

A large newspaper chain recently editorialized against the growing noise levels by suggesting a "national shut up campaign" in which the population cumulatively and individually must attack the sound generated at the source. Then manufacturers would make it a regular policy to include the sound output of their products in the specifications.

PRINCIPLES OF NOISE CONTROL

For the most part, common sense and knowledge of a few principles will effect adequate noise abatement procedures.

1. Noise is sound, and sound is composed of one or more individual frequencies. The more complex the sound, the more numerous the frequency elements that make up the sound.

2. Sound absorption varies with the frequency of sounds. Sound absorbing materials are much more efficient with high-frequency sounds and considerably less effective in reducing low-frequency signals.

3. Just putting a box over or around a noisy device will not necessarily improve the noise situation. The physical law of the conservation of energy states that energy can be neither created nor destroyed; so it is necessary to convert the sound energy to another form. When sound is absorbed, acoustic energy is transformed into heat and is rendered harmless; hence an enclosure for sound-generating devices must have sound-absorbent linings, or sound will find its way out.

4. Room noise is reduced when room reverberation is reduced. As long as sound can bounce from one surface in a room to another, an additive effect is achieved when the reverberated sound combines with the sound the noise source has just made. Absorptive surfaces reduce the ability of sound to stay alive in a room.

5. Generally, it is best to pay the greatest attention to the noise levels in middle and higher frequency (pitch) ranges. The ear is less sensitive to low-pitched sounds; thus somewhat more low-frequency noise can be tolerated than can high-pitched sounds. If, of course, the sound is too great in amplitude and is composed almost entirely of low-frequency energy, the low-frequency influence must be engineered out of the situation.

6. Sound is defined as the propagation of vibratory energy through an elastic medium. Most commonly the medium is air. Since vibrations play an essential role in the creation of acoustic forces, it is vital to consider the contribution a device is making to the noise by its vibratory characteristics. Often the transmitted noise can be dramatically reduced by shock-mounting the offending device to reduce the vibrations it imparts to the surface on which it rests.

7. Numerous noise problems, the result of careless planning or layout, can be corrected by attempting to remedy the faulty conditions in which the noise is allowed to occur.

Some of the most inexpensive building materials are also among the most sound-absorbent. A combination of glass wool insulation and wood fiberboard (commonly referred to by the trade name Celotex) can be used quite effectively in building a sound baffle or enclosure. Usually such materials can be reinforced with plywood for skeletal strength. Two sound-treated booths in which experimental animals receive their sound treatments at the laboratory are constructed of these materials and have served very well. Figure 11.1 shows an overall view of the large double enclosure booth. Figure 11.2 is a closeup view of the sound-isolating materials used.

Sound insulation is best effected when the fiberboard layers are doubly thick. With just a little imagination, one can conjure up designs of very effective enclosures, baffles between sound

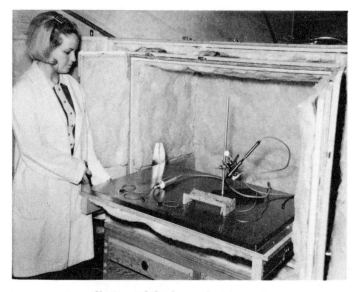

11.1   Overall view of the large double enclosure booth.

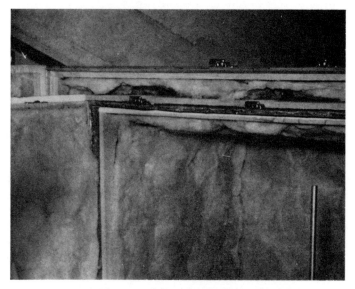

11.2   Closeup of sound-isolating materials.

sources, dividers between use areas or for wall linings. One important word of caution, though. That the use of plywood and fiberboard in combination might constitute an excessive fire hazard should be given careful consideration. Glass wool loses some of its sound-absorptive quality if it becomes glutted with dust, moisture, or grease, and it tends to flake off and can become a skin irritant on contact. Often this problem can be overcome by using a cheesecloth covering over the glass wool.

In some instances a wood structure with fiberboard and glass wool linings will be insufficient. Then one may be forced to install specially designed prefabricated sound enclosures constructed of steel, which understandably are quite expensive but extremely effective.

Remember that a sound reduction of 50 percent is not a great improvement. Depending on the environment, an improvement of that magnitude will be between 3 and 6 dB. In many situations sounds must be halved several times over to bring them to an acceptable level.

MODIFICATION OF OPERATIONS

Quite often it is absolutely impossible to quiet devices currently in use and economically infeasible to replace all the noisy units; so acoustic engineers are turning to a different form of abatement, which is augmented by changing the operation of existing devices. Some machines or tools need only slower operating speeds to reduce overall sound output; others require somewhat greater modifications.

The village of Oberbolheim, Germany, located in the vicinity of a large airport, provides an extreme example of modification. The West German government decided that the most appropriate solution to the village's noise problem was to simply design another town, Neu Oberbolheim, and move the slightly more than 200 residents away from the noise source. What can be done for 200 persons with comparable ease is vastly more complex when huge populations around other airports are considered. Because the new town solution is absolutely out of the question, and the air transportation industry has not quieted the jets to an acceptable neighborhood level, operational variations for aircraft are coming into use in an attempt to minimize the disruptive effect of takeoff and landing noise. The landing profile—the slope at which an aircraft approaches the landing strip—is being redesigned. In some areas it is safe to consider a 6° profile in place of the 3° one most carriers use, thereby lowering the landing sound by as much as 8 PNdB because the plane is over housing areas at a higher altitude. Progress angles greater than 6° generally are considered outside the bounds of appropriate safe operations. Currently, and unfortunately, the airlines are not regularly using this method.

The FAA has produced modifications in the takeoff procedure so that ascending aircraft follow a four-stage operation, allowing for more gradual climb over residences nearest the airport. This "standardized noise takeoff profile" has been successful in reducing ground noise level by nearly 9 EPNdB.

Considerate operation of aircraft apparently can result in rather dramatic reductions in the noise in airport communities, but if the airlines continue to avoid a good neighbor policy federal agencies or local legal action will force costly alterations of their planes. Much has been written about aircraft noise and the various methods of quieting airport communities. Much of the work to be done lies outside the sphere of individual action and hence outside the scope of this book. Suffice it to say that efforts are being made to reduce the whine and roar of commercial jet aircraft, and much more effort must be extended to get the job done.

A very different type of noise to which considerable numbers of persons are exposed is the rattle and clunk of various pieces of office machinery. A television documentary noted that because the personnel in a check-processing department of a Manhattan bank had become quite bothered by the noise of computers, the bank began to hire deaf people who had been trained to operate the equipment. These persons handle their work with little interruption and distraction from the noisy environment because they simply do not hear the sounds.

This unique form of operational modification has been found to work in other places as well. Deaf persons have been operating printing presses for many years, chiefly because they can handle the job well, but secondarily because the noise is of no concern to them. Recently the manager of a graphic arts department for a large university hit on the idea of using deaf typesetters in a small, reverberant room. Although the room noise was extremely disturbing to the normally hearing employees, the deaf paid no attention to the noise and continued unhindered. It is not possible to fill every noisy area vacancy with a deaf person; thus this solution has considerable limitations. For certain situations, though, it is a valuable option to consider.

It seems that much has been said in the mass media about the problems of traffic noise; yet at present little is being done to make sure that drivers can hear emergency vehicle warning signals. As noted earlier, numerous conditions preclude the operator of a moving vehicle from hearing sirens, whistles, horns, or bells; so other means of alerting drivers to road hazards are needed. Perhaps the warning must be put to the receiver through another sensory channel, such as vision.

1. *Emergency vehicles.* On a recent trip through South Carolina we encountered a Columbia fire truck making deliberate albeit not irrationally fast speed through traffic by means of not a siren but, rather, a very bright flashing white light mounted atop the cab of the truck. Although the scene took place at midday in full sunlight the vehicle apparently was easily seen and avoided. Perhaps that use of flashing lights in place of blaring sirens will become more widespread, although cars from side streets could not have the benefit of seeing the fire truck and might rush headlong into trouble. Possibly the truck could radiate an activating signal that would cause all traffic lights to turn red, thus stopping traffic; but then traffic could jam, making the emergency vehicle unable to navigate to its destination. A more plausible concept would be the use of flashing lights situated immediately under traffic light boxes or on street corners. These warning signals would be activated by the radiated beam of an emergency vehicle as it came within a two- or three-block radius of the light boxes.

2. *Railroad crossings.* A claim agent for a southern line has expressed concern about crossing accidents that occur because warnings apparently are too little and too late—a situation

that suggests consideration of crossing signal alterations. Three conditions must be satisfied: (1) the device must be fail-safe; (2) it must provide an early warning at all times of the day; (3) the cost must not be prohibitive.

The following proposals are not to be construed as final versions of track crossing warning signals but are simply ideas that employ a different warning mode and may provide groundwork for ultimate warning devices. Figure 11.3 shows a typical crossing sign whose X crossing bars are outfitted with very bright flashing lights like those used for advertising. The lights, activated by an approaching train, would flash randomly so that they would not be inadvertently ignored. Random signals are more disturbing than are periodic or rhythmic ones, and in this case the driver *should* be disturbed and thus alerted to impending danger.

A second railroad crossing system shown in Figure 11.4 also incorporates flashing lights, but a support post bedecked with the lights bridges the crossing. The bar, of course, must be high enough to allow adequate passage of tall vehicles. This type of signal would be seen for greater distances and would be free of interfering trees, shrubs, and other roadside items that

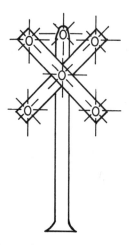

11.3   **Railroad crossing signal with X crossing bars.**

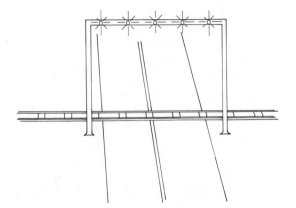

11.4   Railroad crossing system that bridges the crossing.

might hide the crossbars in Figure 11.3. The widespread use of either crossing signal would reduce the need for loud train whistles.

3. *All warning devices.*   A third type of warning signal detector system is an integral part of a proposed vehicle ignition system. This detector could activate a warning light on the top of the dash or cause a sound inside the vehicle to alert the driver to an approaching emergency vehicle. Such devices could be signaled by a radiated beam from the siren, horn, or whistle. This system could prove very effective once appropriate ranges are calculated for each type of warning signal to assure that only vehicles in the vicinity of the emergency vehicle or train are alerted. One problem stems from the apparent hesitation the automotive industry has demonstrated in providing safety features in their products. Seat belts were forced on them by governmental and economic pressures. For some time afterward car manufacturers spoke disdainfully of the belts as "spaghetti." It appears, however, the car designers are seriously considering the need for other internal devices to alert drivers of approaching warning signals.

It is much simpler to offer a plethora of suggestions than it is to determine the best system, and most important, to put the system into use. These ideas thus are intended as leads for persons in the fields of auditory and visual perception who can combine to determine the proper direction for warning signal system modification. The only sure thing at this point in time is that such modification is necessary and is already considerably behind schedule.

Any move as drastic as these suggestions might be considered will call for massive reeducation of the public. The resources of the National Safety Council, automobile clubs, insurance companies, and myriad other organizations must be mobilized. Legislation in conjunction with elements of the final system must be enacted. For example, if the flashing white lights are used as warning signals such lights in advertising signs and other places should be prohibited. Changes such as these would cost money, but considering the value of human lives and the large sums presently being paid in claims that result from accidents directly attributable to failures in audible warning systems, the cost might be greater if appropriate modifications are delayed.

CHANGING TECHNOLOGY

Robert Alex Baron, chairman of the New York organization, Citizens for a Quieter City, has said:

> I believe that there is enough known about the science and technology of noise that most of the noises that are disturbing modern man can be eliminated or minimized. And in cases where a given device cannot be designed for whatever reason to be compatible with the human environment and human existence, then I believe we must give up the use of such a device. I don't think we can afford the luxury of any more excessive noise stress.

These sentiments are echoed by an ever-increasing number of persons who "have had it with noise!" The technology of this age is magnificently challenged to overcome the noise problems of existing and future devices. Certainly the invectives against technology are misdirected; the real culprits have been the users of poor technology that is so narrowly goal-directed that the residuals are not considered.

In a presentation to a state meeting of educators Jules Bergman, science editor for the American Broadcasting Corporation, pointed out that the only salvation from the mess of recent pollution will come from good use of advanced technology. To abandon technology and return to the caves is tantamount to poking man's collective head in the sand. The problems just won't go away if ignored. It stands to reason that through technology new materials will be developed to reduce the vibration of machinery, new designs will bring about quieter units; and new techniques of construction will eliminate acoustic cross talk between apartments.

The Wall Street Journal has reported that an increasing awareness of the health menace in noise has prompted a growing market for noise abatement equipment. Annual sales, growing at a rate of 15 to 25 percent each year, indicate that noise control will command a significant portion of the future economy. If the upward trend in the use of sound-fighting materials and equipment continues, projections for an acoustic holocaust by the year 2000 will be proven false.

In developing new products, goal-directed design engineers can create monsters. For example, in developing a processing machine for a paper mill in the Pacific Northwest a huge steel drying drum, 12 feet in diameter, was added to the chain of machinery to transmit heat to the flattened pulp, dry it out, and then pass the material on to rollers for further processing. In order to pass heat to the pulp it was necessary to perforate the outer edge of the drum where contact was made, but the very evenly spaced holes in essence created a siren. When the machine was placed in operation, the rapidly revolving drum set off an extremely high-intensity wail that workmen could not tolerate; so it was necessary to revise the scheme of perforations to break up the siren effect. In this situation a little foreknowledge of acoustical conditions would have spared time and expense. Poor or short-sighted technology always is a very expensive item.

Rectifying poor planning and design of houses also is expensive. For homes in the $20,000 to $30,000 price range, sound treatment costs begin at $3,000 and depending on the amount of sound insulation can reach as high as $12,000. The technology for adequate internal sound treatment is becoming better known to home builders; so future homes should have fewer problems from outside noises.

The Department of Agriculture suggested a somewhat promising addition to man's armamentarium against noise encroachment in pointing out that trees and grass absorb noise and diffuse sound waves. These barriers can effect a 65 percent noise reduction, which means a decrease in noise levels of between 6 and 10 dB. The department advocated planting trees (evergreens) close together with a grassy area nearby. The taller the trees and the wider the bands of trees, the more effective will be the sound reduction. A serious drawback to this plan for noise abatement, however, is that large amounts of land must be available for the buffer areas. Some thought has been given to using this technique to both beautify and sound-treat high-speed highways. At present, the technique is being used only experimentally.

Considerable thought and planning has gone into the development of mass transit systems for the future. Newly designed laminated wheels for trains reduce noise output as much as 10 dB, and further reduction can be made by shock-mounting the tracks with specially designed pads. The acoustic treatment of wheels and car underbodies, using rubber tires in place of steel wheels, exercising vibration control of bridges and girders, and installing sound baffles along the roadbed will promote better transit vehicles that can be used with considerably less noise. Aerospace industries are moving into the mass transit field, and the result can be better, more advanced design of components and a resurgence in the use of mass transportation modes.

Construction equipment is notoriously loud, but developments in the past decade can silence many of the most undesirable construction industry sounds. Silencing packages have been developed for rear dump trucks so that the grinding, bumping, and howling of these denizens need no longer be tolerated. Similar packages are available for loaders and other construction machinery. A major manufacturer of large air compressors has whisperized the product by reducing the noise they radiate by 25 dB, which represents a 26-fold reduction in the sound pressure. New designs for air hammer bodies have caused a dramatic decrease in the raucous noise of these units. While walking in Berne, Switzerland, we heard a strange noise that could be compared only to a woodpecker working away at a soft, rotten log. On rounding a street corner, we found the source of the noise to be a jackhammer covered by a sound-absorptive jacket. The treatment was so effective that the typical jackhammer sound could not be recognized. Even pile drivers and large drills have undergone noise control. Excessive noise from construction gear is inexcusable. Considerable sound reduction can be occasioned by routine maintenance and the use of some of the retrofit packages that assure better muffling of the sound these devices generate. Hopefully the construction industry will deem it important to become a good neighbor before civic and legal action forces expensive penalties on them.

It is impossible to keep current with the development of new materials that absorb environmental sound or dampen equipment vibration. Several firms have developed a method for spraying a sound-absorbing material on ceilings, walls, panels, and elsewhere in order to reduce the overall sound level in large rooms as much as 12 dB. These products also increase thermal insulation and meet requisite specifications for the Class I fire code. On large installations the cost was no greater than the cost of installing acoustical tile. The material is being used in airport hangars, school gymnasiums and swimming pools, church sanctuaries, cafeterias, office buildings, machine shops, and almost any other type of reverberant room. Since it is available in numerous colors appearance need not be sacrificed for acoustic treatment.

One large manufacturer of wallboard materials has worked up several designs for walls to meet various purposes. Each design specifies how thick the wall will be and, most importantly for consideration here, what sound reduction the wall will provide. These sound-reduction figures are given as sound transmission class (STC) data according to the standard method for calculating the degree to which a barrier will resist the passage of sound. The higher the STC number, the more effective the wall is in sound-isolating one room from another. A company brochure lists a large number of wall, floor, and ceiling designs with STC ratings from 31 to 71, depending on the construction. No longer is it necessary to take acoustic potluck in wall construction, because sound transmission characteristics can be specified and a wall built to suit. Competent acoustical firms can aid in the selection of materials, and many of them will construct the walls as well.

Some developments have benefited small tools and appliances with a few moving parts that create disturbing noises. One of the largest chemical firms recently marketed a new plastic called Adiprene, which can be laminated to metal to cut down noise by severely reducing vibrations in the unit's parts and jacket. A coating of the material on circular saw blades greatly reduces the whine. In a television demonstration of the product a muscular man wielding a huge mallet slowly winds up to strike a large Chinese gong while the announcer describes the material. When struck, the gong emits a dull thud rather than the usual resounding clang.

Often the best method for reducing noise and vibration is to shock-mount a device on a special support structure. New mounting materials and gadgets coming onto the market range from simple foam pads to highly sophisticated hydraulic feet. Acoustic consultants or tool supply outlets will be of considerable help in finding a sound-isolating mount to meet specifications.

A muffler manufacturer has begun to employ a complex engineering principle in muffling exhaust noises in various types of machinery. In a before-and-after test of a muffler on a motorcycle, noise reduction could not be measured because the muffler hushed the output of the vehicle to a level below that of the dynamometer (power measuring instrumentation). The development engineer stated that before the tuned muffler was installed he dared not get his ear within three feet of the motorcycle, but after installation he could place his ear within three inches of the exhaust and hear only motor noise. If this type of development is possible, a major breakthrough in controlling exhaust noise has been made and much will be made of it. At this writing the mufflers have not been sufficiently tested to know whether they are as effective as the design engineer's optimistic report indicates.

LEGISLATION

Over 80,000 units administer the laws and regulations of federal, state, and local governing bodies, and to some extent each agency has some stake in the noise problem. Since noise is such an all-encompassing factor no single regulatory body can hope to control any major portion of the multifaceted problem; in fact, the problem is so broad that no agency appeared to have done much to solve it. The Office of Noise Abatement and Control (ONAC) of the Environmental Protection Agency was created to undertake a coordinating function. To date, the ONAC held a series of hearings around the country, compiled a 15-volume report of the proceedings of those hearings, wrote a health and welfare criteria document, brought together a host of leading noise specialists at an international congress in Yugoslavia, prepared regulations for truck noise, and is currently preparing noise regulations concerning noise emission of many products and vehicles. As a result of the Noise Control Act of 1972, this office was given additional clout in providing regulatory guidelines for sound outputs of certain motors and appliances. The effectiveness of the Office of Noise Abatement under the leadership of Dr. Alvin Meyer will set the tone for future elements of the war against noise. Hopefully, the next decade will see noise abatement efforts on a large scale.

Considerable legislative action has been directed toward control of noise at the source. Laws have been scattered and fragmented, and any similarity between laws in different states and communities is largely the result of chance. Such variety really is understandable, however, since awareness of noise grew quite rapidly, and efforts for legislative controls have been rapidly contrived, with little time given to learning what neighboring communities had done.

Some of the older codes and laws are somewhat strange in

light of modern-day activities. Several laws in England and Wales exemplify early attempts to control irritating sounds.

Music near houses, near churches and hospitals. No person shall sound or play upon any musical or noisy instrument or sing in any street or public place within 100 yards of any dwelling-house or office, after being requested to desist . . .

Organs. No person shall in any street or public place, use or play . . . any steam organ or other musical instrument worked by mechanical means, to the annoyance or disturbance of residents or passengers.

Noises at night. No person shall in any street or public place between the hours of 11 P.M. and 6 A.M. wantonly and continuously shout or sing or otherwise make any loud noise to the annoyance . . .

Wireless sets, gramophones, etc. Any person who by operating or causing or suffering to be operated any wireless set, gramophone, amplifier, or similar instrument—

   (a) in or on any street or public place . . .
   (b) in any other premises . . .
shall be guilty of an offense.

Noisy hawking. No person shall, for the purpose of hawking, selling, distributing, or advertising any article, shout or use any bell, gong or other noisy instrument in any street or public place so as to cause annoyance . . .

Explosive bird-scaring devices. No person shall cause or permit any device for scaring birds by means of periodic explosions to be in operation during the hours of darkness.

Noisy animals. No person shall keep within any house, building, or premises any noisy animal which shall be or cause a serious nuisance . . .

Legal control of noise has been attempted since as early as 1829, when a London law allowed for seizing stagecoach horses that disrupted church services. Later the Red Flag Law was enacted to reduce the number and hazard of horseless carriages. This regulation, as described earlier, required that a man carrying a red flag precede any self-powered vehicle. During the Roaring Twenties public school teachers issued a request for noiseless pavements because schools were disrupted by the incessant passing of carts, wagons, and cars on the rough-surfaced streets.

An early attempt to attach a fine schedule for noise offenders grew out of an ordinance developed by the city of New York in 1925. Considerably later, after the development of appropriate sound-measuring devices, communities began to set limits for allowable noise. In 1954 Milwaukee established that no vehicle could exceed a 95 dB level when measured from a distance of 20 feet from the right rear wheel of the vehicle in motion—a very important concept in that the specific distance for measuring sound and the location of the measuring equipment made possible adequate enforcement. Not infrequently proposed laws that set down exhaustive lists of sound regulations and noise limits cannot be enforced because no direction for taking sound measures is given.

Also in 1954 Switzerland established certain sound limits as measured from a distance of 24 feet. Trucks and buses were restricted to 90 dB, autos 80 dB, 4-cycle motorcycles 90 dB, and 2-cycle motorcycles 85 dB. Motorbikes were held to 80 dB.

The National Institute of Municipal Law set 89 dB as the maximum level that should be allowed by any municipal code. Further, the institute called for state vehicle noise inspection stations to be operated in a manner similar to state weighing stations.

Perhaps the landmark vehicle noise regulation is the California code, enacted in 1968, which established allowable noise levels for various types of vehicles and then challenged vehicle manufacturers by indicating that in subsequent years the regulation would be made more stringent. The California law also approved a section that would prohibit the sale and resale of vehicles found to emit excessively high sound. Unfortunately the law is difficult to enforce, even though a detailed protocol for setting up sound-measuring equipment has been developed.

The state of Connecticut, in conjunction with CBS Laboratories, has tested equipment designed to pinpoint and intercept noisy vehicles. With a camera and integrated sound-measuring system the device simultaneously indicates the peak sound level and photographs the offending vehicle so that the dB scale shows in the upper right-hand corner of the photograph. Such evidence probably would be hard to refute in a court of law.

Many vehicle noise codes are intended to be preventative rather than punitive; so some arresting officers issue warning citations that state an allowable period of time for correction of the problem. If the owner fails to comply, the citation reverts to a fine, often rather large. Whether such regulations will be successful in removing noisy vehicles from the streets and highways cannot be determined yet, except to note the anguished cries of some trucking interests in response to the periodic lowering of sound levels.

Some of the most recent and sweeping noise control regulations were put into effect July 1, 1971, in the city of Chicago. The project to silence Sh-h-h-h-icago has brought numerous environmental sounds under control. In one highly publicized incident that involved the ringing of church bells, a resident of the neighborhood of a church complained to City Hall, the noise ordinance was brought to bear on the priest, and the bells were silenced.

The Chicago ordinances on noise also set forth a schedule for the continuing reduction of various noise sources. For example, no motorcycle made after January 1, 1980, can create more than 75 dBA as measured from a distance of 50 feet. This is a 12 dB stiffer regulation than the one in effect for motors built prior to January 1, 1970. Similar restrictions are placed on cars and medium-weight vehicles. Large trucks manufactured after January 1, 1980, must meet an 80 dBA criterion as compared to 94 dBA allowed for present-day trucks and construction vehicles. In a note to a southern truck motor distributor a Chicago representative commented on the Chicago law. "This is a very tough noise law, and we're not sure they can enforce in '80." That inference hints that some members of the trucking industry may be counting on putting pressure on the governmental agencies to relax enforcement of these stringent laws. If the public proves lethargic toward noise control, the plan probably will work.

Lawmakers currently are concerned about which level of government will be responsible for enacting and enforcing noise codes. Presently there appears to be a sort of moratorium on new legislation until that question is resolved. Prior to this development I made several recommendations to the State of Tennessee Legislative Council Committee Hearings for the purpose of considering noise legislation. The recommendations and personal comments were as follows.

Because I fear I am often guilty of pointing up only the problems in this area of concern, I offer a few suggestions for state and local legislation which would serve to establish permissible noise levels and to determine the fate of excessive noise generators whether they be humans, machines, musical instruments, or other acoustic devices. I will briefly suggest 10 areas of concern which I submit can, and eventually will, be controlled with respect to noise output.

1. *Discotheques.* My research, and that of others, has pointed out the extreme hazard created for the sensitive and delicate ear tissues occasioned by exposure to the intense sounds produced in high school social functions, teen halls, discotheques, cabarets, etc. These establishments must be required to reduce the intensity of the sound environment to a much more acceptable level—e.g., 90 dB as measured on the "A" scale of a sound level meter. Enforcement of this code could likely be affected by agencies which issue cabaret licenses, food and drink certificates or some such established regulatory board. I have been told by the musicians that they do not wish to play loudly, but that they cannot find a job if they do not. Cabaret owners have told me that they can't see how the patrons can stand the noise, but they groan, "If

we regulate the musicians, we can't get them back for a return engagement." It appears that each side is pointing a finger at the other; thus, there is need for legislation which will attenuate the excessive sound present in these establishments.

2. *Traffic noise.*   The state of California Assembly recently passed a bill (#2254) which establishes the maximum allowable sound produced by a moving vehicle as a function of its speed. The New York legislature (Bill #3974) has provided for the regulation of horns and other warning devices stating that horns, for example, should have two volume levels, one for use in congested areas and the higher volume allowable on the open highway. Some cities, including Memphis, have enacted vehicle codes which prohibit the use of automobile horns altogether.

3. *Provision for adequate mufflers on moving vehicles.*   Quite related to the previous suggestion is an appeal for reduction of engine noise through the use of effective muffler (e.g., N.Y. Bill S.4167—an act for prohibiting operation in large cities of motorcycles with inadequate noise muffling devices).

4. *Industrial noise.*   Last year, the revision of the Walsh-Healy Government Contracts Act initiated federal regulation of noise levels present in the plant environment of nearly all suppliers to the U.S. government. These same regulations should be incorporated into state law so as to protect not only the workers in plants with government contracts, but all workers throughout the state.

5. *Aircraft noise.*   The state of California has created an advisory committee for the Public Utilities Board in order to suggest airport noise standards (Bill #645). The bill provides that two of the advisory board members be representative of homeowners concerned with aircraft noise. It is important to establish basic criteria for airport noise as soon as possible before the further expansion of existing facilities precludes such regulation.

With the future addition of supersonic transports, some states have begun to anticipate the sonic boom problem (e.g., California Senate Resolution No. 7, dated June 9, 1969, urged the President and his staff to forestall overland flights at supersonic speeds). In reply to a letter sent to President Nixon and Transportation Secretary Volpe, B. J. Vierling, Acting Director of SST Development assured me, "It is the Administration's policy that flights of commercial supersonic aircraft, at speeds that would produce sonic booms, will not be permitted over the United States." It is essential that the citizenry hold the government firmly to this commitment.

6. *Ear protection in recreational shooting.* The singlemost destructive sound has been found to be impulse (impact) noise. This is sound which reaches peak intensity in a very brief time span (e.g., the crack of a rifle). It is suggested that legislation be introduced to protect the sports shooter by requiring firing ranges to provide and enforce the use of good-quality earmuffs for all persons on the firing line. Further, protection should also be extended to the employees of such facilities.

7. *Neighborhood industrial noise.* Many cities have codes which are designed to limit the intensity of sound produced by a manufacturing plant. This sound is measured at the boundary limits of the industry and must not exceed a prescribed level. I know that our county has such a code, but I also know that it has not been brought up to date since the methods of reporting sound levels were revised by the American Standards Association. I am a firm believer that industry should be a good neighbor, both in the amount of noise it broadcasts over its surroundings and in terms of the amount of foul matter it disgorges from its smokestack and fluid waste system.

8. *Building codes.* There is a great deal which needs to be accomplished in the realm of multiple-dwelling noise, including: regulating the noise of machinery such as air conditioners, etc. (N.Y. Bill S. 3035—A. 4771), construction standards (N.Y. Bill S. 3049—A. 4770),

noise from construction activity (N.Y. Bill S. 3033—A. 4769), and regulation of the amount of noise which is generated within the building (N.Y. Bill S. 3566—A. 5406). In this time of high-rise apartment living, it is vastly important that the acoustic environment be given as much consideration as the interior design and decor of the residence.

9. *Construction noise.* Construction machinery is among the most noisy of all sound-generating devices. Much of this sound can be reduced with the implementation of efficient mufflers, proper maintenance to reduce the squeaks and squeals which result from metal rubbing against metal, and better design. Further reduction of the irritating quality of construction noise can be introduced by regulating the work hours for construction equipment which exceeds a predetermined sound level (e.g., N.Y. Bill S. 3566—A. 5406, which delimits the permissible work hours of construction conducted near multiple dwellings).

10. *Environmental quality control.* Last year, California amended the government code relating to environmental quality control to include noise as one of the factors depreciating the quality of the environment. This is a necessary addition to our state and local codes which define boards, committees, consultants, etc., for the purpose of preserving the environment.

I realize this list will never be complete, but it constitutes a beginning. The representatives in our state legislature who are now fervently attempting to conduct the business of our state government are urged to lend an ear (no pun intended) to these suggestions, make appropriate additions, and design appropriate, meaningful, worthwhile and enforceable legislation directed at the noise problem. I am confident that I speak for the rest of the persons in the hearing health community when I say that we stand ready and willing to assist in every way we can.

The subsequent report of the Legislative Council Committee adopted most of the suggested forms of action against noise.

During the fall of 1971 the Environmental Protection Agency Office of Noise Abatement hearings touched on many aspects of the noise problem. The resulting summaries are available in 15 volumes from the Superintendent of Documents. One volume, *Laws and Regulatory Schemes for Noise Abatement* (NTID 300.4), summarizes the status of legislative action in an excellent manner. The following statements have been abstracted from the introductory portion of the report.

> The existing Environmental Noise Regulatory Structure is fragmented in organization and *ad hoc* (specialized) in operation. Abatement functions are distributed among federal, state, and local government levels but are largely uncoordinated.
>
> The environmental noise problem context is composed of a wide variety of discrete noise sources and noise environments. Numerous partial efforts have been made to regulate "excessive" or "unnecessary" noise through regulatory schemes directed to abatement at the source, reduction of the effects of noise, and to remedies (by private action) to abate the source or to reduce the effects.
>
> Regulation by the federal government has been slight.
>
> Regulation by the states has for the most part been limited to selected noise sources. . . .
>
> Most noise abatement regulation has taken place at the local level by means of general noise ordinances directed to specific noise sources or by the creation of "quiet zones."
>
> Both state and local governmental levels are handicapped in police power regulation of some of the more critical noise sources as a result of preemptive federal legislation (aircraft noise) or by the threat of impinging upon a national interest in maintaining the free flow of interstate commerce.
>
> Very little attention has been given to construction

equipment or site noise, or to domestic noise sources.

Enforcement of noise abatement state statutes and municipal noise ordinances has been notoriously spasmodic and uniformly weak. . . .

Certain trends point to a substantially increased level of effort for federal and state governments.

Federal level:

Occupational noise abatement (OSHA)

Construction site noise abatement under the Construction Safety Act

Highway design to reduce noise effects

State level:

Enactment of comprehensive environmental quality statutes which include noise

Enactment of vehicle noise codes

Local level:

Initial efforts to enact comprehensive Environmental Control Noise Codes

Growing sophistication at all governmental levels in noise abatement and control techniques. . . .

Increasing disposition to broaden coverage of noise sources and noise environments by regulatory schemes and to disseminate through labeling or by other means useful information on noise dangers and abatement techniques to the general public.

The report listed some of the continuing problems in the regulation of environmental noises.

Lack of official and organized public interest in aggressive noise abatement programs.

Conflict of the social interest in noise abatement with other social values such as safety or free expression, which are accorded higher priority in the scheme of social interests.

Intensification of the stress between federal efforts and the state/local noise abatement efforts, especially in those regulatory contexts where federal preemptive legislation is involved.

Continuing difficulty of state or local authorities to regulate noise to the satisfaction of local conditions and needs where such regulation requires control over the noise source or effects of vehicles, equipment, and appliances regularly moving in or operating in interstate commerce.

Continuing difficulty, due to the multiplicity of noise sources and noise environments, of determining what noise sources or effects are to be controlled by what level of government with respect to the setting of standards or to operating procedures, having appropriate regard for the need of uniformity of regulation in some areas and the need for diversity of regulation to suit unique local conditions in others.

Indeed, the legislative problem has become a tangled web that makes little sense. However, this confusion can gradually be resolved, specifically at the federal level, with adequate and aggressive leadership from the Environmental Protection Agency and with the cooperation of Congress.

INDIVIDUAL ACTION

The cry "Let George do it" may work in some sectors, but that attitude will be the kiss of death to effective noise control. Each person must be considered an integral part of the plans for attacking unnecessary and controllable noise, because the extent of individual involvement in combating all environmental pollutants determines the ultimate success of the programs. A man who curses the motorbikes in his neighborhood but will not replace his own car's worn-out muffler is a hypocrite. The businessman who prays in church for peace on earth and sends a fleet of trucks into the city streets to stir up dust and broadcast excessive noise is no better than the fool who blasts his car horn at the slightest provocation. The contractor who receives an

award for developing an attractive addition to the city is decep-
tive if during construction dozens of people have been forced to
move from their homes or have been inconvenienced by the stir
and noise. Airlines that promote their "friendly skies" as they
make unfriendly passes at residents of communities below are
guilty of gross misconduct.

While it is self-satisfying to vent our anger by citing such
examples, accusation does precious little toward getting the job
of noise control done. In the final analysis we control our own
environment largely by our own behavior and movement in that
environment; hence we can, and must, act positively to quiet our
own little corner of the world. Individual action multiplied
many times over constitutes highly influential mass action.

As an example, one miniskirted lady in a music hall goes
unnoticed (acoustically); yet, according to Dr. Vern Knudsen, a
concert hall full of miniskirted women causes a dramatic alteration in the acoustics of the room. In fact, the distinguished
designer of more than 500 auditoriums, including the Hollywood Bowl, has indicated that the increase in exposed skin
surfaces and commensurate reduction in absorbent clothing
would "disturb the balance of sound designed into an au-
ditorium." Thus if each woman acting individually would wear
more skin-covering clothing the acoustical balance would return. Parenthetically, in personal correspondence Dr. Knudsen
has stated emphatically that he does not want these statements
to be interpreted as an expression of dislike for the abbreviated
body coverings. "Quite the contrary," he says.

Most people are aware that Noah Webster compiled
America's first dictionary, but not so many know that he did it
with nine children running about the house. In order to concentrate Webster designed a "quiet room" in his second-story study
by constructing a wall one foot thick with cork lining. Result—a
dictionary. One man, the governor of Georgia, silenced
emergency vehicle sirens in Atlanta. After having been narrowly missed by a racing police car en route from the Atlanta
airport, a taxi driver angrily related that because a loud siren had
awakened Governor Maddox one night, he had issued, the next

day, an executive order to stop the use of sirens in the capital city. Of course, not all persons are in a position to issue executive orders to silence undesirable sound sources; so most people must develop their own quiet places much as did Noah Webster. The task is not necessarily so complex and expensive as one might think.

Naturally, for large projects a competent sound engineer or one of those rare architects who has some knowledge of acoustics will be of great assistance. On the smaller jobs, however, one's own imagination and ingenuity are the primary tools. Near miracles can be wrought by the appropriate and imaginative use of glass wool (home insulation), fiberboard, acoustic tile, sound-absorbent partitions, draperies, and similar materials that are both readily accessible and relatively inexpensive.

A slick-cover magazine has suggested some ways to reduce noise in one's surroundings by not making it.

1. Use plastic garbage cans.
2. Keep your electronic vibes—from radio, TV, stereo—within reason.
3. Check out decibel levels of appliances before you buy.
4. Train your dog not to bark indiscriminately.
5. Keep your hands off the car horn.
6. Don't shout.
7. Carpet your floors.
8. Walk—don't stomp.
9. When rearranging furniture, lift if possible—don't drag or push a chair along the floor.
10. Slip out of your Guccis—don't drop them—bear in mind there's little more nerve-racking in this life than waiting for the other shoe to fall!

Indoor noise in apartments and houses can be reduced, first, by reducing sounds at their sources when possible, or seeking out quieter appliances to replace old ones; second, by using foam pads under noisy appliances, such as blenders; third, by abundantly using sound-absorbent materials that are only moderate in cost but may be well worth many times as much in making a more liveable environment. These suggestions are quite general. Some will require very little time and will cost nothing; others will require considerable time but very little financial outlay; still others will cost money, and a value judgment must be made on how dearly to pay in order to provide a quieter environment.

1. *The kitchen.*   Already crowned the noisiest room in the house, the kitchen can be stilled with a bit of thought and ingenuity. Several operational changes might prevent exposure to the louder noise sources if they cannot be made to operate more quietly. A dishwasher or clothes washer can be turned on after the kitchen chores are completed and the kitchen doors are closed, which also reduces the amount of sound broadcast into the rest of the house. An exhaust fan that at high speed causes a sizable addition to the sound level often does an acceptable job when run at slower speeds and consequently lower sound levels. Certain noisy jobs—vacuuming, for example—might be less bothersome when one is in a better frame of mind or fresh —say, early in the morning after a good night's rest.

Replacement appliances should be assessed for their quietness. Many manufacturers are seeing the market value of "whisper quiet" devices, but a buyer should be braced for slightly greater cost since more expensive craftsmanship or additional materials often are required to make an appliance operate with less noise. It is wise to determine why a quieter device costs more. An engineer related that a manufacturer of construction machinery was adding on huge amounts to the price just because the unit was considerably quieter; that is, price was based on buyer interest, not cost-plus-profit. Be sure that changes in pricing of quieter units are because additional work has been done. Be sure that the appliance is demonstrated to be more quiet. Ask for specifications and noise measurements.

Finally, some form of ear protectors could be used during noisier activities. Although many persons not jarred by the sounds of kitchen activities consider such a suggestion worthless, one need not suffer from nervous exhaustion that can be laid to certain noises. Adequate earplugs now on the market are both inexpensive and effective and are easily inserted and removed. Many department stores carry earplugs in the notions, housewares, or sporting goods department. If noise is a bothersome part of household activities and some of the noise sources cannot be silenced, earplugs offer a type of solution.

Most mechanical devices in need of maintenance become noisier, so routine care of home appliances can reduce the sound levels they create. If the refrigerator fan seems noisier the problem may be a dirty intake or accumulated grit on the fan blades. The exhaust fan also may be in need of cleaning. Screws and bolts that hold appliances together or mount them to the wall need periodic tightening. Vibrations in the operating unit cause the attachments to loosen, allowing for additional clatter.

Noise should be considered in appliance installation. A dishwasher mounted to the cabinet system should be sound isolated by placing absorbent mats wherever the appliance will come into contact with cabinets, work surfaces, or the floor. Be sure that the gasket on the front door is in good condition after the washer has been used for some time. A worn gasket permits both water and sound leakage. Garbage disposals should be installed with a rubber gasket between the disposal unit and the sink, not just a layer of putty around the junction—a method that keeps water from leaking under the sink but is a poor means of reducing vibration and noise.

First at the time of delivery and installation, then at periodic intervals, at least once a year, each appliance should be checked to be sure it rests squarely on the floor. Wobbles add to the noise, especially if the appliance is touching another part of the kitchen assembly. Most large appliances have adjustable legs to assure secure placement, but internal vibration of the unit can alter the setting of the legs over time.

The kitchen poses some problems in sound treatment. The ceiling can be covered with acoustic tile, but vapors that arise from the stove and sink eventually will deposit on the surface of the tile a greasy coating that tends to stain the tile as well as render it less effective in absorbing sound. Thus it is important to use a washable tile, which might also be used on the back surfaces of work counters to reduce the amount of sound reverberated from the hard surface of the wall into the kitchen. Outdoor or the spot- and stain-resistant carpet is a good choice for the floor. A recent study of school floor surfaces indicated that cork flooring material came very close to nylon carpeting in sound absorbence; so it might also be considered for the kitchen.

Sound and vibration isolation in the kitchen can be accomplished by abundant use of pads and mats. A thick rubber foam mat under the blender and mixer will reduce the noise level about 6 dB. Mats and pads on the work surfaces do away with the clang and clatter of pots and pans; cork tile on the surfaces and backs of cupboards reduce dish racket. Cupboard doors with magnetic latches usually require less push to close, thereby reducing the need for an irritating bang to close the door.

2. *Living rooms.*   This discussion includes all of the family living areas, where perhaps the greatest variety of sounds in the house may be found. Sounds of play, sounds of entertainment, and sounds of conversation consistently blend into an array of sound that for the most part is entirely pleasant but occasionally is simply noise—unwanted sound. Relief, however, lies in several possibilities for acoustic treatment of family rooms.

A major source for family conflict is the use of entertainment equipment, specifically radios, televisions, phonographs, and musical instruments. Headsets (earphones) sometimes may be an adequate solution to the disturbance but, as noted in Chapter 3, it is very unwise to lean too heavily on headsets as a means of reducing the overall volume in a room. Mom and Dad may be able to watch their television shows in a much less noisy sound environment, but then they cannot know whether Junior is blowing his ears along with his mind with the big sound. Considerate use of headsets can lend periodic grace to potentially unhappy situations. When one family member is interested in using a form of entertainment that is of no interest to the other members, a headphone may be the answer, but we cannot emphasize too strongly that the use of such devices is not without danger if the volume is high.

The best solution to family noise is the acoustic treatment of rooms. Often the expense involved can be written off as interior decorating as well as sound reduction. Acoustic tile on the ceilings, drapes along at least one wall, carpet on the floor, and well-upholstered furniture not only enhance the appearance of the rooms but sound-treat them as well. Remember that soft, porous materials absorb sound best; so the more of these materials in a room, the better the sound absorption. Just as a sponge soaks up water, so soft materials soak up sound. Anything can be overdone however. Too much sound-absorbing material will give the room a heavy look and make it acoustically dead—a most undesirable quality for a room.

Lower-floor recreation areas present a particular problem as the noise that originates there finds its way upstairs by a very direct route—the ceiling. A good baffle to sound transmission is thick glass wool between the rafters of the ceiling and gypsum board on the rafters, topped with a final layer of decorative acoustic tile. This operation is somewhat expensive if done as a remodeling job, but if finishing a basement is part of the plan the double sound insulation (glass wool and gypsum board) is a good investment.

Because basements normally are constructed of solid-surface foundation materials, such as cinder blocks or poured concrete, they tend to be quite reverberant. Acoustic tile on the ceiling is a good start, but alone the tile cannot help much in cutting down the excessive live quality of the room. Indoor-outdoor carpet or soft resilient floor covering is helpful. Attractive, acoustically pleasing, and inexpensive wall coverings include colored burlap and carpeting, which can be low in cost because wear is not a factor.

3. *Bathrooms.*   Sound treatment of bathrooms might at first glance appear to border on the impossible. The necessary hard-surface walls and ceiling pose a severe problem to the homespun acoustician's ingenuity. However, several steps can be taken to reduce the sounds that come into and emanate from the bathroom.

A layer of special carpeting on the floor is a good beginning.

It must be of a type that can withstand repeated exposure to moisture, the thicker the better. Not only does it feel good between the toes on a cold morning but it is also helpful in damping the sound in the tiny room. Few places show the acoustical impact of shoddy workmanship as does the bathroom. Cracks in the junctions of walls, gaping holes through which pipes have been run, and heating duct openings all make bathroom walls acoustically transparent. Soft insulation material, such as glass wool, pressed into pipe holes and packed around pipes often produces amazing results. If the medicine chest is in a wall that adjoins another room, one can easily remove it, pack insulation around the opening in the wall, and replace the unit.

Attention should be given particularly to the bathroom door. Privacy can be better assured with a thick, well-situated door that provides a good acoustic seal. The doors in many houses have cracks under the bottom surface as much as a half to one inch in length.

4. *Bedrooms.* Many of the steps suggested for other rooms hold for the bedroom as well. Drapes, carpets, and thick furniture will reduce the sound generated in the room but will be of little consequence in cutting down the sound that enters the bedroom from other portions of the house. Closets full of clothing provide a reasonably good sound buffer, but they often lose some if the closet doors are louvered. Solid closet doors are much better sound barriers. If a new house is being designed the architect can be asked to give special consideration to bedroom walls. A fibrous blanket inserted into the wall during construction makes a significant difference in the amount of sound absorbed by the wall and hence cuts down the transmission of sound through the wall. If sound transmission into the bedroom is a serious problem, consideration might be given to adding another layer of wallboard to increase the absorptive quality of the wall.

5. *Other considerations in the home.* Volumes could be written about the various aspects of noise control in the home, but such detailed treatment is not appropriate here. Several additional factors deserve mention, however.

Poorly fitted and/or thin doors are best replaced by heavy,

well-located ones. The acoustic difference often is remarkable. Weather stripping around the periphery of doors ensures a good seal. In some rooms it may be desirable to use an adjustable threshold gasket to reduce the possibility of sound transmission under the door.

Stairs can be a source of recurring noise as they are used —especially by children. Carpeting runners are a good solution, as is safe use of the stairs, which not only reduces the likelihood of a bad fall but also is considerably quieter.

Noises from the pipes usually are a sign of the need for home maintenance. Suspension of the pipes may have become somewhat feeble over time, but additional suspending brackets are easily added where the pipes are exposed. Often, plumbing noises are directly related to worn faucet washers or seats, which usually can be replaced by the home handyman. Excessively loud rushing sounds when the water is turned on can sometimes be attributed to the pressure reduction valve, which occasionally needs replacement.

Doorbells and light switches often are acoustically unattractive. They can be replaced with relative ease by quieter or pleasanter-sounding units.

Most telephone bells can be adjusted by means of a volume control on the bottom of the telephone. If the bell is still unpleasant the telephone company may have an acceptable replacement bell.

Central-heating and air-conditioning ductwork is enclosed quite early in the finish stages of house construction; so it is difficult to be sure the sections are properly mounted and made vibration-free. If rattles remain in the system sound-absorbing material sometimes can be wedged along the ducts to cut down the problem. Acoustic treatment of the interior of the area that houses the central unit will stop a good portion of the noise radiated to adjacent rooms.

Noise from window air conditioners may be a result of inadequate care to shock-mounting during installation or a sign of maintenance need. Window units can cause a sounding board effect if good pads or gaskets do not separate the body of the air conditioner from the windowsill. If the filter is excessively dirty, the fan is forced to labor and can generate more noise. Attention to cleaning and lubricating the parts will pay dividends in a more quietly running unit.

Outside noises can be combated by adding weather stripping to the windows and keeping them closed to the extent that climate control heating and cooling units permit.

Outside barriers, such as brick walls, hedgerows, or tree lines, usually are inadequate. Control of noise from the source is by far the most desirable means.

COMMUNITY ACTION

Individual initiative can be translated into community action if the idea has merit and the leader has sufficient strength. One idea that grew into a sizable project came from James Ogul, a member of the staff of the Museum of Atomic Energy in Oak Ridge, Tennessee, whose hobby was dabbling in electronics. During his evening hours he designed and constructed devices for sampling water purity, air quality, radiation, and sound. Of particular importance here is his noise meter, which could not be regarded as a precision measuring device but was accurate enough for such measures as traffic and other environmental noises. Under a grant from the National Science Foundation, the device, organized in kit form to be constructed by high school students, was supplied and several workshops were held. The workshops, in which students built and then learned to use the meters, provided a shakedown test for the kit so that the problems of kit construction could be ironed out before going into large-scale distribution.

After the trial run, kits were sent to a large number of high schools. When the instruments were constructed, the students took traffic noise measurements and sent the results to Mr. Ogul for compilation. (The figures are not yet available, but they should give an interesting cross-section of the traffic noise levels in a number of cities.) Now more than 20 colleges are evaluating the kit project as a teaching aid.

The project accomplished several things: (1) many students learned the construction ramifications of sound measuring devices; (2) they learned ways to measure sound; and (3) by completing the noise measures they gained insights into the breadth of the traffic noise problem.

As the project continues, one man's idea will not only acquaint a large number of people with noise measurement techniques but also will provide a bank of data unlike any other related to traffic noise.

THE RACKET SQUAD

Civic clubs have a stake in the environmental quality of their city; so let us suggest a project in which organizations form a type of vigilante group to combat the encroachment of community noise. Club projects taken on simply because of a need for something to do are not necessarily well motivated and so may fail. Therefore, we have outlined some general considerations before making specific suggestions on the organization of a community racket squad.

1. Learn about the problem.
   a. Is it a problem?
   b. What is the scope of the problem?
   c. What is currently being done about the problem?
   d. Where are the needs?
2. Decide on the club's willingness to take on the project.
   a. Set up priorities.
   b. Make a commitment.
3. Take action.
   a. Organize well.
   b. Act on only one circumscribed area of the problem.
   c. Set realistic goals.
   d. Follow through.
4. Evaluate the program.

Any project so conducted can be successful. A community racket squad composed of club members can operate sound level meters at various locations around the community to note particularly intense sound sources, and then send diplomatic letters to persons responsible for the noisemakers. The letter would note that interest in community welfare necessitated the racket squad's formation, and it would ask addressees to summon their civic pride and do something about the situation. Noisy trucks could be pointed out as several tons of bad advertisement rumbling along the city streets. Factory noise could be referred to as around-the-clock bad-neighbor policy. Construction noise could be described as public relations in reverse.

Follow-up can be easily augmented with mass media assistance. Radio, television, and newspaper coverage of racket squad activities will give credence to the group. Special recognition can be given to individuals and industries that take steps to correct the noise problem pointed out to them. Such positive reinforcement is better than the negative method of citing those who ignore the suggestions. A local civic organization each month presented the CLAW award (CLean Air and Water) to the industry deemed to make the greatest contribution to the pollution problem. Because it found the positive approach much better, the club shelved the CLAW award and continued to recognize industries that were making a concerted effort to rectify their problems.

Imaginative project chairmen can infinitely vary the racket squad's work, but the idea is worthy of consideration. It will bring noise problems into public focus and hopefully will provide the motivation to solve noise problems by means of individual action.

A line in a popular Sunday school chorus urges: "Brighten the corner where you are. . . . " In light of the emphasis here on individual action to correct noise problems, it might be well to recommend to concerned citizens: "Quiet the corner where you are. . . . "

·12·

THE SHAPE OF THINGS TO COME

The future is purchased by the present.
Samuel Johnson

It has been said that shallow men speak of the past, wise men of the present, and fools of the future. That warning notwithstanding, let us attempt to look into the future.

In an old tale a mischievous boy in order to fool the village oracle planned to approach the wise man carrying a tiny bird, and ask if the bird was alive or dead. If the elder said the bird was alive, the boy planned to crush the little creature and make the old man the fool. If the oracle responded that the bird was dead, the boy planned to release the bird, assured that he had the old gentleman either way the contact was made. Wisely, the elder looked into the eyes of the lad and responded to his question: "Whether the bird is alive or dead is entirely up to you." So it is with the future of noise control. Individual action is the key, and any future trends or possible developments must begin largely with the willingness of many individuals to take the initiative.

As noted earlier, noise has been a part of man's life for many centuries and has been increasing as a function of growing technology and more persons who use the products of that technology. Noise will not just go away if ignored; concentrated efforts must be directed toward its control, abatement, and eventual rollback.

291

The time schedule is not an advantageous one. Noise has a commanding lead over abatement, and the gap seems to be widening. Discouraging words come easily, for myriad problems must be overcome in clearing up the environment and reducing the high sound levels. It can be done, however. Further, *it will be done!*

The narrator of a documentary on noise concluded with this statement about the need for adequate noise control in the future.

> Compared to America's medical, housing, and pollution crises, noise can be easily solved. Noise needn't be the price of progress. Any nation that can quiet its nuclear submarines and aircraft can harness its technology to perfect quieter autos and trucks and factories at home. We aim to get the noise-reduction program started right here and now. With a farewell moment of silence for us all to rest our ears and nerves while the decibels descend to zero on our battered noise meter.

The silent conclusion to the program rested ears across the nation and perhaps encouraged a desire for more such moments.

We have become so accustomed to the noise in our world that adjusting to a quiet time may be difficult. The quiet time experience during camping outings, retreats, and at other times is so new to some people that it is actually frightening—at least, until one begins to adapt to the strange new sensations of silence.

Silence is a rare commodity in the civilized world. Even periods of silence in worship services are unattainable because the hush that falls over the congregation precipitates an epidemic of coughs, throat-clearings, and squeaks in pews caused by fidgety people. Hopefully we have not totally lost our ability to seek out and enjoy peace and quiet, but some reorientation must be undertaken.

Let us reconsider, in relation to the future, the major themes emphasized throughout this book.

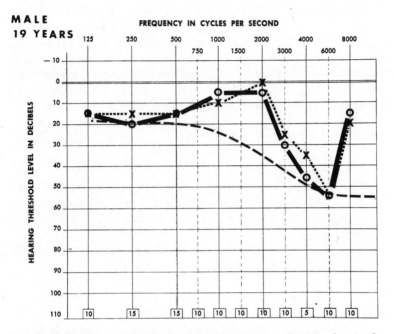

12.1   Audiogram representing the hearing condition of a rock musician.

EAR DAMAGE

That considerable numbers of young persons seemingly have undergone some degree of hearing acuity alteration has been documented. Whether this condition is a result of noise in the environment must still be proven. The future for these young persons hinges on the extent to which they escape additional insult to their precious and irreplaceable hearing sense.

The audiogram in Figure 12.1 represents the hearing condition of a 19-year-old male who had been a rock musician for several years. The maximum hearing impairment was found to be 55 dB for the 6,000 Hz test tone—a sizable reduction in hearing for the high-frequency range (right side of the chart). If his hearing were at the 55 dB level for all frequencies in his hearing range, communication would be virtually impossible without the use of a hearing aid, but, fortunately, his hearing loss was restricted largely to the high test frequencies. In relation to his initial complaint about misinterpreting orders in his job at the takeout counter of a drive-in restaurant, a rather large decrease in his ability to repeat test words was noted. The speech discrimination score of 88 percent does not represent terribly bad hearing, but a person with normal hearing should score 100 percent rather than 96 or 88 percent.

To give a sense of perspective to the audiogram the dashed lines represent the average hearing level of persons between ages 60 and 69. In effect, this man is entering his occupational life with retirement-age ears—unfortunately not an isolated situation. The 1969 college student survey at the University of Tennessee revealed that 14 percent of the men between 16 and 21 had hearing similar to that of the man whose audiogram is shown here. That represents a prevalence figure of one man in seven with ears more than three decades older than the chronological age.

Evidence that hearing ability among the young is being reduced many years before one would expect certainly causes concern and leads to the fearful statement that the current population of young persons will encounter much more serious middle-year hearing problems than those of present 50- to 60-year-olds. Although high-level noise cannot be singled out as the only factor in this apparent auditory epidemic, it must be considered a potential contributor to the sizable amount of auditory deficit in persons who only a few years ago comprised the subjects for current audiometric norms.

Dr. H. Schmidt, head of the sound technology division of a large German corporation, told the Royal Society of Health in Edinburgh, Scotland: "Technology can be civilized only if people are prepared to pay the proper price. Failing this, people will pay for technical progress with their health and there will be one day more people wearing hearing aids than there are today wearing spectacles."

Knowing that hearing aids in no way restore normal,

natural hearing causes one to shudder at Dr. Schmidt's speculation. An old midwest farmer who had been working in his fields all day in the summer heat returned to the house so hot and dehydrated that he was sick. He didn't want to eat; he didn't want to read; he just wanted to soak in the tub and get some sleep. Apparently, though, he was too tired to go to sleep, for when the clock struck 10 he was still awake, as he was an hour later when it struck 11. He was still awake when the timepiece on the mantle rang out 12 times, but an hour later when he heard the clock strike 13 he sat up in bed, startled, and shook his wife, saying, "Ma, Ma, wake up!! It's later than it's ever been!"

For many young people whose hearing has already decreased it is "later than it's ever been." The challenge to future technologists and citizens is to ensure that the increasing spiral of noise does not endanger even more young adults.

FUTURE TECHNOLOGY

The noise-control market was $200 million in 1969 and has been projected to be around $3 billion in 1980. Along with this economic expansion will come technologic developments that will surpass the materials and methods noted in Chapter 11.

Houses now can be more effectively insulated against the encroachment of outside noises, but the alterations are extensive and expensive. Future houses probably will have built-in acoustic controls and greater attention will be paid to the amount of sound present in each room.

Innovative approaches to noise control will hush once noisy devices to a whisper. Human ingenuity and genius for overcoming challenges has been proven many times over. Although noise has been late in receiving attention, now that many persons are making concentrated efforts toward its reduction an astounding number of noise abatement and control breakthroughs probably will occur in the next decade.

POLITICAL FACTORS

Populations in most industrialized nations are beginning to oppose noise-producing equipment and gadgetry. People are becoming less tolerant of technologic developments predicted to raise the overall noise level and, on several political fronts, are demanding that the continuing upward spiral of noise levels be not only stopped but also rolled back. A classic example is the controversy over the supersonic transport (SST), discussed in detail in Chapter 8. In speaking against the SST continuation funds, Senator Proxmire (Wisconsin) stated:

> ... the SST is the clearest example of private power and capital versus the public interest that I have seen in my 13 years in the U.S. Senate. No one wants or needs the SST except big labor, big industry, and big politics. The public interest is the decided underdog. Whether it can prevail against such overwhelming odds remains to be seen.

Shortly after Senator Proxmire made that statement the SST project was abandoned, along with the jobs of several thousand aerospace workers. Perhaps a major reason for such a response from federally elected representatives was the large number of letters and telegrams from constituents who insisted on stoppage of a project that might produce another noisy device.

Political indicators of environmental noise can be seen in the increasing interest of government regulating agencies in curbing the noise various objects emit. In December 1970, the Federal Trade Commission listed noisy toys in a group of playthings that should be seriously reviewed prior to their widespread manufacture and distribution.

The Walsh-Healy Revision of 1969, and later the Williams-Steiger Occupational Safety and Health Act of 1971, defined the allowable noise exposure for employees in nearly every type of occupational pursuit. Work to combat noise has now become politically favorable.

Few other areas of public concern have the overwhelming political support that antinoise interests presently enjoy. Certain political indicators—witness the SST rejection and other similar reversals in national policy—signal a good future for environmental noise control. These indications are impossible to quantify and are subject to revision by succeeding administrations, but they are quite evident in government at all levels.

ECONOMIC FACTORS

The estimate, offered earlier, that as a direct result of noise American industry loses as much as $4 billion annually through noise-related accidents, turnover, quality control problems, and absenteeism can hardly be overlooked. In addition, other economic indicators might be suggested.

A few years ago a vacuum cleaner marketed as a quiet appliance failed to receive consumer acceptance. Housewives couldn't believe that it was sweeping effectively if it made so little noise. At about the same time a typewriter that had a special roller designed to absorb the clatter of keys against paper also was rejected. Secretaries were afraid that without the tell-tale clangor of the typing machines they could be accused of not working efficiently. Thus noise apparently is equated with power and effectiveness. A motorcyclist chooses to strip his machine of the muffler in order to vicariously sense the motor's power through his hearing sense. The hot rodder does the same. Musicians have begun to use amplification systems that give a heretofore unrealized acoustic power output.

In the past the economic cutting edge has been in the direction of sound-producing equipment, with little consumer interest in paying slightly more to purchase a product with reduced noise emission. Because of political action in the late 1960s and early 1970s this trend may be reversed so that production and marketing of noisy items will be more expensive because of taxes or penalties against products that do not meet noise specifications.

TRAFFIC NOISE

Motor vehicle noise will be significantly reduced only when something quieter than the internal combustion engine is developed. Exhaust noise is the major problem, and alternate solutions presently are being worked out. One possibility for quieter engines appears in Figure 8.2. This listing of current automobiles includes the Mazda, a small car found to be second in quietness only to a plush, luxury automobile. The heart of the Mazda's power system is the Wankel rotary engine, an old designing concept being resurrected and proposed for future cars. If the emission factors, durability, and cost features stand up, the Wankel engine may provide significant relief from noisy automobile exhaust noise.

Another possible trend might be reduction of the automobile population—a proposal that has significant economic ramifications. In their future plans for downtown areas many cities are including walking streets where the passage of vehicles is forbidden or severely restricted in order to provide more alluring shopping centers apart from the maddening roar of traffic noise. If this trend becomes significant the need for private passenger cars will diminish.

A related future development would be more desirable and efficient forms of rapid transit. City planners presently are considering numerous proposals.

A change in delivery procedures will reduce the number of noisy trucks and delivery vehicles. One plan calls for the installation of underground tubes to carry capsules of goods by air or fluid pressure, much like the old money-changing tubes once prominent in large department stores. At Disneyworld near Orlando, Florida, all deliveries to the various park areas are made via underground passageways. This installation might serve as a model for larger programs of a similar nature in crowded cities.

SELF-REGULATION

Citation of some exemplary positive action should obviate an anti-industry interpretation of this book. These actions do not constitute all of the known examples but will indicate that many branches of the industrial complex are working diligently to reduce noise problems.

For the most part these forms of action call for a basic reordering of special interest group priorities. There is a need to move away from power expression and hunger to the milder style reflected in quieter products. Not many industries have spontaneously undertaken noise control projects but, rather, have determined that the least desirable future conditions would be obtained if no concerted effort were made in the direction of product noise control.

1. *Motorcycles.*   In 1971 the Motorcycle Industry Council (M.I.C.), the organization that represents manufacturers, importers, and distributors of cycles, agreed to meet a 92 dBA standard by January 1, 1972. Further, the council decided that the muffling system was to be made an integral portion of the exhaust system. In effect, the muffler would be tuned to the engine so that alteration of the muffler would result in loss of power. New motorcycles carry the warning that tampering with the exhaust system—say, gutting the muffler—will result in automatic cancellation of the warranty.

For one industry group to require that such sweeping conditions be brought into effect within a period of less than a year is both remarkable and commendable, but even more satisfying is that many of the new motorcycles not only meet M.I.C. standards but also exceed them. One 1972 model was found to be 25 dB quieter than its 1971 predecessor.

As the motorcycle industry moves toward continuing noise control the M.I.C. slogan, "Less sound—more ground," may be realized. Where landowners had been restricting the use of their properties because of motorbike noise, areas soon may be opened as the raucous racket continues to diminish.

2. *Construction noise.*   One manufacturer has developed a program for quieting air compressors, jackhammers, drilling rigs, and similar devices, partly out of a need to meet stringent New York City construction codes. These developments could be added to some pieces of equipment but for some types of gear are available only on new units. One resident near Central Park said that construction firms still are resisting inclusion of the quieter equipment on quotes and specifications for construction sites though the equipment manufacturer has offered to provide the equipment on a cost-rental basis to the construction companies. Apparently a good deal of reeducation among construction personnel is necessary.

3. *Plant siting.*   Before beginning work on a quarry site a local extraction company sought out advice and opinions on the seismographic, dust, water, traffic, and noise concomitants of the proposed site. Each consultant's specifications were incorporated into the proposed use of the property so that a minimal

impact on the environment will be experienced in the location of the quarry.

This forward-looking action is to be commended, and hopefully other forms of industry will follow the lead. Placement of a manufacturing plant or other portion of the industrial complex deserves full consideration, including noise estimates. In past times zoning ordinances and city codes have been circumvented in order to locate at certain sites, but increasing citizen displeasure should forewarn industry to consider the impact of their proposed sites.

4. *The automobile.*   Details of the automotive industry's success in reducing the interior noise of their product are contained in Chapter 11. More can and will be done to reduce the amount of noise in the environment, however.

5. *Aircraft noise.*   Aircraft design engineers have been inclined to throw up their hands when the subject of quieting jet planes is broached. Their response generally is to ask people to wait on the development of a new generation of jet engines designed for noise control from the ground up. To be sure, future engines will be more quiet, or no market for them may exist.

FINALE

Noise is a common problem whose impact cuts across nearly every facet of human existence. The complexity of the problem defies circumscription into a small number of universal indicators, at least, as we now know noise and its effects.

Human correlates of noise response come largely after the facts. Because of a time delay the physiological effect may accumulate over years and later result in one or more physical problems. Neither does the loss of hearing occur immediately on exposure to high-level sound but becomes conspicuous as the bits of structural damage accumulate to cause a severe communication problem in later life.

Probably never will man's environment be free of annoying sounds. The best that can be hoped for is a reduction of noise to universally tolerable levels. It can be done; perhaps it will be done.

A favorite saying observes: "All the flowers, for all the tomorrows, are in the seeds of today." In like manner, certainly the steps taken in the next few years will establish the type of life future generations will encounter. With adequate and appropriate action in the next decade perhaps the tomorrows of countless human beings will be extended. Thus man is challenged to overcome the dehumanizing and degrading influences of his advancing technology so that the flowers of tomorrow can bloom freely.

Appendix ·I·

The following scripts, prepared for a local radio station as spot announcements in community service time slots, may be used in other communities as part of an ongoing public education program on noise. Reading time for each comment is between 40 and 50 seconds.

CAR STEREO EARPHONES

Perhaps you have seen persons driving their cars and listening to music with earphones on quite obviously enjoying their music as they wheel along the streets of the town. The first time I noticed this, it was truly a shock, for I began to determine just what was going on in that driving situation. By using headphones, drivers are making themselves a distinct safety hazard. In effect, they become functionally deaf, but without the keen dependence on the visual sense of the truly deaf person. Further, the audible signal coming from the earphones distracts one from using his other valuable senses, especially vision and touch. This serves to reduce the likelihood that such a driver will respond with quick and appropriate action in case of a crisis. Stereo headsets on automobile drivers are totally unwarranted.

AUDITORY AWARENESS

The other day, I watched a police car, its siren blaring, follow a car over a mile on a narrow street before the driver of the car was aware of the presence of the patrolmen so that he could pull over and allow the emergency vehicle to pass. He just had not heard the siren! This is one of the unfortunate side effects of the move by the automobile manufacturers to provide us with vehicles that protect from the bothersome road noises. Unfortunately, we are also shielded from warning signals such as sirens, horns, and train whistles. Persons in a car traveling at moderate speed with the radio playing and the heater or air conditioner operating have virtually no chance of hearing an audible warning signal. This is reason for us to be especially alert visually in our automobiles—for the warning signals can scarcely be heard.

STEREO EARPHONES

The boom in hi-fi, stereo, and tape player sales has brought with it a new popular item—stereo earphones. Parents, bedraggled by the booming sounds of rock music, have welcomed the phones on the heads of their teen-agers in order to maintain a quieter household. But the headsets pose a severe danger to the ears of users if they are coupled to an amplifier set for high levels. We measured the sound of music coming through earphones and discovered the sets were able to drive the ear with sound levels exeeding 140 decibels. That is equal to the sound level 10 feet behind a jetliner at full takeoff velocity. The sound levels in stereo headsets must also be monitored in order to prevent unnecessary and irreversible damage to the ears.

ROCK MUSIC

Even with repeated warnings about the damaging effect loud rock music has on the ears, there has been no reduction in the sound levels at dances and rock concerts. Jack Casidy, bass player for Jefferson Airplane, has stated, "Our eternal goal in life is to get louder." And they are doing just that! Unfortunately, the undesired side effect is irreversible ear damage—with a terrible price to be extracted—not now, but in later life when the accumulated destruction within the ear becomes sufficient to restrict one's communication ability. It makes good sense to conserve and protect the precious hearing sense by avoiding extremely loud sound both at work and at play.

CONSUMER APPEAL

The test of the effectiveness of consumer action lies in the ultimate selection buyers make in their purchases. Much has been said about the noise generated by appliances and other popular consumer goods—including the automobile. Soon the consumer will have an opportunity to select a number of items that have been rated according to their noise output. Hopefully the quieter devices coming into the stores will meet with better success than did early attempts to manufacture quiet products, such as the quiet vacuum cleaner that was a marketplace disaster, or the quiet typewriter that was rejected by secretaries because people equated power and effectiveness with sound output. Household sound levels have been on the increase; thus buyers will be wise to seek the products developed to be effective—but quiet.

PHYSIOLOGICAL EFFECTS

Noise is a stressor. Prolonged exposure to sounds may damage the ears—but other effects can also be noted. We have conducted some experiments using noise as a stressing agent. Some of the results have been quite revealing in that our laboratory animals that receive noise stimulation over prolonged periods of time develop stress ulcers in the digestive system and manifest a large number of other physical symptoms that are dangerous to the health of the animals. Research has given some additional indications that the body takes a severe beating in the presence of sustained noise. Dr. Rosen of New York states: "You may be able to ignore noise, but your body will never forgive you."

EARS NEED REST

Recent surveys of high school and college-age young people have shown an alarming trend toward early hearing loss. The fact that we can observe some loss of hearing sensitivity in youth is a cause for concern. Environmental noise levels have never been higher than they are today for the majority of our population, thus, noticeable hearing impairment in young persons must be a natural by-product. However, the noise in our community is not sufficiently intense to cause ear damage, with the exception of certain recreational or occupational areas. Perhaps the problem stems from the fact that young ears do not get much opportunity to rest any longer. Years ago one could seek out a quiet place and rest—presently such areas are hardly available, and our ears may be showing signs of fatigue as a result.

OSHA

In 1971 the Occupational Safety and Health Act was passed. The bill required that employers obtain accurate sound measurements to determine if their place of business is safe for the workers. Secondly, the abatement of problem areas is required. In the case of noise the employer is required to embark on an effective hearing conservation program if the work environment is excessively noisy. These are the requirements for the employers—but there are also requirements for the employees. They must cooperate by using the safety devices provided for them. If you are working in a noisy environment, explore the advantages the new act offers you for protection.

FUTURE IMPLICATIONS

I received a letter from a girl in California in which she asked what the world would be like in 30 years if environmental noise levels continue to rise. Of course, our life would be greatly affected if such would be the case. In fact, within the next decade the environmental noises in most large cities will reach dangerously high levels. It seems, however, that public awareness of the noise problem, federal controls on noise-producing devices, and the developing technology of noise abatement will allow us to anticipate that the sound in our environment 30 years from now will be significantly less than we now experience. The achievement of this goal, however, will require that we as consumers and users of noisy products take into account the need for us, individually, to reduce the sound we are creating.

EAR PROTECTIVE DEVICES

The question is often asked, "What type of earplugs should I use?" A second question naturally follows: "Where can I get them?" Ear protective devices have developed through the use of modern technology and the understanding of acoustic principles so that nearly every person can be protected from ear damage by consistent use of earplugs or earmuffs. If the noise levels to which one is exposed are extremely high, acoustic earmuffs are generally recommended. In moderately noisy conditions, good earplugs will suffice. Swimmers' plugs and cotton are ineffective in protecting one from loud sounds. Many sporting goods stores and safety equipment distributors have good ear protectors in stock, and they are a good source for advice on the best type of ear protection for you.

INDUSTRIAL NOISE

Former member of the U.S. Supreme Court and prosecutor in the Teapot Dome scandals Owen J. Roberts has said: "The constitution does not secure to anyone liberty to conduct his business in such fashion as to inflict injury upon the public at large, or upon any substantial group of the people." Justice Roberts's comment well describes the underlying principles of the recent Occupational Safety and Health Act. This massive system of regulations includes the control of noise in industry. Under the provisions of the act, workers in an industrial setting are not to be excessively exposed to noise. There are indications that these regulations are improving the work environment and will continue to do so.

CONTROL OF MOTORCYCLE NOISE

Few noise sources cause the severe criticism brought about by the roar and pop of poorly muffled motorcycles. There are some indications that this unfavorable community noise is coming under control. The enactment of vehicle noise laws includes regulations which must be met by individual cycles. More important, however, is the fact that the Motorcycle Industry Council—the national organization of manufacturers and distributors of these vehicles—has embarked upon an active program of cycle noise control. The mufflers and exhaust systems are being made an integral part of the motor. Tags on the cycle warn against tampering with the muffler, lest the warranty be canceled. The slogan, "Less sound, more ground," is being used to encourage cyclists to enjoy their hobby or mode of transportation more quietly.

CONSTRUCTION NOISE

Historically, construction has hailed progress; therefore, the noise and inconvenience has been tolerated by persons whose life-style is radically altered in the wake of construction activities. This tolerance is reducing, however, and an increase in angry outcries has necessitated the development of quieter construction machinery. A new technology is evolving whereby jackhammers can be scarcely heard when outfitted with a sound-absorbing jacket. Large drills and heavy machinery are being designed to operate at significantly quieter levels. The noisy air compressors—so much a part of the picture of most construction sites—are also being redesigned with a resulting noise reduction of as much as 25 dB. These developments give the hope that construction sites of the future will be less noisy.

EPA ACTIVITIES

In 1971 the Environmental Protection Agency held a series of meetings around the country with invitations to all citizens to present a statement regarding the noise sources which they felt needed control. Naturally, a large number of such noise sources were cited. As a result of the hearings, the Office of Noise Abatement for the EPA is now undertaking to write noise specifications for a number of products. Such items as household appliances, power tools, utility equipment, heavy machinery and many other products will be assigned a maximum allowable noise output. All products built after the regulations go into effect must meet the specifications, or their sale will be prohibited. The end result of these actions will be less noise in the home and community.

PLANT SITING

A local company applied for permission to establish a quarry site in an area east of town. Prior to filing the petition, they wisely took account of all of the environmental problems which might have been caused by the establishment of the quarry. One of the considerations was noise. Baseline noise measures were made before the quarry was established in order to know if the sound of the plant operation would be bothersome to neighbors. This is an example of industry taking care that they do not disrupt new sites unnecessarily. There is little question that the environmental impact of this new quarry will be minimal because the industrialists made adequate provision in their plans to locate the facility. Hopefully, this signifies a trend in plant siting for the future of our community.

QUIETER CARS

Cars are getting quieter! With the use of undercoating, the development of improved suspension systems, thick carpeting, acoustic treatment of the top liner, insulation and padding of specially noisy areas, today's passenger vehicle is considerably less noisy to the occupants.

Recent sound measures taken by members of a class on noise at the University of Tennessee support this claim. Seven 1972-model cars were borrowed from local dealerships and driven at a speed of 60 miles per hour on an interstate. All seven of these vehicles proved quieter than the 1970 or 1971 models. Improvements from nearly 5 dB to as much as 10 dB. A 10 dB improvement means the sound intensity was reduced to one-eighth the original level. Hopefully, this trend will continue.

SOUND-TREATING HOMES

The time to sound-treat a home or office is during construction, not afterward. It is estimated that the cost of acoustic treatment of completed structures is 10 times greater than would have been the case if consideration had been given to sound treatment during the planning stages.

Contractors should find out about the most recent developments in sound absorbent materials from an acoustical materials distributor. With the greater emphasis on reducing undesired noise in buildings, a market has developed for acoustical building materials. Recent developments have included thermal acoustic blankets, spray-on materials, and compounds which reduce vibrations of objects. With the growth of acoustic control products, new buildings can be expected to provide an increasingly better sound environment for us.

NEW JETS

Recently, we attended a wedding and became very aware that the church was located in the flight pattern for an airport. Several times during the service, jet takeoff noise drowned out the ceremony. Experiences such as this are not uncommon to most of us. For this reason, there are multibillion-dollar lawsuits pending against most of the large commercial airports.

A new generation of jets has begun to make inroads into the noise problems faced by the airline industry. The giant Boeing 747 creates considerably less noise than the much smaller 727 during both takeoff and landing. The new Lockheed Tri-star and Douglas DC-10 also have engines which were developed to operate much more quietly. These planes will make less noise and thereby reduce one serious source of community noise.

INFRASOUND

In England, researchers have found that drivers can become "drunk" without touching alcoholic beverages. Low-frequency infrasound encountered while driving a vehicle can blur vision, affect the balance sense, slow reaction time, and interfere with following and tracking other vehicles. Scientists have attributed these factors to some of the otherwise unexplained highway accidents they investigated.

At NASA, they have studied how low-frequency sound can cause one to develop headaches, begin to gag, develop nausea, or become extremely fatigued. Not all persons react in this way to low-frequency sound, but if you seem to tire easily while driving, it might be a warning that you should avoid driving long distances without considerable attention to rest stops.

MAGIC SOUND DEVICES

A lady wrote to ask about ways community noise could be kept out of her house. She observed that her TV antenna was able to pick out all the signals from the broadcasting stations; thus she wondered if a special "antenna" could be placed on or around her house to do just the reverse—reject all unwanted outside noise interference.

It is not possible to construct some magical type of sound warden to screen out all undesirable noises. In fact, sound-isolating a home from community noise would necessitate en-casing the structure in a very forbidding and expensive enclosure.

The best way to avoid excessive community noise in the home is still to work toward reducing the sound generated by such devices as vehicles, power equipment, and planes. That will make our homes the way we want them to be—quieter.

Appendix ·II·

REFERENCE BOOKS

No single book can be expected to cover such a broad area as noise; so the serious student should consider reading additional sources of information. The following list is an annotated description of a few books generally considered to hold worthwhile information.

American Academy of Opthalmology and Otolaryngology. *Guide for the Conservation of Hearing in Noise.* 1970.
Probably the most universally used reference on damage-risk criteria—exposure experiences above which hearing is in jeopardy. The small booklet's value is great.

American Industrial Hygiene Association. *Industrial Noise Manual.* 1966.
Contains most of the rules and guidelines for conducting an effective hearing conservation program in industry. It is must reading for the industrial team charged with noise control in their place of business.

Baron, Robert Alex. *The Tyranny of Noise.* New York: St. Martin's Press, 1970.
An angry book written about a subject that has caused its author considerable distress. Written by a layman for laymen, it spells out one man's feeling about the gravity of the noise problem. Baron is founder of Citizens for a Quieter City in New York.

Beranek, Leo. *Noise Reduction.* New York: McGraw-Hill, 1960.

Not intended as casual reading but as authoritative reference material for the serious student of sound.

Berland, Theodore. *The Fight for Quiet*. Englewood Cliffs, N.J.: Prentice-Hall, 1970.

One of the best organized and researched general treatments of noise, oriented to the layman. Berland has prepared a useful academic reference book that is also an extremely well-written text for the interested reader.

Bragdon, Clifford R. *Noise Pollution–The Unquiet Crisis*. Philadelphia: University of Pennsylvania Press, 1971.

Two books in one, the first half devoted to a well-conceived, overall review of the breadth of environmental noise, the remainder a detailed study of community reaction to aircraft noise emanating from the Philadelphia Air Terminal. Some sophistication on the part of the reader is assumed; thus the book may not be a first reference source for many interested in noise.

Burns, William. *Noise and Man*. London: William Clowes & Sons Ltd., 1968.

Valuable, and recommended highly, to the more advanced reader. The book was written in order to provide detailed knowledge of human reaction to sound.

Chalupnik, J. D., ed. *Transportation Noises: A Symposium on Acceptability Criteria*. Seattle: University of Washington Press, 1970.

A not quite successful attempt to summarize the transportation noise problem. Much of the information is also in *Noise as a Public Health Hazard*, for many of the participants were the same. Nonetheless, it is valuable resource material for the person centrally concerned with traffic commotion and the resulting sounds.

Committee on Environmental Quality, Federal Council for Science and Technology. *Noise–Sound without Value*. Washington, D.C.: Government Printing Office, 1968.

From the committee charged with evaluating the status of the noise problem, assessing the level of research completed, and establishing areas wherein federal programs should provide research funds. The conclusion of the booklet gives an excellent picture of the role governmental agencies should play in studying and controlling the noise problem.

Environmental Protection Agency. Reports on hearings. 1971. Available from the Government Printing Office.

NTID300.1 — Noise from construction equipment and operations, building equipment, and home appliances

NTID300.2 — Noise from industrial plants

NTID300.3 — Community noise

NTID300.4 — Noise laws and regulations

NTID300.5 — Effects of noise on wildlife and other animals

NTID300.6 — An assessment of noise concern in other nations (two volumes)

NTID300.7 — Effects of noise on people

NTID300.8 — State and municipal nonoccupational noise programs

NTID300.9 — Noise programs of professional/industrial organizations, universities, and colleges

NTID300.10 — Summary of noise programs in the federal government

NTID300.11 — The social impact of noise

NTID300.12 — The effects of sonic boom and similar impulsive noise on structures

NTID300.13 — Transportation noise and noise from equipment powered by internal combustion engines

NTID300.14 — The economic impact of noise

NTID300.15 — Fundamentals of noise measurement, rating schemes, and standards

Harris, C. M. *Handbook of Noise Control*. New York: McGraw-Hill, 1957.

Size and scope nearly defies description. Not read casually, the book serves as a massive and high-quality reference source for most theoretical and practical aspects of the study of sound.

Hewlett-Packard Company. *Acoustics Handbook*. Palo Alto, Calif., 1968.

Written for the person sophisticated enough to use some of their instruments; a readable and informative introduction to sound and the measurement of sound.

Hosey, A. D., and Powell, C. H. *Industrial Noise—A Guide to its Evaluation and Control.* U.S. Department of Health, Education and Welfare, Public Health Service Publication no. 1572, 1967.
Contains much of the vital information needed to understand the more technical aspects of the industrial noise situation. The text is clearly written, and very little is assumed. It is highly recommended for the safety engineer or other members of the industrial staffs that control noise in their plants.

Kryter, Karl. *The Effects of Noise on Man.* New York: Academic Press, 1970.
From an author almost without equal in the study of noise. The book consists of data gleaned from hundreds of research projects, but unfortunately for the novice it may be exceptionally difficult in that Dr. Kryter has not introduced concepts but has assumed that the reader's background is sufficient to grasp them.

Navarra, J. G. *Our Noisy World.* Garden City: Doubleday, 1969.
A worthwhile beginning for the newcomer to the subject of noise. The concepts treated are quite basic and do not take one much beyond the beginning level of understanding the noise question. The illustrations are especially numerous and interesting.

New York City, Mayor's Task force on Noise Control. *Toward a Quieter City.* Report, New York City, 1970.
From the New York Board of Trade. The report indicates the scope of community noise problems in a running discussion of numerous areas of noise problems of America's largest (and perhaps noisiest) city.

Peterson, A. P. G., and Gross, E. E., Jr. *Handbook of Noise Measurement.* 3d rev. ed. West Concord, Mass.: General Radio Co., 1972.
Largely revised to incorporate developments since 1967. Highly recommended to the person who wants to learn much of the technical information in a painless manner.

Shurcliff, William A. *SST and Sonic Boom Handbook.* New York: Ballantine Books, 1970.

A one-sided (negative) presentation. Dr. Shurcliff, Harvard physicist, assumed the leadership of the Citizen's League Against the Sonic Boom (CLASB). His original intent was to "educate" congressmen, government officials, journalists, and others on the perils of the boom.

Stevens, S. S., and Warshofsky, F. *Sound and Hearing.* New York: Time-Life Books, 1965.

A clear and concise treatment of a complicated subject. As are most of the books in the Time-Life series, this one is recommended to seriously interested persons.

Still, Henry. *In Quest of Quiet.* Harrisburg, Pa.: Stackpole Books, 1970.

One of the most clearly written and most interesting among books prepared for the lay reader. Still is a professional writer who can study a complex subject and present it in understandable terms. As both reference and casual reading, this is one of the best available.

U.S. Department of Commerce, Commerce Technology Advisory Board. *The Noise Around Us: Including Technical Backup.* COM-71-00147, 1970.

Includes many common noise sources and the impact they are making on the lives of Americans, along with the technical background necessary to understand the concepts. A recommended reference book for the student interested in learning details of specific aspects of the noise question.

U.S. House of Representatives. *Noise Control. Hearings from the Subcommittee on Public Health and Environment.* 92nd congress, Serial No. 92030, 1971.

Copies of proposed legislation and testimony on the bills. An interesting aspect to this report is the transcripts of the give-and-take between members of the committee and those testifying during question-and-answer portions of the hearings.

Ward, W. Dixon, and Fricke, James, eds. *Noise as a Public Health Hazard—Proceedings of the Conference.* The American Speech and Hearing Association, ASHA Report No. 4., Washington, D.C., 1969.

Papers and discussions from one of the first extensive conferences on the overall concept of noise as a major environmental contaminant, held in June 1968. Under the joint sponsorship of the U.S. Public Health Service and the American Speech and Hearing Association, the meeting included papers on a wide range of subjects presented by numerous professionals and interested laymen. Although much of the material has been updated since then, the information is still good.

Appendix ·III·

Equipment Manufacturers

The following lists provide a starting point for persons interested in obtaining further information about equipment used in noise study. Inclusion on the list does not necessarily constitute an endorsement of the product; omission does not constitute rejection of the company or its product(s).

SOUND MEASURING EQUIPMENT

General Radio Corp.	West Concord, Mass. 01781
B & K Electronics Co.	5111 West 164th Street, Cleveland, Ohio 44142
Hewlett-Packard	1501 Page Mill Road, Palo Alto, Calif. 94304
Tracor Instruments	6500 Tracor Lane, Austin, Tex. 78721
E. I. DuPont Corp.	Wilmington, Delaware
Bausch & Lomb	465 Paul Road, Rochester, N.Y. 14602
Mine Safety Appliances Co.	201 N. Braddock Ave., Pittsburgh, Pa. 15208
H. H. Scott, Inc.	111 Powder Mill Rd., Maynard, Me. 01754

SOUND-TREATED ROOMS (PREFABRICATED)

Eckel Industries, Inc.	155 Fawcett St., Cambridge, Mass. 02138

General Acoustics Corp.	12248 Santa Monica Blvd., Los Angeles, Calif. 90025
Industrial Acoustics Co.	380 Southern Blvd., Bronx, N.Y. 10454
Wenger Corp.	Owatonna, Minn. 55060

AUDIOMETERS

Ambco Electronics	1222 W. Washington Blvd., Los Angeles, Calif. 90007
Bausch & Lomb	465 Paul Road, Rochester, N.Y. 14602
Beltone Electronics Corp.	4201 W. Victoria St., Chicago, Ill. 60646
Eckstein Brothers, Inc.	4807 W. 118th Pl., Hawthorne, Calif. 90250
Grason-Stadler Co.	West Concord, Mass. 01781
Maico Hearing Instruments	7375 Bush Lake Rd., Minneapolis, Minn. 55435
Mine Safety Appliances Co.	210 N. Braddock Ave., Pittsburgh, Pa. 15208
Tracor Inc.	6500 Tracor Lane, Austin, Tex. 78721

EAR PROTECTORS

Adcomold, Inc.	1558 California St., Denver, Colo. 80202
American Optical Corp.	14 Mechanic St., Southbridge, Mass. 01550
Bausch & Lomb	465 Paul Road, Rochester, N.Y. 14602
David Clark Co.	360 Franklin St., Worcester, Mass. 01604
Flents Products Co., Inc.	103 Park Avenue, New York, N.Y. 10017
General Electric Co.	Med. Systems Div. Bldg. 5-105, Schenectady, N.Y. 12345

Human Acoustics, Inc.	P.O. Box 14400, Portland, Ore. 97214
Mine Safety Appliances Co.	210 N. Braddock Ave., Pittsburgh, Pa. 15208
Sigma Engineering Co.	11320 Burbank, Blvd., North Hollywood, Calif. 91601
Tull Environmental Systems	285 Marietta St., Atlanta, Ga. 30302
Willson Products Div.	2nd & Washington Sts., Reading, Pa. 19603

Appendix ·IV·

NOISE TERMINOLOGY

Numerous words have been used in describing noise. In the interest of decency some of the more testy terms have been omitted from the following list. Each term cited can be or has been used before, after, or in place of the word *noise*.

abatement	bump	creak
aural sodomy	burble	din
babble	buzz	ding
bam	cackle	dingdong
bang	cacophony	drip
bark	chatter	droning
bash	cheep	drumming
beep	chime	eek
bellow	chirp	fiz
big	clack	flap
blap-blap	clang	flopping
blare	clank	glub
blaring	clap	gnashing
blast	clatter	gobble
blatt	click	grating
bleat	clickity-clack	grinding
bloop-bleep	clink	groan
bombardment	cluck	growl
bong	clunk	grumble
boom	crack	grunt
brak	crackle	gurgle
bray	crash	high-decibel

hiss
honking
hooting
howl
hubbub
hum
intense
intruding
jangling
jargon
jarring
jerking
jingle
jumbled
klunk
knock
loud
mew
moan
moo
murmur
neigh
Niagara of sound
ominous
patter
peal
peep
ping
plop
pockata
pop
pounding
pow
powerful
prattle
pulsing
purr
quick

r-r-r
racket
rap
rat-tat-tat
rattle
ringing
riotous
rippling
roar
row
rumble
rustle
screaming
screeching
scrunch
shock
shouting
shriek
sizzle
slam
smashing
snap
snarl
snort
sock
sonic
sound
splash
splat
squall
squawk
squeak
squeal
squish
stamp
stomp
swish
tap

tattoo
throb
thud
thump
thunder
tick
tinkle
toot
trauma
trill
twang
twitter
ubiquitous
unmuffled
unquiet
vr-r-room
wail
wheeze
whimper
whine
whirr
whistle
yap
yelling
yelp
yodeling
zap
zip

·Index·

Note: Italic page numbers denote illustrations

anatomy, *36*

damage, 12-13, 17, 45-71, 97-114, 191, 292-95

development, 34-36

function, 36-39

introduction to, 31-34

muffs, 112-13, 119, 275

plugs, 85, 112-13, 119, 196, 283

protection, 85, 112-13, 119, 275, 282-83, 307, 320-21

wax, 40

Eardrum, 32, 35, *36*, 233-34

Earphone, 123-25, 194, 284, 303-4

Ecocatastrophe, 6

Economic factors, 296-97

Ectomesodermal insufficiency syndrome, 68-69

Effective perceived noise level (EPNdB), 26-27

Electric heat pump noise, 230

Electric toothbrush, 193

El Mofty, 35

Emerson, Paul D., 114

Engström, Hans, 212

Environmental Protection Agency (EPA). See Office of Noise Abatement and Control

Equipment manufacturers, 319-21

Equivalent energy, 27, 124

Equivalent loudness (Leq), 27, 124

Erythrocytes, 65, *66*, 67

Eustachian tube, 36, 40

Exhaust fan noise, 191, 193, 282-83, 297

Fan noise, 196-98, 287-88

Federal Aviation Agency (FAA), 152-54, 260

Federal Council for Science and Technology, 199

Ferrell, Jack, 247

Firecrackers, 120-21

Fosbrooke, 8

Frankfurt, 154

Freeway noise, 16

Frequency, 14, 22, 49, 234, 256-57

Fricke, James, 9, 317

Fuller, Buckminster, 5

Future considerations, 248-49, 291-301, 306

Galvanometer, 75

Garbage disposal noise, 17, 144, 183-84, 283

Glass wool, 257-59, 281, 285-86

Glorig, Aram, 19, 121

Goethart, B. H., 147

Graham, Bill, 123

Graham, Billy, 132

Gross, E. E., 316

Gunshot noise, 18, 56, 83, 115, 117-20, 128, 139-40, 275

Hair spray, 244

Hardin, Garrett, 159

Harris, C. M., 315

Hawking, 270

Health, 92-96

Hearing aids, 50, 98, 133, 244-46

Hearing conservation, 105, 109-13, 140

Hearing loss, 50-59, 89-90, 157-58, 305-6

Hearing tests, 44, 52-59, 64, 70-71, 109-12, 128-29, 255

Heaters, 194, 287

Heat furnace noise, 17

Heathrow Airport, 86

Heat transfer, 68

Hertz (Hz), 14

High-frequency impairment (HFI), 43, 44, 52, 54, 55-56, 58

Home construction, 198-203

Horace, 9

Horn honking, 169-71, 177, 279, 281

Hosey, A. D., 316

Hospitals, 270

Household noise, 16-18, 189-205, 265-66, 282-88